ME AND MARIO CUOMO

ME AND MARIO CUOMO

CONVERSATIONS IN CANDOR

ALAN S. CHARTOCK

BARRICADE BOOKS INC.

NEW YORK

Published by Barricade Books Inc.
150 Fifth Avenue
New York, NY 10011

Printed in the United States of America.

Library of Congress Cataloging-in-Publication Data

Chartock, Alan Seth.
    Me and Mario Cuomo: conversations in candor / Alan Chartock
    p.   cm.
    ISBN 1-56980-062-6
    ISBN 1-56980-056-1 (pbk)
    1. Cuomo, Mario Matthew—Quotations. 2. United States—Politics and
government—1945-1989—Quotations, maxims, etc. 3. United States—Politics
and government—1989-   —Quotations, maxims, etc. 4. New York (State)—
Politics and government—1951-   —Quotations, maxims, etc. I. Title.

F125.3.C86A25 1995
974.7'043'092—dc20
[B]   95-706
                                                                 CIP

Book design by LaBreacht Design
First printing

TABLE OF CONTENTS

ACKNOWLEDGMENTS 7

INTRODUCTION 9

CHAPTER 1: *Excerpts from the Last Show* 21

CHAPTER 2: *Progressive Pragmatism* 31

CHAPTER 3: *Religion* 67

CHAPTER 4: *Family* 103

CHAPTER 5: *A Sense of Humor* 131

CHAPTER 6: *Cuomo and the Media* 167

CHAPTER 7: *Friends and Enemies* 195

CHAPTER 8: *Character* 231

CHAPTER 9: *The Cuomo Dialectic* 269

EPILOGUE 299

INDEX 301

ACKNOWLEDGMENTS

This book was a long time coming and a lot of people put considerable time and effort into making it happen.

There were all the teaching assistants at SUNY who helped transcribe so many years' worth of broadcasts. Their work was exceptional.

Selma Kaplan deserves an awful lot of credit for reading, editing and typing the manuscript in several versions. To put it mildly, no Selma, no book.

Lyle Stuart, the publisher, has a reputation for going where others won't and Marc Jaffe, one of the great figures in contemporary publishing, led me to Stuart who took a chance on this project. Marc edited the book and guided me through it.

Of course, it is to Mario Cuomo that I owe my greatest debt of thanks. He encouraged me on this work from the very beginning. He kept his distance from the project, which couldn't have been easy for him. He is a generous and true friend and I am sure that I shall never meet another like him.

As always, I couldn't do anything without my wife, the lovely Roselle, who serves as the rock and foundation of my life. Along with her there are son Jonas and daughter Sarah, who always help remind me, as Mario Cuomo so often did, that I am "no more than a walnut in the batter of eternity."

Naturally, anything that is wrong with this book is my fault.

INTRODUCTION

On February 26th, 1987, a few days after he announced he would not be a candidate for president of the United States, Mario Cuomo wrote me a letter. With it, he enclosed a copy of a letter from a listener to *The Capitol Connection*, our weekly public radio show. Said the governor:

"Dear Alan: You will have to write another letter to Ms. Ellen Vierick, one of our more enthusiastic fans. As I said last week, I will not be a candidate for president. Maybe you are our second choice. Sincerely, Mario."

Every one of us has had those dreams. We have all imagined what it would be like if we were somehow miraculously thrown into a relationship with a great public figure. More often than not, such thoughts remain fantasy and are never actualized, but I got lucky, perhaps through no fault of my own. I met Mario Cuomo.

This simple book is about a political science professor whose wires got crossed with those of an extraordinary man. We will leave it to others to write those books detailing what laws he signed. This one is a chronicle of sorts about the man; his intellectual strength, his capacity for humor, and his love of life.

It hasn't always been easy. I have been at the receiving end of telephone admonitions at home and at work. I have, on occasion, offended him. At times he has offended me, so hard-hitting has been his criticism. But the more I got to know the man, the more I respected and, frankly, loved him.

This book is also the story of a radio show with two mythical listeners named Harvey and Ethel (and, according to the governor, "Ethel dropped out.")

It began about eighteen years ago, when I started a small newspaper in Albany which was to serve as a workshop for student journalists from the State University College at New Paltz. That newspaper, *The Legislative Gazette*, has proven to be far more successful and long-lived than any of us ever suspected it would. But it almost didn't make its first birthday because many of the powerful Albany political bosses tried to kill it. They almost succeeded. As one of them said at the time, "We never had it, why should we have it now?"

Thanks to the good offices of a few newspapermen who didn't like the spectacle of some big shot Albany pols beating up on a student newspaper, a bunch of students who didn't want their project killed, and even a few legislators with moxie, the *Gazette* didn't die. The kill order issued by the then-Comptroller Arthur Levitt was rescinded.

About a year later, as I was still shaking in my boots from their previous attacks on the newspaper, one of the students, Anne Erickson, decided to hold a fundraiser for the *Gazette* and invited all the state's senior politicians to attend. The idea was to generate enough money to pay for some darkroom equipment.

What we didn't know when we were setting the date for the fundraiser was that it was the same night as the annual Senate dinner, the gathering of the state's most powerful solons—people like the Senate president, Warren Anderson, and his colleagues.

The fundraiser was held in a little bar, the Lark Tavern, on Madison Avenue in Albany and the kids each prepared something to eat and offered the entertainment. A lot of people came, mostly legislative interns; a few legislators poked their heads in the door. But to the astonishment of all present, an hour after the doors opened, Mario Cuomo, the lieutenant governor of the State of New York walked in, sat down, and started talking to the kids.

The lieutenant governor is the presiding officer of the state Senate and I was sure that Cuomo would be departing in minutes for the Senate dinner. But it didn't happen. He amazed everyone in the place by staying late into the evening. He sat on a bar stool in that dingy place, a man of incredible dignity and generosity, and took on all comers. His interest in the students on the *Legislative Gazette* was obvious for all to see. That kind of interest is very hard to fake. He was a study in class.

About 11:00 that evening, the door to the Lark Tavern flew open and there they all were—Republican Majority Leader Warren Anderson, Speaker Stanley Fink, Minority Leader Manfred Ohrenstein and Republican Party leader Richard Rosenbaum. Even though I believe they were shamed into showing up, the ice was broken and they stayed for hours. The *Legislative Gazette* project was strengthened that night to the point where it couldn't be killed. And Mario Cuomo led the way.

Often, throughout the years, powerful people have been honored or have retired and the governor's people have been leaned on to get him to drop by. He didn't. But when you least expected it, he'd do something extraordinary, like show up at a dinner in honor of a retiring secretary in his office. That's the way it is with Cuomo. He has a real thing for the little people and a healthy cynicism about those on top.

Years later, someone asked the Governor why he came to the Lark Tavern that night. Why did he show up for a bunch of kids when he could have been schmoozing with his Senate colleagues?

"I did it for the girl," he is reported to have said of gutsy Anne Erickson. "I did it for the girl."

So the rescue of the *Legislative Gazette* was how I first came to meet the governor. You might suspect that after Cuomo's kindnesses to the paper, I would be forever in his debt and would only sing his praises. But no, it didn't happen that way. In fact, I had just started writing a syndicated column about New York State politics and in 1981, with the 1982 gubernatorial election looming,

I wrote a column predicting that while Mario Cuomo was a bright and good man, Ed Koch, the mayor of the Big Apple, would soundly defeat him. One of the newspapers, *The Berkshire Eagle*, published the column under the headline "Meet Governor Koch." Cuomo has that column to this day and regularly reminds me that I wrote it. "Everyone knows that you were with Koch," he'd point out at times when we were going head to head.

Then in the days leading up to one of the closest primary elections in history, something else happened. One of Cuomo's top supporters, Bernie Ryan of the CSEA, Civil Service Employees Association, which was running Cuomo's campaign (probably more against Koch than for Cuomo), made a silly mistake in a graduate class I taught.

Ryan told a story about how Mario Cuomo had thrown a police officer out of his office. The officer had tried to peddle documents purporting to show that Ed Koch was a homosexual. *The New York Post* ran the story and it was the only smoking gun that anyone could show that the Cuomo campaign was up to dirty tricks, portraying Koch as a homosexual at a time when signs were appearing all over Archie Bunkerland in Queens urging voters to "Vote For Cuomo, Not the Homo." Ryan told the class that they could tell that story to anyone they wanted, leaving the impression that Cuomo's people wanted it out there.

There is no question that the Cuomo people thought Ryan had done a foolish thing, but some of them were quick to blame me for the leak. I heard in no uncertain terms from several members of the highest echelons of the campaign that I was in deep trouble. When you are a college professor at the State University and not used to that kind of rhetoric, you lose a few hours sleep wondering what will become of you. One of Cuomo's top advisors at the time told me it was possible that I would never be allowed on the second floor of the Capitol if Cuomo became the governor.

The campaign was close and, as Cuomo won, I saw my life slipping away. On the one hand, I owed a great personal debt to

Cuomo and wanted to see him win. I had never admired Koch but I also knew that a Cuomo win could have some very serious implications for my career. I had heard over and over again that the man had a temper and would get even.

Then one day I was sitting on the floor of my home in western Massachusetts, playing with my son, when the phone rang. My very little boy picked up the phone and murmured something about the governor calling so I grabbed it. It was the engineer on duty at WAMC, the northeast public radio station which I head, who told me that the governor had called and wanted to hear from me. Heart pounding, I dialed the number of the Executive Mansion and sure enough he came right on the line and screamed into my ear that he had just heard a reporter tell a lie about him on a WAMC program that I hosted.

"When can *I* be on your radio show?" asked the governor.

"Whenever you want," I replied, still reeling.

"Tomorrow," came the abrupt answer. "Bring your tape recorder." And that's how it all began.

I showed up with the newspaper reporter and we questioned Cuomo for half an hour. It was a great show. At one point, the governor stopped to take a call and as he was speaking into the phone, the reporter leaned over and whispered to me, suggesting I ought to ask him to do the show every week. "What are you, nuts?" I whispered back. But I did ask the governor and, a day or so later, he agreed.

Subsequent to that conversation, I was told by the governor's people that he had decided to do the show against the advice of his principal assistants. They quite correctly predicted that some members of the reportorial corps, known in Albany as the Legislative Correspondents Association or LCA, would be furious at the unparalleled access I would have with the governor. What's more, both he and I were told that the fact that I was an academic would be perceived as a slap in the face by journalists who prized the exclusivity of their club.

The Capitol Connection turned out to be unlike anything any-body else was doing. The very existence of that program says more about Mario Cuomo than you might imagine.

One of the qualities I have always admired most about the governor is his ability to take risks and to do the unconventional. His advisors were right—there was general consternation about the show. Years later I learned that the governor had mentioned to a few friends that the reason he continued to do the show for so many years was the "...cruelty exhibited toward Alan by mem-bers of the press corps." Mario Cuomo doesn't like bullies of any size. He has never been afraid to take on the press. What's more, his reaching out to me although I was *persona non grata* to his peo-ple proved once again that Cuomo had no equal in politics when it came to bringing people together. Simply put, his philosophy dictated generosity to political enemies in an effort to widen the political circle.

All the Cuomo charisma, magic and philosophy came out on the radio show that started that day on the floor of my living room when the governor made his call. Perhaps he was doing what he does so well, expanding his circle, and drawing it wider all the time. Perhaps it was his humanity, his brains, his love of fun and dan-ger, his response to challenges, his mistreatment by those who drew him out of *their* circles.

Mario Cuomo is a very complex man. Every sentence, every thought, is intricate. Cuomo would cover his tracks brilliantly, first getting into trouble with his candor, then adding a caveat which could be used to negate what was said in the event that anybody called him on it. He may be best known for his ability to argue the pants off of anyone, but on that first show I began to discover that Mario Cuomo is, above all, a very funny man. Perhaps it's all the old-time radio he listened to in his youth. He can do all the characters, from the Green Hornet to Fibber Magee and Molly. I grew up listening to "The 2,000 Year Old Man," a classic piece of recorded humor by Mel Brooks and Carl Reiner, and I think

Mario Cuomo is right up there with those two guys, and Jack Benny and Fred Allen and Will Rogers. He doesn't tell jokes *per se*, but he sure can tell a story. And each story has a message.

Once I asked him why he made a decision which he knew would eventually be overruled. As his response, he told me the story of the rabbi and the horse. It seemed that a famous rabbi was teaching his student when a king walked into the room and told the rabbi that he would be executed.

The rabbi looked at the king and asked if there was anything he could do to stop his beheading.

"Why, yes," said the king. "You see that horse over there? If you can make that horse fly, I'll spare you."

"How long do I have to make the horse fly?" the rabbi asked the king.

"I'll give you a year," said the king.

"I think I can do it," the rabbi said to the king and the king left.

The rabbi's unhappy student turned to his teacher and asked why he had done such a foolish thing.

"In a year," said the rabbi, "the king may die, the horse may die, I may die, or, of course, I may teach the horse to fly."

Not exactly your typical gubernatorial fare.

Cuomo and my honorary Uncle Jack, whom I really loved, have a lot in common. Relatives would admonish me to listen carefully to Uncle Jack. He'd say the obligatory good things about people in his first two sentences, but "...listen for the third sentence," they would warn. The third sentence was always the zinger, the drop of the other shoe. The subject, who had been lauded up until that moment, was carved into dog meat with a few seemingly harmless words. And so it was with Cuomo. He'd take on his rivals, Edward I. Koch, Hugh Leo Carey, Roy Goodman, first praising them, then verbally excoriating them.

Cuomo's sense of humor and skill at debate, combined with his love of language and artful precision with words, made *The*

Capitol Connection much more than a weekly conversation about New York State politics and government. Because Cuomo is so bright and articulate and because he loves to fight (though he says he doesn't), he maintained some of the highest numbers in popularity polls in the history of the governor's office.

Frankly, I have interviewed many players on today's political scene and I don't think that any of them could conduct a week in, week out radio show, month after month, and survive. Most, like Mike Dukakis, who I had on the show once when Cuomo was busy, are either too boring or try to be too safe. Even though Dukakis's people called and asked how he could replicate the show in Massachusetts, he never did. Years later we found out that he just didn't have the horses. It takes an awful lot to sustain that kind of program. WAMC's listeners from both within and beyond New York State indicated through letters, phone calls and surveys that *The Capitol Connection* with the governor was one of their favorite shows. They'd say things like, "I could listen to that man speak the English language all day long—it's poetry," or "He knows and loves language—a lost art among politicians." Indeed, not since Adlai Stevenson or John F. Kennedy has a politician in either party dealt with ideas and thoughts in quite such a spontaneous and loving fashion.

Mario Cuomo showed such an incredible faith in his own rhetorical capability that he would sometimes take the most indefensible positions, just to see whether he could convince others to buy his point of view. That is Mario Cuomo the lawyer, Mario Cuomo the law professor in a Socratic dialogue with a student, Mario Cuomo the law clerk for the judge, Mario Cuomo at the dinner table, training his children to face life.

The very first regular program we recorded with the governor was beset with technical problems but nonetheless, showed all the elements comprising the Cuomo style—his verbal technique, his gentle self-deprecation and his love of the fight.

We recorded the program in a small conference room next to the governor's office. The problem was, despite the use of the best recording equipment available, the governor's conference room had all the acoustical properties of an underground cavern. Add to that a nervous tape recorder operator who remembered to open the governor's microphone but forgot about all of the interviewers' mikes, and we were not off to an auspicious start.

The size of the room meant that only a limited number of reporters could get in and from the first minute, the taping sessions for *The Capitol Connection* program were the hottest ticket in town.

We knew that the regular press corps reporters were not going to like the special access that public radio had to the governor, so we tried hard to play fair. We had several reporters as regular questioners, we allowed access to United Press International and Associated Press pool reporters, and we found a way to pipe the program into the Legislative Correspondents' room itself. But no matter how hard we tried to arrange things for the benefit of the reporters, nothing ever proved to be good enough. I asked many of these people if they would allow us in the room with them when they had their regular one-on-ones with the governor and they just sneered. Like any institutional group, they called their own shots and didn't particularly like anyone else in on the action.

In New York State, there is a long history of governors leaking material directly to *The New York Times* and bypassing the rest of the press corps. There is a certain irony to the fact that *The New York Times* proved, over the long haul, to be the most irate about the existence of *The Capitol Connection*. Years into the program, one of the *Times* reporters, furious about being excluded from a session because of lack of space, shook his finger at me and in a quivering voice told me, "If the governor croaks on your show you won't read about it in *The New York Times*."

But, to be fair, Michael Oreskes, another reporter who covered Albany for the *Times* during the early days of the show, was always supportive and helpful. He seemed genuinely pleased on those occasions when we asked him to participate. Unlike other politicians, Cuomo was willing to go head-to-head with the press.

He was not afraid to criticize the press and would use every opportunity to do so. Other politicians warned constantly that it is imprudent to get into wars with the press; that it is unwise to "get into pissing matches with skunks," and that "if you fight with them, they'll get you in the end." They may well be right, but for as long as I have known Cuomo, he has rejected that advice, preferring to hold the press accountable.

Although I was a bit nervous during our first outing, it turned out to be an important one. Not looking before I leaped, I asked at one point, "How do you differ from other run-of-the-mill politicians in the state?"

Cuomo, a bit nonplussed, asked if that meant I viewed him as one of those run-of-the-mill politicians. It was the first hint of what was to come in our relationship. As the other reporters in the room laughed, he answered the question. "I am taller than about 40 percent of them, heavier than about 52 percent of them. As for the Republicans—I belong to a different party. Anything more, Alan?" Red-faced, I pursued that point and asked if the office of governor has a different constituency than that of other politicians in the state and whether or not *that* made him different.

"There is one basic standard for me," said Cuomo, "and I believe it is the standard for all political people who think about their role." That standard, said Cuomo, was the opportunity to serve others.

In my early forties at the time, I had grown cynical hanging around the Legislature. I was quite convinced that most politicians do serve their constituents, but only after they themselves were served. I truly wanted to believe in Cuomo, but his detractors had been bending my ear about how pompous he was, how he couldn't get along with people, how he always wanted his own way. To me, that answer provided food for thought.

Unlike almost every politician I have known, Cuomo's mind can grasp both the long range and the immediate. He negotiates all the time but he doesn't cower. He throws out classic political gambits. He thinks three moves ahead. He is not afraid to foul, to muscle a bit and to make his opponents come to him.

Cuomo thinks, he conjures up phrases, and he shares them with others. The speeches that really counted—the speech on abortion at Notre Dame, the speech that rocked the '82 Convention in San Francisco and had men and women in tears, the impassioned speech at the College of Saint Rose suggesting that only God has the right to take a life—he writes those speeches himself.

He recalls so many of his heroes, those from a quieter time; Lincoln, whom he constantly invokes and with whom he clearly shares values; Joe DiMaggio, who played ball with such grace—those are Mario Cuomo's heroes. And, while his opponents would portray him as some kind of way-out liberal, Mario Cuomo is no such thing. Underneath it all, I tell you, the man is an old-fashioned conservative. He values family, order, and religion above all.

We did *The Capitol Connection* together for twelve years. During that time I learned a lot about politics and a lot about life from Mario Cuomo. The programs from which this book draws comprise a unique chronicle of both Cuomo's tenure as governor and the recent history of New York State. But perhaps most importantly, they reflect the full depth and character of the man who, for three terms, served the citizens of New York State as governor.

Take a few minutes and listen to all that *The Capitol Connection* has revealed about Mario Cuomo over the years. You'll be surprised by a lot of what you hear.

CHAPTER

1

EXCERPTS FROM
THE LAST SHOW

It remains one of those once-in-a-lifetime events. It was Wednesday, November 16, 1994. On November the eighth, Mario Cuomo had lost his bid for a fourth term as governor. It was not an easy time for him and he had pretty much remained behind the walls of the mansion.

Two days before, our member–supported public radio station, WAMC, had started its fund drive. Our goal was $250,000. Cuomo had always been willing to help out during fund drives and listeners well remembered his reading poetry and telling stories of his parents and of his childhood.

The sixteen volunteers who were answering phones in the pledge room were hoping against hope that the governor would show up in person to record what was to be his last *Capitol Connection* program. My wife, Roselle, drove over having had a premonition that he might, but until the very end I was told that he didn't want to leave the mansion and he'd talk to us on the phone. I repeatedly called his staff, imploring them to intercede, and with about fifteen minutes to go, I received a call that the governor would indeed come to the station.

I stood on the street in front of the WAMC offices and waited for him. Within seconds, I saw "Major Marty," (Martin Burke) the head of the governor's security detail, strolling up the street. I asked The Major where the governor was and he told me that for the first time in years, the gov was driving himself. I was curious. "What kind of a driver is the governor," I asked, and in response, the Major put his hands over his eyes. The governor's car pulled in across the street, he got out, came into the studio, and was greeted by cheers and applause from the assembled staff and volunteers. I can tell you, there were more than a few tears in the house.

After asking the applauding volunteers in the big room whether they weren't confusing him with Al D'Amato, "because we all look alike," we were off.

For the next thirty minutes, the governor held us all spellbound as he reflected on the recent elections, what they meant for the country and what they meant for him. He spoke of disappointment and of the frustration of losing. He spoke of defeat and of pain. But he also spoke of hope, and of faith, and of turning things around.

The aftermath was really astounding. As soon as this incredibly poignant program concluded, the governor stood up and walked over to me, hugged me for the first time in twelve years, and asked, "Is this our last show?"

"I hope not," I responded.

"Well, it is," he said, and with a kiss to the lovely Roselle, he was off.

I walked him to the door, then returned to the microphone and the volunteers. It was about 2:30 in the afternoon, traditionally a low point in our radio listening day, and I told the listeners that they had just heard the "Valedictory" of Mario Cuomo. It would be available to anyone who wanted it for a pledge of .... and then I looked up at my colleague, David Galletly, and held up three fingers—meaning thirty dollars. Galletly vehemently shook his head and held up five fingers and I waved him off, believing that we'd never get it. He shrugged, indicating that it was my decision. In the end, I went with his suggestion and finished my sentence, "... for a fifty dollar membership in WAMC." I really didn't expect much at that hour of the afternoon.

There and then, fund raising history was made at WAMC. It may have been the fact that a lot of people were still grieving over the governor's recent loss or the election of Newt Gingrich, but all hell broke loose. There are sixteen phones in the pledge room and just as a great forest fire consumes everything in its path, that's how the phones rang. First one, then a second, then every phone in the room, then every phone in the building. Twenty-four phones were ringing all at once. As a result, no one could call in or out of the building. The phones rang for more than seven hours and I don't mind telling you that in all my years of doing this kind of fund raising, I've never seen anything like it. I was an emotional wreck. The tears were streaming down my face. When I couldn't go on, David would step in and pick it up. Nobody can remember anything like it. I couldn't help myself— I picked up the phone, dialed the mansion and said, "Listen to this!" to the out-going governor.

We were asking for two hundred fifty thousand dollars in the drive and we needed a little less than a hundred thousand more to make our goal. We expected to be there for several more days but it was soon clear that the drive would be over on the strength of this one tape.

People called in and lamented how stupid the electorate was. They called from Massachusetts and Connecticut, New Jersey, Vermont and New Hampshire to say how much they would miss listening to this great man. Many of the callers were crying. Lots of Republicans called in to say that while they hadn't voted for him, they were making a contribution to salute this premier politician.

Sitting at the computer, tallying it all up, was our diminutive engineer, Jim "Sparks" Scholefield. I noticed as he feverishly entered the pledges that every so often he would hold up a finger and go "bing." With a shock I realized that each of the "bings" indicated a thousand dollars over and beyond our two hundred fifty thousand dollar goal.

When the smoke cleared, we had exceeded our goal by $50,000. We were up to three hundred thousand dollars! Not only that, the entire drive was over in three days. We never saw the likes of it in all our years of fund raising and we probably never will again.

In the past twelve years, I've spent many hours across the microphone from Mario Cuomo. I've read his books and listened to his speeches. But as time passes, this valedictory, in all its spontaneity, will probably be the thing I remember most clearly.

These are his words, exactly as we heard them on that final show:

AC: Are you ready?

MC: No, I'm not.

AC: You're on the radio, you know that? See that red light over there? That means you're on the radio.

MC: Listen, you told me that we were going to talk to the public. You didn't tell me I'd have to listen to you for a half hour. The truth is, I don't need this aggravation. I've had a very tough week. So, can't we just talk to them? You have nothing to say to me. I've been listening to you for so long, but go ahead, we may as well. I'll just offer this up with the rest of the other seven days of the week.

AC: One second.

MC: Do I get coffee?

AC: Yeah, will someone get the governor a cup of black coffee? Is that right? Here we go.

AC: It's *The Capitol Connection!* With Governor Mario M. Cuomo!

[Applause]

AC: Governor, you are a guy who has waxed philosophical over the years about all of this. You've just gone through a tough time. Is it tough? Is it—how do you handle disappointment? What does one do with disappointment? I ask you that because we've been getting a lot of telephone calls here at Public Radio from people who are disappointed, and I want to know what you do when you're disappointed. How do you make it all right?

MC: Well, I think first, you have to know what it is that disappoints you. If people are disappointed because what they believed, or what they thought they believed has been rejected, then that's one thing. I think no one ought to be disappointed because Mario Cuomo is not going to be the governor, because that really isn't the important thing. The important thing is, what is it that we believed, what is it that we were trying to do and if you believed the same thing and you're disappointed because you think that's been rejected, then the appropriate response is to fight a little bit harder to make sure that it gets restored even in the new administration. I would not give up on the possibility that the next governor will come to see things a little bit differently in the course of being governor. For example, I don't think it's realistic to believe that he can do the tax cut he said he would do in the campaign. That's just not in the cards. So I think if the disappointment is "gee whilikers, all those things that I felt so deeply now have been rejected, and I feel rejected," therefore, I think your response is let me get out there and tell the story again. That's what I'm going to try to do, nationally, and in New York State. I believe that a lot of the things that I feel and have stood for personally have been rejected around the country. I'm very disappointed at that, so I'm going to fight a little bit harder to make the case.

AC: How are you going to do that?

MC: Just seize whatever opportunity is given you to talk about things. What is it that the country needs? Are we being offered by the radical right in the House, are we being offered real solutions or are these parodies. Everybody knows that crime is a problem. Is the death penalty anything more than a travesty or a parody? I mean, does the death penalty make you safe? Why is Thomas Grasso, even in *The New York Post*, pleading this week "Let me die" and "If I were free I would never kill another person, not because I've changed, but because I would hate the idea of coming back to face life in prison." Well, that's what we've been saying over and over. Are you really going to tell us now that the death penalty will make us safe, when in five of the seven states that have brought it back the homicide rate is growing faster than here, when in Texas where they're killing them casually almost, forty-six percent increase in violence, where all the evidence is that it has become an instruction in brutality? You offer this solution to our economic problems, a tax cut that can't occur all over the United States of America; and now the Republican Contract saying we're going to cut everybody's taxes, we're going to balance your budget in five years, but they won't tell you how. Is that anything but a parody or a travesty? Isn't this really Reaganism with a harsh face? Reaganism without the benefit of the lovely non-menacing, beguiling, charming Reagan? Isn't that what this is all about? Aren't they trying to con you? Go deliver the message. Make the case. That's what I'm going to do. Also, I have to make a living which—I have a problem here—we ought to talk about this.

AC: Do you think there will be a doctoral dissertation written on the works of Parkinson at some point?

MC: I may do one myself. I may do the works of A. J. Parkinson. He's one of the pithiest of all my favorite authors.

AC: Pithy was he?

MC: Indeed he was.

AC: Governor, what is it that progressive pragmatism means, which you share with Parkinson? This is the philosophy of progressive pragmatism. What does that mean?

MC: If you look closely at the new so called contract with America that the Republican House has advanced, it really is a kind of top ten or top twenty from focus groups and polls. What it is, is going around to the people of the country and saying, "What concerns you most?" and they say crime, and then you ask them "What would you do about the death penalty?" and they put that down, death penalty very big, and then—well, taxes, and then they put down tax cuts, very big; "Politicians are all at fault" and then they put reform government, so these are down by polls and that's why it produces parodies and travesties. Can you imagine Moses coming down the mountain? Can you imagine him with the tablet saying "Okay, now before we try to make this policy, we're going to take a poll. How many people here in favor of banning adultery?" You know, this notion of having the talk show hosts in—did you hear this? I think the speaker-to-be-

AC: Yes, Mr. Gingrich—

MC: Yes, that he's going to call in Rush Limbaugh and the Bob Grants and the other talk show people and ask them what they're hearing from the population. And presumably they will report the predictable. Well, they hate this, they hate that, they curse this, the heck with the immigrants, the heck with this, and then you make policy. Why don't you just call Blockbuster? Why don't you say, what cassettes are you selling, and then push pornography. Why don't you go to a book store and say, what are the people asking for? And when they tell you this is what they are asking for, well, that's what we're going to give them back, even if it's wrong. What happened to leadership? What is this? Get the people angry, bottle their anger and then dispense it? Is that what you're offering me? Is that what you're telling me your rationale is? But this is, this is part of the polarizing politics that we've gotten accustomed to. You're two hundred years old. The

strongest nation the world has ever seen. You're also one of
the youngest. And in that youth comes immaturity. We're
not mature yet as a people. We haven't developed our own
culture yet. You know we don't have the stability that comes
with homogeneity for a thousand years. We're made up of
parts from everywhere; we're still assembling parts—178 eth-
nicities in this state alone. We have this teaming diversity
constantly jolting itself, you know, by rubbing against one
another. We're still finding out, wait, what is your music?
What is your philosophy? Write me on a card, the American character. What is it, after two hundred years? And we
have this habit of lurching the way children do from one
polar extreme to another. We take the country over, we blow
away the native Americans, we are the most violent people
in history, we treat blacks like property, we go through a
period of macho individualism. Why, we do indeed leave
people by the side of the trail as we're moving west. Why,
we're tough, we're individuals. Then comes the Depression,
and a hero steps forward and changes everything and moves
you to a paternalism that nobody ever imagined possible for
this band of rugged individualists. And now you have a government that takes you under its wing and says we'll do
everything for you. And then you go through a stage of
excessive bureaucracy because that leads to a—you know—
the Johnson years, etc. So you go from one extreme to the
other. Now you are at one extreme. Death penalty, cut the
taxes, the heck with the immigrants. You put together a series
of parodies and travesties—death penalty is surely one—we'll
cut the taxes in New York 7 billion dollars. Forget about it.
Incidentally, they're not even talking about that tax cut anymore. Now they're calling it a 25 percent income tax cut.
That was only part of it. What the Republicans offered you
in this state was a 7 billion dollar tax cut. Don't forget it.
No way that's going to happen and everybody knows it.

Another parody. Take the money away from the children on welfare, punish their mothers. This way they'll stop making babies. Foolish. The bishops were right and I applaud the bishops of my church. They don't always agree with me but they were right when they called on the Republicans and said this is monstrous; this is stupid.

AC: The idea of taking the children away and putting them in an orphanage?

MC: Oh, my God! And who is going to build the orphanages? I thought you wanted less government. Now you're going to have government orphanages? Or will the thousand points of light build the orphanages for you, and who will watch the children with AIDS? Travesty! Parody! Exaggeration! Lurching to the right, a kind of pandering. What we need is a more mature, more intelligent consensus that brings people together, people like your audience. Frankly, they're the core, the most intelligent people, not all geniuses, but the most intelligent people, the most thoughtful people, people who say, hey, look, let me think about this a little bit more. It must be more complicated than that. People who have an impulse that says there must be more subtlety to this thing than we're being told. There is. We need a politics that is reasonable, a politics of common sense. That's where progressive pragmatism came from. In 1985 I did the Fellowship at Yale and it was after 1984 and all that had happened in the Reagan years and I said, look, forget all about Democrat, Republican, Conservative, Liberal; you people are choking on labels. You know, you're developing a myopia here. You are assuming that Conservatives stand for the— throw away all of the labels, take every issue, apply reason and common sense to every issue. And what would I call myself? A progressive pragmatist. What does that mean? That means I want to learn, I want to grow the way the whole Universe is growing, upward toward the light. And I want it to make sense, practical common sense. That's pragmatism, progressivism, that's intelligence and practicality, that's compassion and common sense. Put it all together; that's the politics that you need. That's going to be the Clinton politics. That's what will make him president again.

CHAPTER 2

PROGRESSIVE PRAGMATISM

On the wall of Mario Cuomo's press office was a huge framed poster containing the heart of the famous philosopher A.J. Parkinson's entire body of work; a truth it had taken the philosopher years to come to. The poster proclaimed: "Reason with them, it makes them crazy"—A.J. Parkinson."

Of course, there is no philosopher, A.J. Parkinson. He is one of a group of colorful characters created by Mario Cuomo. But make no mistake about it: what Parkinson says, even in humor, is what Cuomo thinks. And "Reason with them, it makes them crazy" has always been central to the thinking of Mario Cuomo.

Closely related to A.J.'s admonition is Cuomo's self-proclaimed philosophy of 'progressive pragmatism.' What that means is to do what works—not to be married to an ideology that will fence you in as a politician and destroy you. For twelve years, Cuomo drove his political opponents crazy because just when they thought they had him boxed in, he would turn from the pursued to the pursuer. To this day, he is not married to a political party but to the principle of using what will work. That, combined with his incredible oratorical skills, is what made him so effective.

As governor, Cuomo would bash a president when he thought he deserved it, but when the same man did well, Cuomo would be quick to praise him. That, in itself, made him a different kind of politician. Progressive pragmatism is two words. It is not just pragmatism but a pragmatism with ethical and moral limits. In other words, it's pragmatism within strict boundaries.

Mario Cuomo has always genuinely hated to have anyone attach a label to him. I think that was the basis of progressive pragmatism. The whole thing really may have started as a joke. Based on what I have heard on the radio show, I suspect that Cuomo just got tired of being labeled as a liberal and was continually frustrated by all those people who asked him to label himself. But this time I think the joke grew into something more meaningful.

While some would call him a classic liberal, I would swear the man I spoke with on the radio each week was a personal conservative. Cuomo clearly felt sympathy for those who were excluded from society's benefits. That is probably because he himself was raised in a family which had little in the way of material benefits and because he learned first- hand what the sting of discrimination can feel like. He came from a household where one's personal integrity, the worth of a man's word, and morality were preached constantly. He knew that many would attach the label "free spending liberal" to him and fought very hard not to let that happen. There were days on the radio show when he eschewed all labels, there were days when he defended classic liberalism, and there were days he just had fun with the whole thing.

"I said that I am a liberal," he said once. "The whole matter is in the definition.

"I am a liberal in the sense that Roosevelt was a liberal, in the sense that John Kennedy was a liberal, in the sense that Harry Truman was a liberal. I am a liberal in the sense of those who used government progressively and affirmatively to help the free enterprise system by giving land to people to build railroads, by bailing out Chrysler to keep them in place and by helping the savings and loans so that the depositors would not be damaged. I am a liberal in the sense that the liberals are the ones who created the social security and Medicare and Medicaid programs and the GI Bill of Rights and affordable housing. I am liberal in the sense that I am the one that spoke for civil rights, for human rights, for freedom, for the end of oppression. In that sense, I am very much a liberal yet people would regard me in other ways in my insistence on a legally required balanced budget."

What's more, suggested the governor, the fact that "...I insisted on tax cuts, I insist on controlled spending, my discussion with the State University about fiscal accountability. This would make me a fiscal conservative."

In fact, Cuomo on occasion joined forces with the state's conservative business leaders in calling for less waste in government.

"It is plainly wrong," he said, for example, "to have a situation in some parts of the state where you can have a county park and town park side by side on the same block offering the same facilities. But because of two jurisdictions you duplicate, replicate costs.

"So what I call myself is 'progressive pragmatist,'" said the governor. But what he worries about is that all the labels don't "become encumbered by media misunderstanding." If that happens, said the governor with that characteristic lilt to his voice, "I will call a new party the 'neo-progressive pragmatists.'"

Progressive pragmatism has one other crucial element: faith in the ability of people to reason for themselves—for the people to decide. Cuomo didn't always follow it, as in the case of the death penalty, but he did where he could. Of course, Cuomo believed that people had to know what the facts were before they could make up their minds. Once, when I was talking about the Cuomo magic on the podium, he told me, "Elocution is not the important thing. The important thing is: can you explain things clearly enough to people to educate them, illuminate them, at least communicate with them and get approval?"

When President Reagan tried to eliminate state and local taxes as a deduction from federal income tax, it was Cuomo who led the way against Reagan's plan. It wasn't easy because most people didn't understand the issue. But Cuomo was, if nothing else, a teacher. And, in the end, he prevailed.

"It was that people began to understand it. It showed in polls, it showed in mail, it showed in letters, it showed in non-letters. The president of the United States did an extraordinary thing. He said after the summer, I'm going to launch a new campaign and he went out to the people of this country and he said, 'Call your congressman.'

"And you know what happened? Nobody called nobody. That non-response was as loud as any congressperson could wish a message could be from the American people. Now, what happened here, and it's very significant, is that without television, without a president to deliver the message, with only a whole lot of anonymity scurrying around, getting it around every way they could, the American people heard it and were smart enough to figure it out. That's the message here. This is a very smart people."

But Cuomo's brand of progressive pragmatism involved more than taking the pulse of the people and following that.
"Sure we get fooled from time to time, the way a jury does, but basically the consensus wisdom in this country, I think, is very strong. In a way, that's why our politics is cyclical. It's because the people are smart. It takes them a while..., you make some statements as a campaigner, you sound attractive, you sound right, they give you four to eight years, they catch up to you... you're out and they go in the other direction. The cyclical aspect of our politics is not so much a sign of our arbitrariness as a people, but a sign of our intelligence, that's what happened here. How does it feel to be with those Americans who reached the right judgment? It feels comfortable, but I think it would be a terrible mistake to try to personalize it, to try to take credit or blame for it."

Cuomo's liberalism and pragmatism were learned at the knee of his beloved parents. That explains his compassion for those who have experienced the kind of discrimination they suffered. Many of those people formed the central group to whom he as a Democratic politician had to appeal. But while he claimed to hate words like "liberal" and "conservative," they are not without real meaning.

So here's my understanding of the man. He believed that government can and must do for the little people. But he knew there were limits to that activity and he knew that some of that activity could be both destructive and dehumanizing. As he put it to me:

"I think the point is we need to do a lot more. The work force of the twenty-first century is threatened. We've got too many illiterates, too many kids dropping out, too much drugs, too much AIDS, too many homeless. We must acknowledge that we need to do better. It is not enough to say 'status quo.'"

And if Cuomo talked about Roosevelt and Truman he also invoked the name of his political hero, Abraham Lincoln, another self-made man, who, he pointed out—a lot—was a Republican:

"I see government as doing for people what they cannot do sufficiently, or at all, for themselves. Incidentally, I look for comfort and consolation in that definition. I find it in Abraham Lincoln, a Republican who cared."

He said government is a coming together of people to do things for themselves they could not do at all, or as well, individually. Build a road, defend yourself against the Indians, defend yourself against the Soviets, give a child who needs special care the special care, give care to elderly people. The extended family doesn't exist the way it used to. Not everybody can take in Mom and Pop the way they used to.

"That's government's role: taking care of poor people who, without us, would be without shelter, without food. That's an obvious obligation of government."

This is a theme Cuomo reiterated again and again. He preached that we cannot be so short-sighted that we don't rescue our least fortunate kids from lives in hell. We must give them a chance. It is ethically correct. It is morally correct. But more than any of that, it is the only way to save the society from drugs, billions spent on prisons and from a devastated work force. The

Cuomo problem that plagued his stewardship in New York was how to do all this. He tried it through liberty scholarships that would guarantee a college education to every high school graduate making the necessary grades. He put massive amounts of money into the state's educational system. But he also tried to teach values. He said this of the students who were failing:

"How do we get people to make better choices? How do we educate them, give them more incentive to make good choices? Give them opportunities in life so that the baby the teenager has isn't the best thing she can do for herself; give her other avenues to dignity. Give a young person growing up surrounded by the temptation to take drugs, the clear vision of a path for her or him: you can go to school, you can graduate, you can go to college, you can graduate, you can get a good job, you can live a good life."

A very pragmatic approach to a very serious problem.

Mario Cuomo sees himself as a self-made man. In his family life and in his individual values he is a conservative. He is as far from a libertine as anyone I have ever known. He is a funny man but he is a formal man. So when he says that he is a progressive pragmatist, I suppose one could accept it. To me, he is a moral pragmatist. He does what is possible in any situation. He knows that there are things that couldn't or shouldn't be done. But he sees himself as a positive rather than negative person and believes in a "can-do" approach to government:

"There is a temptation to destroy instead of to build. It is easier to be negative than to be constructive. It is easier to show the fault in your speech than to write a good speech. It's easier to point out your failure in designing a proper house than to design a proper house. It has always been true. And you develop the habit of attack, instead of constructive criticism. My advice to all [New York City mayoral] candidates is, as one who has been through it, and who was himself too negative on occasion, my advice is give the people your simple, clear description of what you think the major problems are and your simple clear description of what you think the solutions are. Don't spend a lot of time attacking your adversaries because they will not vote for you because your adversaries are weak. They will vote for you because you are strong. And if you all wind up attacking one another, what you are liable to produce is no vote at the polls, or very few. So come forward affirmatively, and state what you believe in and what you have done and what you will do. I think that works best."

At the end of one of our radio shows I asked him how he would go about filling the last thirty seconds of the program. His reply:

"I'd say, 'Governor, one thing that we should remind everybody of on the way out of this program, and you and I have talked about it a lot, is that there are two ways to look at life: positively and negatively. It is better to look positively. It is better, instead of counting up your enemies in the morning, to count up your friends and the friends you can make. Instead of worrying about all the problems you have, worry about all the wonderful things you can do—the children you can educate, the elderly people you can take care of, the taxes you can reduce—if only you work together. Governor, I'd rather smile than frown, I'd rather be happy than sad, I think we agree on that and I think the people should, too."

His reliance on conventional and widely accepted notions of justice could occasionally come down to a personal judgement call. I disagreed with Cuomo on the Bernie Goetz case. (Goetz was the subway gunman who shot down several thugs who he said, and I believed, were trying to rob him.)

In that case, the state could not protect Goetz and I believed that the man had a right to protect himself. Cuomo worried about what would happen if everyone started blasting away in the subways and raised those questions with me. Years later, we had another twist. This time it was a black man who saved a white victim who was being robbed by two thugs. This time, when I asked Cuomo about it he said that he thought about the so-called "Good Samaritan." This time Cuomo said he thought the man had a "wonderful instinct." He went on saying that he didn't have all the facts but that "...from the general description, the idea of a person risking his own life to help someone else to do justice as he saw it on the spot, yeah, that's a good instinct. It can be overdone, it can be misapplied, of course, but it's a good instinct."

"But what about that?" I asked him. "What if the guy didn't want to do it? Two thugs were beating up somebody, knocking the hell out of him, taking the money out of his pockets. People were standing around looking. The guy (the 'Good Samaritan') gets up and says 'We're not going to have this any more. Pulls out a knife and kills one of them?'"

The governor responded by saying, "Is it necessary force under all the circumstances? Almost the same test you apply to a policeman. Difficult in the application."

He said that on the one side there was the famous case of Kitty Genovese, killed while thirty-eight people "ignored her."

"Can it (the urge to help) be overdone? Of course it can be." In other words, there will always be limits and hard decisions to be made about what can be done in a particular situation. Bernie Goetz went too far; the so-called "Good Samaritan" may not have. Progressive pragmatism.

Take his position on the legalization of drugs. In the late '80s, several top names in the country offered the advice that we had lost the war on drugs. Several "heavy hitters," including former Secretary of State George Schultz, federal judge Robert Sweet and William F. Buckley, spoke out in support of the legalization of drugs. Their line of argumentation was that we had to recognize the fact that people would get drugs if they wanted them. According to this thinking, we were only forestalling the inevitable in continuing to dump money into the prohibition of drugs. Each, in their own way, was calling for some form of legalization.

While some might describe such an approach as "pragmatic," Cuomo wasn't buying.

"This new madness that says that you ought to legalize drugs is one of the great dangers," he told me. He quoted an upstate woman who said that state monies should not be used until we could see whether drug treatment worked.

"I wonder if they would say that" he asked, "if it were their own children that you were talking about? I wonder what would happen if all the people that were talking about legalization were talking about a child in their own house? It's their fourteen year old daughter who will now be able to go to the corner and get crack because there is a sign that says, 'free heroin.' I wonder if they thought in terms of their grandchild being born to a cocaine-addicted mother? One of the three hundred and fifty thousand born addicted with no say about it at all. I wonder if they knew it was their grandchild, whether they would say, 'Yes, let's legalize.'"

Cuomo's approach to allowing dangerous privileges to the citizenry could go either way depending on how important he felt the consequences would be. One of the funniest conversations I ever had with him was not about drugs but about beer in ball parks.

AC: Governor, a couple of Democratic assemblymen, as I understand it, have come up with a plan in which certain areas, like smoking sections in restaurants, would exclude alcohol. You couldn't have alcohol or beer in those sections. Do you think that makes sense? I do.

MC: Why do you think it makes sense? Maybe I can learn something from you, Alan.

AC: Well, if I have a choice sitting next to a drunk or not, I prefer not to.

MC: Well, are you going to have a section that says no drunks allowed?

AC: Yes, no drinking allowed.

MC: Excuse me, you mean drinking and drunkenness are the same thing?

AC: No, but one certainly, Governor, leads to another.

MC: Oh, just a second. Then you are going to provide that no one who takes a sip of alcohol should be seated in a public place?

AC: In that public place. In that particular location.

MC: How about in restaurants?

AC: Wait, wait, wait, wait...

MC: Would you provide in restaurants that if you are going to drink alcohol then you are going to get rowdy, and I don't want my family to sit next to a rowdy table. So you should have a corner next to the no smoking section that says no imbibing?

AC: Actually, that is not a bad plan, Governor, as far as I am concerned. As you know, I happen to be a teetotaler.

MC: No, I didn't know that you didn't drink. And frankly, I didn't think that the evidence would have indicated it. So go ahead.

AC: But in these ball parks, we do start with a problem. The problem is that you do have, you know, some people who get drunk out of their skulls.

MC: No, excuse me. In my understanding of the ball park problem, and I am not telling you that Senator Dunn and Assemblyman Brodsky are wrong, but my understanding of the ball park problem as described by these legislators is that some people are rowdy.

AC: Yes.

MC: Well then, why not have a section that excludes rowdy people. Because you can be rowdy without drinking. Isn't that correct? Have you ever seen a rowdy child?

AC: Do you know the difference between necessary and sufficient?

MC: Did you ever see a nine year old who was rambunctious and rowdy? And has never taken a sip of Smirnoff's.

AC: Yes. Even around my house it has been known to happen.

MC: Well, why don't we have an anti-rowdy section?

AC: Because you see, Governor, we think some things lead to other things. For example, you signed a bill providing that one had to be twenty-one to buy alcoholic beverages in this state.

MC: Why don't we eliminate food on the grounds that it will produce obesity?

AC: That's not a bad idea too, especially food with sugar in it.

MC: Alright, I don't have an opinion.

AC: It sounded like you have an opinion. Why am I so fooled by this?

MC: Because the bill is dead. Why should I have an opinion on a dead bill?

AC: Because you are a leader, Governor. And leaders...

MC: I don't lead on dead bills. I lead on live bills. This bill has been withdrawn.

But if Cuomo didn't like permissiveness, including giving up on the war on drugs, he certainly had major fears about some of those who would take away constitutional rights to win that war. He put it eloquently.

"I'm afraid if things don't change, if people don't perceive a strong and effective response from government on crime—I underscore 'effective'—they will begin to demand other things. Like the erosion of some constitutional privileges.

"Why should drug dealers be entitled to the same fair trial that everybody else is? The heck with the search and seizure rule—this is war, and in a time of war, you don't worry about search and seizure. In the time of war, they broke down doors and they dragged spies out and hanged them in the public square. They always have because it's you or them. It's survival.

"And that mentality takes over. There's no telling what walls it will tear down and what protections, and so what we need now, as a federal government especially, is strength married to reason. Strength married to reason. Because the people want strength and have a right to it. They want a strong response to crime. I think they're mistaken when they think that the death penalty is a strong response. Police, courts, prisons, rehabilitation—all of that is a strong and intelligent response. Short-term and long-term. Add to all of that law enforcement, education, other avenues to dignity, value-construction or reconstruction in the society. Change things long-range, change the attitudes, the judgments, the decisions being made by people. Avoid these avoidable disasters of drugs and teenage pregnancy, all the things we are doing to ourselves now. That's strength married to reason. We had better prove that we can respond that way or the people will demand something worse."

And how *should* we protect the society and the police in particular? The answer, says Cuomo, is to make the criminal justice system more efficient.

He was talking about it years ago: "The best response to crime I can make as governor, and we've done it: better police, better courts, better jails—the whole system has to be improved from the beginning, in order to arrive at a tougher punishment at the end. You have to beef up the entire system, including making the laws more effective."

More recently, Cuomo put it this way: "I think police need the protection of a more effective criminal justice system. They need more police, more judges, more courtrooms, more prison cells, a swifter, surer, more efficient system to honor the arrests they make. They're making plenty of arrests. The problem is that people can get arrested twenty times and never get convicted. And so the most support we can give our police is to make the system more effective."

Cuomo the progressive pragmatist looked at a situation and summed up the total danger to the society. In the Goetz case it was clear to the governor that guys running around with revolvers in their pockets looking for trouble were not in the best interests of the society. In the case of the legalization of drugs, we saw a governor who believed legalization meant total capitulation to the drug craze.

Mario Cuomo, the child of immigrants, knew what prejudice felt like, and would do anything to ameliorate racial and religious tensions.

Cuomo once laid all of that out for me.

"We have been guilty of all sorts of inhumanity to one another. We have been guilty of slavery. We were born with a country committed to slavery. I would not argue that there is no anti-Semitism, that there is no anti-Black feeling, that there is no anti-Italian feeling. All these things exist. They are the product of our diversity and our insistence that people may remain different in this society.

"Our challenge must be to deal with these realities through intelligence, through patience, through education, through expression, even through simple talks like this one. Try to get people to understand better and live better."

Mario Cuomo walked a dangerous road in his insistence that the government provide a safety net for those who would otherwise do without.

Cuomo clearly recognized what prejudice and bias are all about but believed that the more insidious enemy was social class. In the '80s, for example, there was consideration given to a separate Black and Puerto Rican political party.

Cuomo told me, "I don't think it's a matter of color or race as much as it is a matter of economic condition. I think the operating distinctions are mostly those of economic class. Poor people have a great deal in common, whether they are the white people upstate who happen to be on welfare, are out of work, or white women with children without a spouse upstate, or black, or brown, downstate. It is their economic condition that affects them in uniform ways more than it is their color.

"The implications of this? It is appropriate to have a Black and Puerto Rican caucus, but you see that caucus addresses mostly problems of economic condition, not problems of color...when you look at their agenda: housing, jobs, Medicaid—they're talking about economic conditions, they're talking about helping people who need help economically. And it's because such large numbers of Blacks and Hispanics find themselves in that situation that they attempt to organize."

Cuomo saw bias and prejudice as problems that had to be treated separately, at least in the short run. He consistently sponsored programs and legislation that would stop the more insidious acts of discrimination and bias. Perhaps the centerpiece of this program was his bias-related crime bill. In its simplest form, this legislation would have added more jail time to crimes motivated by race and sexual orientation. The sexual orientation issue, principally gay bashing, was consistently opposed by the Republican majority in the State Senate who were willing to include religious, racial and ethnic bashing but not violence against gays. I worked hard to get the governor to try to tell me why some groups should receive the extra protection under the proposed legislation and why others shouldn't.

"We believe that we should make a statement as the great state of New York, that if you beat someone up because he's a Jew, if you attack somebody because he's gay, if you assault somebody because he's Black or Italian, you should be punished in a special way. And the bias-related crime bill says that. If we prove in a court that you not only committed the crime but that it was motivated by that kind of bias against a person's religion, or race, or sex, or sexual orientation, than you should be punished more severely for that."

Then there was Cuomo's pragmatic approach to medicine. For example:

AC: Governor, true or false—there's going to be a special session this year?

MC: False. There will be a resumption of the regular session.

AC: And when will that be, Governor? For those of us who have been hanging on your every word week after week we know that there has been an attempt to come to grips with [medical] malpractice. There doesn't seem to have been a decision up until now...

MC: I think generally there has been an impression of tentativeness but there has not been any tentativeness. Since July it's been clear we wanted to go one further step in dealing with malpractice, understanding that this is a developing problem and that medical malpractice is only a small part of the overall liability insurance difficulty. While we understood that there would be no total solution to medical malpractice or the overall problem, we did say, I did say, specifically in July when I signed the bill, to the doctors and the world if you will, that we'd come back in a resumed session to take another step to do more, and we have been working ever since to come up with that second step.

Obviously, Alan, when I signed the bill we didn't know what the changes were going to be. I was just confident that we had the ability to improve on what we had done in July and that if we worked hard enough we would be able to. I think we have worked hard and I think we have something that is a very definite improvement. Nothing is going to satisfy everybody, few things do. But we do have a bill that I have discussed with the Democratic leadership. I will discuss it tomorrow with the Republicans, and I think it's good. We'll await the response of the Republicans. It's certainly an improvement on the July bill, and I suspect frankly that there will be other improvements as we learn new things, and as developments occur in the months and years ahead of us. This is an evolving problem. This is a new time in our history. This is a new situation and one that is changing and evolving daily. So we need to have current responses and that means that we can't do it, and that we can't package it all nicely and neatly, snap the lid shut, and say, 'There it is, up on the shelf, now let's move on to the next problem.'

AC: For any of our listeners who might be paying attention to either of us at this stage...Governor, there is a question about what you're actually telling us. It sounds pretty general to me. What seems to be the sticking point? What particular issue?

MC: Well, there's more than one. There are many, many issues. The one basic question is how much should a doctor pay? Should you measure it by his wealth? We haven't even suggested that. Is 100,000 dollars a year too much to pay in insurance for a doctor? Well, it is if he makes 110,000 a year. What if he makes a million or two? What about the problem of getting liability insurance? Is it available? What if a company won't sell insurance above a million dollars?

Should a doctor who has worked hard all of his or her life have to risk their possessions because they can't get insurance? If you asked the hospitals to get involved, who pays the hospitals? All the taxpayers, by reimbursing the hospitals? I could go on and on. Isn't the problem of malpractice a problem because some doctors make mistakes and hurt people, or kill people? The answer to that is 'yes.'

And so, how do you reduce the overall level of incompetence? How do you discipline? Will discipline do it? What about capping the rewards? Doctors have said we should limit the awards to two hundred fifty thousand dollars.

Let's assume that a doctor has butchered some person—has been negligent or grossly so—leaving that person who was fifteen and beautiful, blind for a lifetime. Would you say that two hundred fifty thousand dollars would take care of that? Seventy years of darkness. Would you say, 'Well we didn't want the doctors to pay too much, two hundred fifty thousand is the cap, that's that.' 'You lose, doctors win.' And so on and so forth. So Alan, it's very, very difficult and easy to be demagogic on either side, frankly.

AC: California's governor, not to interrupt you, Governor, but California just—the courts just—upheld the constitutionality of a two hundred cap in that state. A) How can California have it and we don't? B) Does it make sense?

MC: California doesn't have the other things that we have. And California is willing to say to that blind child, "SORRY, we took care of the doctors." We're not. We think we found other ways to do it and better ways to do it. I don't like California's brand of justice here. That it is constitutional is irrelevant. It's constitutional to be unfair, many, many times.

Remember for a long time it was constitutional to enslave people. So, the Constitution is the measure at a moment in time of what is allowable, and it is not the measure of what a society should say about what is right and what is just. Because it is constitutional does not mean it is acceptable.

From the day he became governor, Mario Cuomo fought to preserve the quality of air and the general environment. But he was able to prioritize his values when it came to that important fight. Cuomo saw the protection of the environment precisely the way he saw the protection of his body.

"I like to exercise because I feel I have an obligation to take care of this body, such as it is, because it was on loan to me. You are supposed to keep it in the best shape as you can. The way you are supposed to care for the environment. I try to do that. I don't do that enough. I think the American people should arouse themselves, too. It is easy to fall into bad habits. We are falling into bad habits personally, we are falling into bad habits nationally. While we slouch on couches and watch television, we have let our economy go flabby, our educational system go second-rate, our roads and bridges deteriorate, our environment become polluted. We are couch potatoes in the largest and most dangerous sense of the word."

But the Cuomo pragmatism has an application to his approach to the environment. Here, too, it is a matter of balance. In order to achieve something good for the environment you also have to put limits on how far you go. During one interview, I told him of an argument I was having with an environmentalist friend of mine. The fight was over open spaces.

"Some of these very people who have a certain amount of what I could call 'noblesse oblige,'" I told him, "are saying 'buy it' [forever wild land] but then 'don't let anybody on it.' In other words, don't make it accessible to the public. I don't know why you have hundreds of thousands of acres and don't let people use them. I wonder how you feel about that."

He answered, "Generally, there probably are areas that have to be preserved against traffic for particular ecological reasons. But the point of preserving the environment is to make it available and useful to all people for all time."

Cuomo was careful to say that there were different ways to use open spaces. "Some environments are to clean the air. Trees do that for you, they gobble up the bad things in the atmosphere and put out the good."

But the overriding concern, said Cuomo, is "sharing."

"We wish to share God's gifts to us or nature's gifts if you prefer, for generations to come." Cuomo was a sensible environmentalist.

Cuomo once reflected on a major world conference on global warming. The conference, said the governor, was important because it made two important points.

"It was an important coming together to say two things: One, this is a real problem, this question of the greenhouse effect and global warming, it's not make-believe. And two, we'd better do something about it. We have an obligation to this world and to the life in it to preserve it, and this is a serious enough concern for politicians to get together right now to start making plans."

The word "pragmatist" is to Cuomo clearly a double-edged sword. I have seen him use it in a way that could mean a person who knew how to compromise and I have seen him use the word to signify an opportunist.

There was, for instance, that time we were talking about George Bush. In that conversation, a tongue-in-cheek Cuomo fixed the pragmatic label squarely on Bush. But now the word "pragmatic" was hardly praise but a word that signified a member of the world's oldest profession.

In this particular discussion, held in the first year of the Bush administration, Cuomo began to speak about the differences between Bush the president and Bush the candidate.

"There is more pragmatism than principle in politics generally," said the gov speaking of Bush's performance to date. "They say what they have to say. President Bush is now saying that the federal government has an obligation to deal with clean air in the environment. He did not say it for eight years as vice president. President Bush is now saying that government has an obligation to help out with day care. He didn't say it for eight years as vice president when President Reagan was contradicting it. And President Bush is now convening all the governors for a summit on education and [has] said that more resources have to be spent."

Another time in 1989 before Bush's inauguration, I asked the governor to predict Bush's success. Once again he labeled Bush as a pragmatist. This time, Cuomo gave us a little insight into what *he* would had have done if he were wearing Bush's shoes.

He predicted that Bush "...would start very strongly and very well with the new and conciliatory attitude that is the kind of thing that we have been pushing in the state of New York for a long time." Cuomo the Democrat then went on to specifically mention the names of "Roosevelt, Dewey, I blush to put myself in the same company." He said, "We all have the same approach to politics, a combination of social progressivism and fiscal conservatism, the words used by Roosevelt when he was governor."

Cuomo said that arch-Republican "Tom Dewey said, 'a heart and a head.' I say 'progress and pragmatism.' It's altogether the New York idea." Cuomo predicted that "it's the kind of thing that Bush appears to be striving for. He will remove himself from the radical positions of the campaign and he will content the conservatives by saying that 'I have Sununu in the staff and Quayle as the vice president. What else do you want?'" Events, from treatment of Gorbachev to the bail out of the savings and loan associations, bore all of that out.

Before Bush was inaugurated, Cuomo was flat out predicting that "all the policies will be moderate. Sununu will be radical-conservative. Quayle will be conservative. The policies will be moderate. Even if he [Bush] proposes radical-conservative policies they won't go anywhere because the congress will be moderate. So you can look forward to a moderate presidency, unlike the Reagan years."

Cuomo predicted that Bush's brand of moderation would even extend to his appointments to the United States Supreme Court. Even here Cuomo contrasts the Bush approach to the Reagan conservatism. "I hope that what appears to be President Bush's move to be conciliatory, moderate and pragmatic produces a willingness to select judges for their competence and their integrity instead of their ideology."

Just as we were speaking, the phone in Cuomo's office rang and he quipped, "I think that is President-elect Bush calling to say that he likes this direction. It's the Washington hot line but I won't answer it 'til 1992." As always, Cuomo took every opportunity to imply that he would run against Bush. No matter how many times he said that the press wouldn't leave him alone about the presidency, little remarks like that one that kept the scribes coming back for more.

But even if Bush was pragmatic, Cuomo made it clear that Bush's brand of pragmatism was unacceptable. In this particular conversation he said that the Republican approach was that "...you make money by cutting taxes and you cut taxes and it produces wealth. It didn't work. It's the poor people who took the brunt of all of the social programs: women who needed day care, the people who needed job training and the illiterates who needed education, hungry people who needed nutrition.

"And to them for eight years what you [Reagan] said was, "Oh, no. What they needed is a little incentive. Don't give them too much. So the poor people needed incentive, the rich people needed tax cuts. That was the philosophy for the last eight years. You give the poor incentives by giving them no benefits that will make them run out and work. You make the rich people invest by giving them more benefits that will make them even more benefits."

When it came to prescribing ethical standards in office, Cuomo had his limits. He recognized that politicians had to be free to make deals, that they had constituencies which needed to be satisfied. And when someone, especially when that someone was me, got too sanctimonious about political behavior he was always ready to argue the point.

Take the case of court reform in New York. The courts had been a mess for years and needed serious streamlining. But the pols, particularly those in the Legislature, always resisted because some of their greatest patronage and sources of power came from the courts.

It shouldn't be surprising, then, that one of Cuomo's biggest fights was over court reform. He knew that along with the streamlining would come more control for the governor and less for the hack politicians who had been making their homes in county court houses for years.

According to Cuomo, the Republicans in the Senate refused to go along with the desperately needed court reform deal, unless they got to name the new judges on Long Island. The governor told me that he had "...been pushing the proposition for a long time." We discussed the subject several times but once I suggested to him that the whole thing had fallen to a bunch of politicians with "grubby political concerns." I figured that Cuomo would use my remarks as a point of departure for his own with the legislative politicians who had been refusing to work with him on court reform.

This time Cuomo was even more brilliant than ever. Not only were the politicians chastised but I came in for some criticism as well. Like the legendary Plunkett of Tammany Hall ("I seen my opportunities and I took them"), Cuomo seized on the opportunity to let the others know that he was watching them, all the while giving it to me for having gone too far in insulting the honorable political pastime, thereby having it both ways.

"You merge courts so that instead of having different types of courts you have courts that are streamlined." Those opposed to his way of thinking, he suggested, were concerned with their own political turf. But he said for me to use the term "grubby political concerns," was unacceptable. If I wanted to talk about "grubby political things," said the governor, "I should extend my political sights all the way to Washington."

That line of argumentation from the governor suggested that other wrongs were far worse, an old variation of two wrongs somehow make a right. "What's the difference between that and politics at the very highest level? People are fighting for patronage all the time. They are fighting for their people to be in and other people to be out."

The argument became a teaching lesson on conventional politics. From grubbiness we were taken on a tour of the system as it really works. He started with those who voted on the basis of party, right or wrong.

"I understand that there are lot of people who vote that way. 'I vote Republican no matter what.' 'I vote Democratic no matter what.'"

The governor said that "you can go upstate and find places where the Republican is almost a sure thing to beat the Democratic candidate if neither is known, because the people will simply vote the party. The same will happen in downstate areas in reverse. And that kind of thing happens all over the country. Is that good or bad? You can argue forever but it is a fact of life.

"I don't necessarily approve of it. I would like to live in my own Utopia. I would like things to be perfect. As a matter of fact this does not get written about. I have not seen a single piece on it. We have spent perhaps ten years pushing for a new kind of politics. I wrote a speech ten years ago that called for a new family kind of politics with a deemphasis on party labels, that invented a new label, 'progressive pragmatism,' just to make the point that there were truths that go high above the traditional perception of the ideological differences between Democrats and the Republicans. You have seen in these past ten years the development of a whole new politics. Call it various things. I call it the 'New York idea,' in one State of the State we call it 'progressive pragmatism.'"

To make his point, the governor took pains, as he often did, to demonstrate that labels don't work. The Republicans, he said, are "the big spenders. They can deny it and send out literature that denies it but they are the ones who are asking to spend. It's the Democrats who are asking to spend less. It is the Democrats who seek to deregulate the financial industry. I want insurance companies to be able to compete with banks and vice versa. I want all the financial institutions, banks and insurance companies, to have free enterprise. It's the Republicans who are stopping us, who are saying 'No, you have to protect the insurance companies.' Why?! Even the politics here is in reverse. In many, many, ways we are fighting very hard to keep spending down in order to avoid taxes. We are insisting, the Democrats are, on balancing the budget and avoiding deficits. The Republicans spent us into deficits since 1982 and from '59 to '74, so the political labels don't mean as much here as they do somewhere else."

In a recent program, the governor went even farther to suggest that he was never a party man. He pointed out that his own party had rejected him for years before he challenged them and won political office.

Even earlier, following the same theme, Cuomo told me, "The fact that you prefer one side to another does not mean that you have to condemn one side. That is an important lesson. I have said very good things about President Reagan and I have disagreed with him. Good things about President Bush, not disagreeing with him as much, yet, but I may before his four years are over. Richard Nixon wrote me nice letters about the things I was doing and I said some kind things about him. Why not? Why is it that because your ideological position may be different that you get to condemn the other person to be bad or evil."

Concluded Cuomo, "I take my side but I'll try to make a contribution to civility in campaigning." Indeed, even in losing to George Pataki, sponsored by Al D'Amato, I never saw Cuomo take a personal cheap shot.

Over the years, I have often asked the governor to comment on someone whom the legal system has exonerated or found guilty. Each time, he has said the law isn't perfect but it is the best legal system in the world. When it was Leona Helmsley's turn, when she was found guilty of massive tax evasion, I asked him about it. I was concerned, I told him, that the law was making an example of an unpopular woman for two reasons: 1) to get others to pay their taxes and 2) to make a scapegoat of her in order to make the judiciary more popular.

To that he replied, "Those are natural concerns about a system run by human beings, which is our democracy. And of course, there are human failings. There is liable to be jealousy and bias and shortsightedness. But over all I believe that our judicial system certainly must be the best ever constructed. It is not perfect, it makes mistakes. But as Churchill, or somebody, said about democracy, I can't imagine a better way to do it than the way that we're doing it."

But then he went on, "I think what the Helmsley conviction shows, I'm not going to comment on the sentence or whether or not she was guilty—how would you know unless you were in the courtroom and read all the evidence and heard and saw all the witnesses?—what this proves is that the law is the law and that they will bring the law down on the head of a president and that they will bring the law down on the head of a governor, a politician, a wealthy person just the way it comes down on the head of poor, middle class or struggling people every single day. That is the one continuous, confirming cohesive value we have in this society. Think of it."

The cardinal principle, said Cuomo, is that the Constitution demands that we "apply the rules evenly to everybody."

Sometimes the governor and I disagreed because when a law or a rule is promulgated, one group has to be the loser in order to protect another, often a minority group. For example, there is the case of sexually transmissible diseases.

In New York State there is a public health law that says that when a disease is named "sexually transmissible," the sexual partners of the person having the disease must be informed. This is called contact tracing. The reasoning behind this procedure is that those who have possibly contracted the disease need to know so that they may get treatment and so that they will not spread the disease to others.

In the case of AIDS, the governor's health commissioner at the time, David Axelrod, had not designated AIDS a sexually transmissible disease because both he and the governor believed that by taking that step, they would drive those who had the disease underground rather than forward to get tested voluntarily.

The governor explained it this way to me when I asked him whether the President's Commission on AIDS was right in suggesting to Bush that he stop the practice of stating on passports that the bearer had AIDS.

The issue, said Cuomo was "a sensitive one. We deal with it in our state all the time. Ought you to disclose to people who might be dealing with people who have AIDS, if they have AIDS. We have come down mostly on the side of privacy. We have a law now that says that a doctor who is treating someone who has AIDS and who, having given the person an opportunity to tell others with whom they may be having relationships that could spread the disease, having given them an opportunity to tell all those others and having been convinced that the person with AIDS was not going to tell the others, then the doctor may do it. That's about as far as we've gone in allowing disclosure. I'm satisfied with the policy as it is now."

Summing it all up, when I asked him where he came down on the AIDS issue, he said, "Mostly for privacy on the grounds that to widely disseminate the fact that the person is a carrier, or whatever you wish to call that person, would only make it more difficult to deal with the problem. It would impose a great burden on the individual which is something that should concern us. It also makes it less likely that individuals will come forward and ask for treatment which is something that we want them to do. So it is a counter productive step to take."

Another time, I read in the press that a group of doctors at Montifiore Hospital in the Bronx had said that they were not about to perform heart operations on those addicts with the AIDS virus in their blood. I asked the governor what he made of that situation. The state was not going to allow that to happen, said Cuomo.

This was one where the governor was not pussyfooting around. "Doctors have legal obligations and have ethical obligations to perform operations and to give care. Doctor Axelrod and the Board of Regents are very mindful of these requirements which they have the right to enforce and which they will enforce. Any doctor who refuses to live up to his obligation should be penalized."

Cuomo said that there "is a general obligation to give treatment even if it is inconvenient or distasteful to you. You can't pick and choose the patients that you want to take care of and mark all the others with a crimson letter and leave open the possibility that no doctor would ever operate on them. That's the same as sentencing that person to death."

Said Cuomo, putting a face on the idea so that people could best understand it, "That means that an AIDS patient with a heart attack would be sentenced to death if he or she needed an operation. That obviously doesn't make sense."

Another example of the man's pragmatism is seen as he described the nation's airline crisis. My question was prompted by a number of airline crashes. I asked him whether deregulation of the airlines was to blame. His answer: "Well, I don't know enough to know whether it has anything to do with regulation or deregulation. I don't think it's that.

"I think that the stock is getting older and I heard somebody this morning, or early this week, saying on TV that the stock is twenty, twenty-two, twenty-three years old and people are not investing in new machines. I guess, trying to adjust to the new regulations, they had to reduce fares and scramble around. With the new competition, people are unwilling or unable to invest the capital necessary to buy new equipment. In the end, the market, I guess, in one way or the other, will take care of this. People will get so frightened that they will start complaining. They will demand new aircraft and some airlines will start producing new and safer aircraft."

Cuomo said that the airlines that respond to people's demands will "get all the business. Eventually the government will respond with stringent regulations." Cuomo said that the whole thing is part of "the eternal cycle."

One day I asked him about a newspaper report that he would help the Democrats take control of the state Senate in the 1990 elections. For the first time it appeared to me that the Democrats meant business about taking the upper house.

There were those who believed that Cuomo had never wanted to win control of the Senate, which always served the purpose of putting the brakes on Democratic demands for more and more services. Did Cuomo really believe that it could be done and was he willing to risk the political fallout from a hostile Republican Senate that would not be pleased to hear of Cuomo's position on stripping them of their power?

But since Cuomo had not really committed himself to such an ambitious project in past elections I wanted to know just how far he would go. I wanted to know whether he would personally lay hands on Democratic Assemblymen and convince them to give up their majority seats, with perks such as chairmanships and extra stipends, to run for the Senate where they might well end up in the minority with much less power.

The governor responded that things didn't work that way. He said that he didn't own the Democratic party and his staff. "I don't possess them. I don't own them. I don't control them." He rejected "...this notion that the governor is there and he snaps his fingers and people adopt his opinion, follow him slavishly. Life is not like that, Alan. I am not going to prod anybody to be a candidate for any office. It does not work. It was done to me once [his ill fated run for mayor of New York] and I became a terrible candidate and

I am not going to do it to anybody else. If you want to be a candidate, fine, I will support you if you are good. I am not going to back a person who is reluctant."

Cuomo said that when a candidate doesn't want to run, when his family thinks "he or she can't win," he isn't going to say "do it for the Gipper." He said that is "not the way to do it if you want to be in public office."

People should serve because they want to serve, otherwise the price seems to be too high for the people who asked them to run, said the governor. People should run who think that such service is "...an immense privilege—that being in public service is all that you want to do at this point in your life. You are willing to work hard, take abuse, not get paid a whole lot. You may not be fully appreciated, you still want to do it you are doing it from your heart. Your family is with you, you know the odds along the way but you are willing to take the chance."

When those conditions are met, said Cuomo, he'll talk to a prospective candidate. "I am not going to talk someone who is reluctant, into being a candidate. That is not useful. The person has to begin by wanting it badly."

Progressive pragmatism even played a part in the way Cuomo approached his political battles. Once when I was interviewing Cuomo during his Cinderella, come from behind, primary fight with Ed Koch in 1982, I told him that people were saying that he, Cuomo, had no record. He told me that was not necessarily such a bad thing, because if people didn't know your record they would project their own values onto your candidacy. He told me on a number of occasions of the people who would walk up to him in the early days of his political life as governor, slap him on the shoulder and say "'Atta boy, Mario, I like your position on the death penalty—fry the bastards." Cuomo, of course, opposes the death penalty.

Mario Cuomo's enemies went out of their way to portray him in a variety of negative ways. First, they said that he wouldn't deal. That he was too professorial, that he talked down to people. They said that he wouldn't know how to negotiate the laws and that he was a quintessential outsider, a law professor who couldn't make the system work.

Then when he was accepted and elected by the voters, these same characters, many of them his disappointed rivals in the Legislature, began to spread the word that Cuomo had no program, no set of defined ethics and that he offered no leadership. They said that he behaved like an Italian Don, that he was mean and vindictive, that he never forgot and held grudges forever. Then, when Cuomo outclassed the Legislature at every turn and was elected by historical margins, came what Cuomo has referred to as the "Dumb Blond Syndrome." So confounded were the Cuomo enemies by his brilliant style and public appeal that they began to spread the word, working assiduously through the members of the capitol press corps, to make the point that Cuomo was all style and no substance.

Cuomo compared this to the erroneous stereotyping that all attractive blonds were dumb. In other words, his opponents were saying of him that because he spoke so well, he was all flash and no substance. If Cuomo is nothing else, he is a child of the law and trained in argumentation. To Mario Cuomo debate is mother's milk. If you can't speak well you can't lead.

Pragmatism involves compromise. He is not only a superb speaker but also a superb negotiator. Week after week as I spoke to him on the show I heard him listen, anticipate what was coming next and give way when he had to. But he challenged constantly.

I learned the hard way, in the context of the show, that those he respected the most were those who would argue with him and let him work his mind at highest capacity. Cuomo's constant problem was that he was like a great tennis player whose single greatest problem is that he can't test himself against a worthy opponent and he fears his skills are slipping away. In a sense, the pleasure and the learning experience were all mine. Believe me, I was the one who had the advantage of playing with someone a lot better than I was. On the other hand, Cuomo's insistence on having me come out and fight when I had a position different from his proved painful at times.

All of this points up Cuomo's character, which is defined by nothing so much as where he was educated and trained among the Vincentians, a Roman Catholic order of educators whom Cuomo himself compares to the Jesuits. To understand Cuomo, one has to look to the family which he adored and where he was a prince and to the Catholic schools where Christ provided the model. Cuomo followed Christ, who believed that everyone is saveable. That those who were not in his church could be brought there by patience, love and understanding. That if the right approach was taken, no one could escape that love and logic.

That's why the governor spent the time and effort he did with negative reporters. But there is still another side to all of this. Cuomo went to school in an order that taught that all were saveable and that persistence and logic often paid off, but Cuomo also saw an order which emphasized the rules for those who were within the church. In other words, Cuomo treated those who worked for him as disciples. His followers were expected to behave as if they were extensions of Cuomo. From the point of view of the public administration, that in itself is not a bad thing. After all, most governors and presidents fail because they cannot get others to do as they would like. To know Mario Cuomo is to know that his life is dedicated to hard work. His capacity for work is legendary and he expects that those who work for him will work hard and follow his lead.

Those who know him best, like the late Assemblyman Saul Weprin, the powerful chairman of the Assembly Judiciary Committee, told me that Cuomo never sleeps. I know that he is constantly working, working the phones, always available. He has tremendous confidence in his own ability. On occasion he recruited first rate talent such as Timothy Russert, his first major media advisor who subsequently went on to become a vice president at NBC

News. Then there were men like the brilliant Thomas Jorling, once his environmental affairs commissioner and one of the best in the nation.

Cuomo's approach to public administration was quite pragmatic. Having those in harness who would do what he said was more important than having an appointee who might have had brilliance but fell outside his individual span of control. The negative side of all of this is that the governor appointed some who would follow rather than contest with him when they thought he was wrong.

I have called him "Br'er Rabbit" and the "Tar Baby," both great characters from *Tales of the South*. Both of these characters confounded and ultimately outsmarted their enemies. Br'er Rabbit did it by begging his enemies *not* to throw him into the briar patch (which, of course, they did) and the Tar Baby kept having his enemies punch him until they were tangled with him and couldn't get away.

Cuomo did it again and again to his political and philosophical adversaries.

At one point we were discussing the coming presidential elections and I asked him to respond to names that I would put forward. The idea was for him to tell me which one he'd like to see as the Republican candidate.

AC: George Bush.

MC: My favorite ticket for the Republicans. The one I'd like to see the Democrats run against. Bush and Bush.

AC: Bush on both tickets because you think he's weakest?

MC: I think he's a nice man and I know him, but I don't think he's going to be a strong presidential candidate.

AC: How do we know you're not playing Br'er Rabbit in this case?

MC: You don't.

AC: What would A.J. Parkinson have said about this conversation?

MC: A.J. Parkinson wouldn't have even listened to this conversation. He would have been busy writing or listening to
music or watching a baseball game or doing something
worthwhile.

Nowhere in his memorable twelve-year term was Cuomo better
than when it came to faking out his political adversaries. Each time
he ran, the Republicans did their best to find a candidate to take
him on. In 1986 it was Andrew O'Rourke, the county executive
of Westchester county. In that election, Cuomo the pragmatist
wouldn't debate O'Rourke, reportedly because the other team had
slandered Cuomo saying that he had "made his bones, (an old
Mafia term) in Queens politics. Personally, I have always believed
that Cuomo was so far out in front and his adversary was so
unknown that it didn't make any sense to give the guy free publicity. In that election a frustrated O'Rourke called up Cuomo at
a radio station talk show and became so caught up in Cuomo's
dialectic that he made the mistake of saying "God dammit, Mario,"
to the governor. Of course, the governor turned the discourse into
a lecture on profanity.

Cuomo, the progressive pragmatist, often said that as long as
the opposition raised money, he would have to do the same thing.
When I read him a long list of all those candidates who said that
they would not run against him, he said that was of no import. "This
is not significant. The Republicans will have a very strong candidate eventually. They will have a lot of money. And that's all you
need. Let's be honest. You can take a person who has never run
before and with thirteen million dollars you can nearly make him
governor. That's what happened in 1982." Pointing to the near win
of Lew Lehrman, Cuomo said that "the truth is that nobody knew
him and he hadn't served in government....With his natural personal
strengths and thirteen million dollars Lehrman nearly became governor." Cuomo said that "Republicans were telling him that they
were going to raise "fifteen, twenty, twenty-five million dollars."

Then, the Cuomo wit took over as he announced that "now the president [Bush] comes and he raises in one visit, what, a million and a half dollars." Then in a highly unlikely but hilarious projection the governor asks, "Well if the president comes and he raises in one visit, what, a million and a half dollars? Well, if the President comes twenty times, twenty times a million and a half is thirty million dollars." Then the governor said that his friend has called him up to tell him, "What do you think of the idea that the vice president is going to come to play golf with people for twenty thousand dollars a round."

So I asked him if he played golf.

"No, I don't play golf. I used to caddy for people, for Republicans who play golf. No, I don't play golf. And I tell you, if I did play golf I'm not sure that I have a lot of friends who would be willing to give me twenty thousand dollars for eighteen holes."

Then Cuomo, the man who raises a lot of money (reportedly two million dollars at one dinner) said, "They can raise, as they said they would, a million and a half dollars for one golf game with the vice president. They'll get fifty people, fifty-seven people, or sixty people to play golf with him for twenty thousand dollars a pop, or whatever it is. That's an awful lot of money. And if I were the candidate there is no way I could compete with that. I am thinking myself of having a one-on-one basketball tournament for five dollars a pop and that'll be a lot of fun. But I don't think I'm going to get anyone to play basketball for twenty thousand dollars a game."

Then there's the fight over taxes in New York state. It's gone on for years. Cuomo almost always took the same approach. He marshalled his facts and then made his political opponents, the Republicans, eat them. He carefully pointed out that the true tax and spenders in New York State were not the Democrats but the Republicans, the party of Nelson Rockefeller, who almost put the state in the poor house.

In the late '80s, Cuomo did what a great running back would do. He reversed the field on the Republicans once again. The state was facing the fourth year of a tax cut program that had been passed in the hey day of Reaganomics when tax cutting was rampant in America. It was unstoppable. Even the Assembly Democrats subscribed to the theory that the way to prime the economic pump was to remain competitive with other states by passing a comprehensive tax cut. Cuomo, recognizing a giant political steam roller when he saw it, went along. In private negotiations with the legislative leaders, he tried to keep the amount of the tax cut lower but when he passed it he kept referring to it as "my tax cut."

But by 1989 the situation was desperate. His governorship had already taken its lumps when it faced a two and a half billion dollar budget shortfall. Cuomo saw it happening again in 1990. He saw Michael Dukakis disgraced in nearby Massachusetts because of his inability to provide services while a leaderless Legislature stood by in fright. Rather than face that prospect, Cuomo launched an initiative to drop the third stage of the tax cut. Some thought it couldn't work but Cuomo the pragmatist, Cuomo the teacher, thought he could.

His strategy was pin the tail on the Republican elephant. They had raised the taxes, and now they were committing the state to a diminution of services while they hypocritically committed the state to more and more programs. They wouldn't dismiss the fourth stage of the tax cut; they wouldn't stop spending so they had to be held up to ridicule and that's exactly what Cuomo did. Once again, he tread where others, like Dukakis, had feared or were unable to go.

Said the governor, "One point six billion dollars [in tax cuts] would go to the people who would make the most money." Cuomo was saying, "Don't look at me. It's up to them, because I can't change it." Cuomo argued that "the Democrats want to change it but they can't without the Republicans. This is a stool that will not stand on two legs. Only the Republicans can change the situation. If they don't they are denying people 1.6 billion dollars of budget money. You know what that would be for? Schools, on

Long Island, constantly saying that they need more money. The local governments who are constantly saying, and the Republicans remember, spent more money than I did last year, and were in the vanguard of demanding more money for the local governments."

On a roll, Cuomo spelled it out: "Money for roads and bridges will be denied. Money for AIDS will be denied. And so the Republicans have this judgment to make. Do we want to take this money for the people who are doing best and then say to the people of this state, 'Sorry, we're short again, we can't help you with the State University, we can't help you with the City University, we can't help you at the county level.'"

The governor yelled it out. The Republicans had actually raised his budget. "The Republicans raised taxes two hundred million dollars more than I asked. I asked for eight hundred million dollars. The Republicans raised one billion dollars in taxes. Will they do it again?

"So let me sum it up for you," said Cuomo. "This decision is for the Republicans. If they insist on keeping the tax cut, and it's entirely up to them, all they have to do is nothing, then they are denying their people 1.6 billion dollars." He went on, when someone raises his hand at a meeting "and that person happens to be a Republican, I will say to them, 'You gave it away. You had it but you didn't want to spend it on schools. You cannot have it both ways.'" He continued: "This is not fantasy land, this is the real world where you have to give to get, where there is no free lunch. Now you want to play your political games and say 'we're the people who believe in tax cuts.' Oh really, you Republicans are the people who gave us the biggest tax cuts in the history of the state." So having made this Freudian slip, saying tax cuts instead of increases, Cuomo did what any good teacher would. He attempted to erase the memory of the words by going back over them with a verbal eraser, not once but three times: "I'm sorry, biggest tax increases, biggest tax increases, biggest tax increases, 1959 to 1974 when you owned both houses and the governor's mansion."

Having established the Rockefeller legacy, Cuomo jumped up to say that "we the Democrats, Carey and then Cuomo, gave you the biggest tax cuts in history." Cuomo, really on a roll, pointed out still again that the Republicans were the big spenders. "I only asked for eight hundred million and you gave me one billion, now all of a sudden you are born again? Now all of a sudden you want to make tax cuts your issue? Really? Have you forgotten the Rockefeller years?"

And Cuomo turned the tables on his opponents.

"It's going to be an interesting question for the Republicans, but let's make it clear. It's for the Republicans, it's not for me. I'm flattered that the Republicans would say that I have the power to change things. I don't. I wish I did, but I don't. The Republicans are the ones with the power. It is the Republican decision. They will be tested by it. They will be measured by it and I can't wait to see how they decide it."

All I can say is, no wonder the man lasted three terms. Now *that's* progressive pragmatism.

A.J. Parkinson would have been proud, had he ever lived.

RELIGION

I believe that there is religion in everything that Mario Cuomo does. It is not only the religion of a Holy Church, it is a religion of the soul; a commitment to a greater spirit. That spirit, according to Cuomo, resides in each of us and, properly channelled, allows each of us to heal ourselves and make ourselves complete. Put simply, Mario Cuomo believes that most of us need religion. Where religion acts as a negative, he criticizes it, including his own Church. Where it is a positive, he extols it.

"When you presume to talk about religion, you don't presume you're good. God forbid. I think most of us feel we need religion because we think we are not good. I think from my own knowledge of it, my limited knowledge of it, from what I read, and listening to people who are older and wiser than I, or just wiser than I, most religions are affirmations. They are affirmations of a deity, our connection with the deity, and the goodness that can come out of that relationship. Most religions do not start with the assumption that there is a power that wishes to hurt us all, and that hurt is inevitable, so the whole world is negative. That is not religion, as it seems to me. Most of the time that is a denial, a rejection of religion. In religions, certainly the ones that we are accustomed to in this country—in Judaism, for example, there is the principle of Tsedakah, one of the fundamental principles of Judaism, the obligation you have to love one another. You find your own best good and the good of the whole community. In Christianity, an extension of Judaism, it says 'Turn the other cheek.' "They sum up the whole law. The founder of the religion sums up the whole law with one answer to one question by a bunch of lawyers who ask, 'What is the whole law?' Here is that answer: 'Love one another the way you love yourself for the love of me.' "'Me' is God, the deity, the beginning and the end, something larger than ourselves. So commit yourself to something larger than yourself, and express it by being good to everybody around you. Yes, you have to defend yourself when they attack you and you have to have justice as well as mercy. That is the complexity of it. The essence of it is, love one another. That is Judaism, Christianity. That is all the forms of Christianity. That is the Hindu religion, Buddhism, Muslims, everybody that I am aware of, in modern religions believes in love, and affirmation."

Teilhard D'Jardin, the Catholic monk who means so much to Cuomo, is a constant source of reference. Once before our show he quoted his theological superstar. "Teilhard says, 'First you start by loving yourself, then loving the person next to you, then loving the whole world around you, even the part that you can't reach. You start by loving yourself.'" That is a theme that we hear again and again from Mario Cuomo.

Cuomo believes in religion. But to him, religion is a great deal more than men in clerical garb telling him what to do. Many of them have tried it and have been pretty unhappy by the time the intellectual and theological smoke cleared. To Cuomo, the only way to make sense out of the world is to recognize a force greater than the human force. That means acceptance of things as a matter of faith.

That belief and/or faith means that you have to go further than what here-and-now evidence would permit. One time we were talking about my dubiousness about some portion of the state budget and I said that I was a Doubting Thomas.

That reference seemed to interest him a lot and he picked right up on the subject with characteristic humor and the concern of true teacher who was interested in sharing something about his religion. It also gave him a chance, as he often does, to speak of his love for his religion.

"Interesting reference you make, Doubting Thomas," he said. "That's a Christian reference."

Not wanting to look like an ignoramus, I agreed with him. "That's right. I believe in borrowing generously from something good."

But my teacher was not about to let me get away with this deception:

"Do you know what the reference is to?" he asked.

"Uh, no," I replied, knowing that the game was up.

"Well, then how do you know it's Christian?" he challenged.

"You said so," I responded.

"How do you know it isn't Thomas from Thomas's English Muffins?" he demanded.

So I tried to recall the little I knew about Catholicism and continued the bluff. "It's from St. Thomas Aquinas, right?" I responded, hope against hope.

"Nope," said he.

"Oh well," I said, throwing in my cards, "that was a bad guess. Go ahead."

Now generous in victory, he said, "Thomas the Apostle."

And I continued, "Thomas the Apostle, who said..."

"I will not believe that he is back from the dead," recounted the governor, "until I put my fingers into his wounds."

The governor told me that the story of Thomas was in the preceding week's readings at church.

"Who so dubbed him 'doubting'?" I asked.

"The ages," he responded. "Because he was one of the Apostles, and he was told by some of the other Apostles that Christ had reappeared after his death, and he said, 'I will not believe it, until I put my finger in his wounds.' And as the gospel has it, St. John wrote this particular gospel, the Lord reappears to Thomas and Thomas says, 'Now I believe,' and the Lord says, 'Well you believe because you put your fingers in the wound, blessed are they who did not see and still believed.'"

Then, said Cuomo, bringing it all home, "It's the way the Christians make the point that the real blessing in our religion is to believe as a matter of faith without being able to prove it by your senses or even by a compelling logic. That's the great challenge of Christian believers, to be able to accept, by faith, which is an acceptance of this truth not contradicted by reason but not proven by reason."

Cuomo's view of God is that He or, as he has put it more than once, She is everywhere. The spirit of God, according to Cuomo, is a positive and liberating one. Cuomo finds that spirit in everything he sees or does.

Just listen to a little talk I had with him when we got onto a simple question about what motion pictures he had seen lately.

MC: I'll tell you what I saw this weekend, *Benji*. I love *Benji*, the Disney movie. I loved it. I admired the photography. The animal, Benji the dog, is a magnificent creature. There's something behind the eyes, there's something in the face, it's as though you can see Benji smiling, sometimes, and frowning. A magnificent animal and a wonderful way to celebrate creation. To see that animal in his setting, and to see how beautiful life is. I enjoyed Benji. He's not a cartoon, he's reality and I like that kind of reality.

I asked him if Benji reminded him of his own beloved dog.

AC: Does he remind you of Ginger?

MC: Yes, Ginger is a wonderful creature too. Also an expression of God's work, the universe, alive and breathing, therefore important and beautiful.

God is everywhere according to Mario Cuomo. It took me a long time to believe that, but after a while I got it.

Once on a Thanksgiving, I asked him what he was thankful for.

"If there is an eternal scorekeeper in the sky I am afraid to go and account right now because I am so far ahead in the gifts I have received compared to the ones I have given out."

Cuomo's thanks to a good, loving God tells a lot about the way Mario Cuomo sees religion. Avenging Gods are for others. Cuomo sees God as something quite beautiful.

Part of that beauty for Cuomo is to see the potential for humans to rehabilitate themselves each day, to start over. In order to do that, each person, using God and religion as a frame of reference, has to study his or her own imperfections.

MC: Does imperfection hurt? Well, of course imperfection hurts but that's part of the great scheme. That's part of life. That's part of Easter. Easter is a renewal. You start again. Every moment is another Easter, every moment is a chance for another renewal, another door opening on a new future, another daybreak, every moment.

Cuomo also sees religion as a positive part of his politics. He will not allow it to become divisive. This does not mean that his political views have been shaped exclusively by the teachings of the Church.

When John F. Kennedy was running for president, his Catholicism was divisive and he tried to avoid making religion a major issue. Unlike Kennedy, Mario Cuomo has made positive use of his religion. He clearly loves it but has never been afraid to test

its outer limits and to urge change in the Church. On issues rang-
ing from abortion to the role of women, he has challenged the
institution to do better.

But while Cuomo continually works at his religion he has
been first among those fostering religious tolerance and respect
for the religions of others. He has been outspoken in protecting Jewish interests, speaking with passion on such subjects as
the Holocaust. Over and over, I would refer to Christmas on the
radio show and he would respond by gently correcting me by
example, saying something about "Christmas and Chanukah." He
is as far from a chauvinist about his religion as one will find in
America today.

While governor, Cuomo actively sought to utilize his position as a lay Catholic leader to explore issues important to the
church. He has spoken at Notre Dame, St. John's University and
the Cathedral of St. John the Divine on contemporary religious
and social issues. On our program he has spoken at length about
such difficult issues as Papal infallibility and about what religious
issues in his church are acceptable for debate and which are not.
This was always risky stuff, likely to produce headlines and trouble with his Bishops.

There was a point in the show when the Catholic bishops were
having their difficulties with the Vatican over a series of social issues.
I asked the governor about it. I wanted to know whether he would
disagree with his Church when he felt they were wrong. It is a subject we had explored on the show on several occasions. The Church,
said the governor, had always experienced turbulence.

"I am a Roman Catholic. I am a member of the Church. I
believe that we who belong to this church ought not to be afraid
of this present turbulence, that the church has always known this
kind of disagreement."

Cuomo told me at the time that much of what the Church
used to believe has been changed. He pointed to simple subjects
like usury and more complex matters like the origins of life.

"It is a growing institution. It has to be designed. It is an institution to be applied to the human condition and the human condition changes." The result, says Cuomo, is that "you have to expect disagreement, discontent as a concomitant of growth. I am not afraid of it. Like all of life, all of government, in all things you need moderation, reasonableness, balance. The Church is an institution. It has to have a form. It has parameters. It has rules. At some point you can't break the rules without losing the form of the Church. So to a certain extent you are confined simply by virtue of the fact that you are a Roman Catholic. To be a Jew you have to believe. To be a Catholic you have to believe. To be a Democrat there is a certain something that you have to believe. To be an American you pledge a loyalty to a certain body of belief and that is true of the Roman Catholic Church. If you disagree very radically it is logical to say that you are no longer a member of the Church."

Always aware of that very fine line, Cuomo might try to change things but at the same time to always put the most positive face on Catholicism. On the American bishops' disagreements with the Vatican the governor only said, "They are not saying that we are defying the Vatican. Just the opposite. They are saying 'We want to sit down with the Pope, who is the rock on which this Church is built, and we ask his holiness, the Pope, to discuss this matter to avoid a fragmentation of the Church.' I see that as a plea for unity."

While Cuomo has fought with the Church over controversial matters he has also supported it. This is no doctrinaire separation of church and state liberal. In that respect, Cuomo has not shied away from certain controversial issues. He has, for example, supported direct aid to parochial school children in New York State. But, on the other side, Cuomo has been the first among lay Catholics to test his church.

Cuomo claimed that he just responded to issues that were raised by Cardinal John J. O'Connor and others but there was a good case that *he* brought the fight to them. Without question he drew a conceptually difficult fine line between himself and the established Catholic clergy. Cuomo the politician understood a great deal about the way Catholics feel about political issues and their church and the way that outsiders feel about the church. The governor was outraged when a group of AIDS protesters took over St. Patrick's Cathedral in New York City during a service and told me that they should be punished. But when the Cardinal told a reporter that he would join the line outside an abortion clinic the governor told me that the Cardinal, like Leona Helmsley or the president of the United States, was not above the law and should expect to go to jail if he broke the law.

And sure enough it happened. In January of 1990, Cuomo was viciously attacked by Auxiliary Roman Catholic Bishop Austin Vaughan, a jailed Newburgh, New York cleric, who had been incarcerated in a local Albany jail over something called "Operation Rescue" in the Albany Archdiocese where he was found guilty of blocking access to Planned Parenthood facilities. The issue, of course, was abortion. It was my view that there was a certain irony in the fact that a member of a non-violent church was using violence in not allowing others to exercise their own free will.

Attacking Cuomo, Bishop Vaughn told *The New York Post* reporter (who called him in jail), "He is in danger of going to Hell if he dies tonight." What's more, the Bishop went further in his rhetoric by suggesting that Cuomo was similar to the Nazi soldier who "may have objected to the Holocaust but nevertheless supported the German government's right to murder six million innocent Jews."

That incredible statement brought swift condemnation from many of the very highest Jewish organizations in the state, including the Anti-Defamation League of B'nai B'rith, whose mission is to fight bigotry and intolerance.

When I spoke with Cuomo on the radio show about the Bishop's remarks, immediately after they were uttered, he could not have been more gentle about the whole thing. The most he would say in characterizing the Bishop's statement was that it was "intemperate." When I pressed him, Cuomo did admit that "one would always have to be unhappy about intemperance."

Nor was the governor willing to leave the theological decisions to the Bishop. In defending his stance, Cuomo said that his "position on abortion has been checked with every theologian of repute that I could find. It's absolutely sound. As a Catholic I have no doubt about that."

When I asked Cuomo whether he "got a shot of negative adrenaline" when someone said that "you could go to Hell," Cuomo could only answer that he had benefited from the days when he played baseball and "the guy curses at you through a catcher's mask."

"Sometimes you learn from that," he said. "If you seek to defend yourself against oppressors of that type you ought first to remove their catcher's mask, which I forgot to do." I had the distinct feeling that the "catcher's mask" in this case was the Bishop's clerical garb. And despite the fact that I believed Cuomo was not happy about what the Bishop had said, the governor went out of his way to deal gently with the Bishop. Cuomo told me that his first instinct is to assess whether your accuser has a point. "Is there anything to it? Maybe the person is right." When you have satisfied yourself that "this person happens to be wrong," you assume that "nobody's perfect. Let's assume the best for everybody. He's following his conscience, I'm following mine, so be it, and that's the end of it. Then you move on to something more constructive, I hope. More affirmative."

But the week following the great "hell" controversy, I asked Cuomo what had developed. He responded, "I can tell you frankly that I've heard from bishops, from nuns, from priests from this state, from this region and from other parts of the country and they have been very supportive and very kind and I'm—maybe overwhelmed is too strong a word—I'm very, very pleased at the compassion, the consideration and the intelligence demonstrated by the people who have written.

"There are some, on the other hand, who frankly agree with the Bishop and who were as harsh as I think the Bishop was. Harsh may be too harsh a word. But overwhelmingly the mail I have received was reassuring, and I'm pleased at that. But it's a regrettable situation. I would prefer not to spend any more time talking about it. I have never been ashamed of my views. As a matter of fact I'm proud of them. That's why I wrote them all out in my speech on abortion at Notre Dame. I don't know any politicians or many politicians who have taken the time and the trouble to spell it all out as specifically I did. Now maybe that's why I attracted some of the criticism."

Later, when I asked Cuomo about a terrible remark made by a homosexual activist on Senator Ohrenstein's staff about Bishop O'Connor (likening the Bishop to Hitler) the governor condemned the man's words but noted that he would have liked similar support from the bishops when he was attacked with the same sort of quotation.

Summing it all up, Cuomo issued what seemed to be a clear warning to the bishops and the clergy who might have liked to go still another round with him. "I'll say what I have to say, if I have to say it."

For weeks after the "hell" event I would ask the governor about it and once he actually brought it up with me. We were kidding around on the show and I told him that I had been in Washington being "deposed" in a legal case. Loving words as he does, he couldn't help but kid me by suggesting that being deposed is "what happened to Ortega [in Nicaragua]. That's what happened to Ceausescu [in Romania]."

In other words, they were "deposed" as in kicked out. The governor took a sharp turn into one of his favorite subjects, the hereafter.

MC: Where is Ceausescu?

AC: He's dead.

MC: No, but where do you think he is?

AC: Where do I personally think he is?

MC: Yeah.

AC: Under the ground.

MC: You don't think he is in an eternal punishment?

AC: No, I think he may deserve it but I don't think he's there. History as a social force may be his eternal punishment. How's that?

MC: You don't believe that there is an existence after this life?

AC: I'd have to say,...[sighing]

MC: Why not?

AC: I don't. That's what I said in my deposition. The lawyer said when you don't know the answer to a question just say, "I don't know."

MC: That's because you don't know. Well, so you don't know that there is none.

AC: Right.

MC: And you don't know that there is?

AC: Right.

MC: You can choose to believe what you wish.

AC: Right.

MC: If you choose to believe that there was a hereafter that would be an act of faith.

AC: Correct. There's no question about that.

MC: That's a pretty good definition of a lot of the religions.

So I tried one more time.

AC: I think that there is a hereafter only in that I think that floating around is...if Alan Chartock were to go, three people or two people might say, "Hey, I remember him, he was nice," or, "he was a rat" or whatever. There would be a residue of my spirit somewhere. How's that?

MC: Well, it will do until we hear something even more vague.

And that was that. But a few minutes later I asked him, after he had been answering questions about the New York State economy, "Governor, do you believe in Hell?" And, boy, did I get an answer.

"I think we ought to talk, not about your religion, or my religion, but the idea of religion and how interesting and important it is for this society. I think it is not simplistic to say, about some religions, and I think this is true of Christianity, what the Benedictines say: the Benedictine order. 'You cannot perceive God as we understand God, you must apprehend God, as we understand God.' Which is to say, you can't do it all with your eyes, your ears, your brain, your calculator. That not everything will reveal itself to those limited faculties. That beyond that there has to be a general acceptance of the notion, which you can do emotionally if not intellectually.

"As long as it's not contradicted by your intelligence, then you can choose to believe. For example, you cannot prove that there is not a hereafter, you cannot prove that there is a hereafter. If you limited yourself to what you could prove, you probably wouldn't believe fully in electricity, either. But you can choose to believe that there is a hereafter, because your intellect doesn't refute it, and because it makes you feel better, because it is compatible with general notions that you've developed about the universe. There seems to be a design. There seems to be a pattern.

"I choose to believe that there is a hereafter. A time of eternal vindication, eternal justice. Why not? Well, because you can't prove it. So what? Can you disprove it? Why can't I choose to believe it? And who said that we should limit our horizons only to the things we're absolutely sure of?

"Some day I'm going to be a movie star. Well, how do you know? I don't know, I just believe it. And those who choose to believe it live supercharged lives, and sometimes they make it. And sometimes they don't. More often they don't. And if they don't make it what have they lost? They had the benefit of a supercharged existence. That's one way to look at religion, I think."

One can almost watch his mind work as he approaches these issues, always aware, I believe, how they will play to those who are Catholics and those who are not. Perhaps the most obvious position pointing up the differences between Cuomo and his Church has to do with abortion, where Cuomo has come down solidly on a woman's right to choose while maintaining that he himself follows the Church's dictates on abortion.

In the late '80s, Cuomo chastised clergy who refused to serve lay Catholics who were politicians because of their pro-choice positions. He literally challenged the bishops in New York State to do the same thing to him. There was no such response until months later in his home diocese in Brooklyn, when the new Bishop announced that Cuomo would not be free to speak in the churches of Brooklyn and Queens. By the time the smoke cleared, the Bishop had modified his remarks to say that he was welcome to speak, but not about abortion.

It is clear to any observer that the Catholic clergy is very wary of Cuomo, though he does represent the thinking of many progressive lay Catholics.

"You see the Catholic Church now has a reform movement proposing that women should be priests, and so on. There is one interesting name on that list, one of my favorites. A man who was on COGI. Maybe you ought to do a profile on him. It's Bishop Emerson Moore. If it's the same Emerson Moore, he is an African-American, Roman Catholic bishop in the Arch Diocese of New York. And he was on COGI, the Council On Government Integrity. I put him on COGI, telling him that I wanted very much to see him get involved in the work of our community. And he did it, and did it well. Well, if it's the same Bishop Moore, then that is an extraordinary signal. This man works with Cardinal O'Connor, and he's talking about dramatic possibilities for the Catholic church."

Most American Catholics have responded in survey research that they do use birth control and many have views that state that abortion under some circumstances is a right to be practiced by a woman faced with an unwanted pregnancy. The Catholic clergy in New York know that highly publicized fights with one of the most articulate of progressive Catholics can only hurt them. They have tangled with Cuomo before and only lost ground because of it, both from the point of view of Catholics and those outside the Church. It is very hard to argue a persuasive case when Cuomo, on our show, continually referred to the injustice of cutting off Medicaid funds for abortion to a "thirteen year old child who had been raped by a drunken father."

Because he had worked so long and hard on his famous Notre Dame speech on the issue, Cuomo, when asked about abortion, would refuse and tell all questioners to read the speech. But once in a while he would come out with both guns blazing on the issue. The whole thing was a brilliant strategy for not getting into trouble except on your own territory and playing by your own rules.

Cuomo and I once had one of many discussions on the death penalty that led into a broader discussion of whether it was permissible for a lay politician to differ with the Church. It was a particularly fascinating exchange because the governor was suggesting that his position was not a moral one. He said that, "I have never made it a moral proposition as you know, nor has my church." It was a clue that Cuomo felt somewhat angry and let down by the fact that the Church had chosen to spend a lot of time on the abortion issue, where he has had his greatest differences with the Church hierarchy, and the death penalty where he has heard little by way of support from the Catholic clergy.

In one of our conversations Cuomo told me that, "The Roman Catholic Church did not speak against the death penalty in 1977, when I was getting hammered by people. They didn't speak against the death penalty in 1982 when I was getting hammered. And in 1980 and 1984, when they were arguing about abortion, none of them, none of those bishops or cardinals ever said a word about the death penalty."

Cuomo was giving as well as he got, as he pointed out that "the Pope said in 1982 that the death penalty was wrong." The governor went out of his way to insist that his position on the death penalty was not a Catholic one. He insisted that the church had been waffling on the issue for years. Despite the Pope's 1982 pronouncement, it took years for the Catholic Church to start adopting his view on the matter. "You didn't hear that from the Roman Catholic Church in 1984, in any great way. You do now. There has been an evolution. So, this can not be regarded as a matter of dogma by the Roman Catholic Church. And it's not. It's not a matter of belief, it's not a sin if you are for the death penalty. So I've never taken a religious stand on it, that's irrelevant."

Cuomo is very good at playing with the clergy. It's almost as if he has decided to play their game. He goes as far as he is allowed to go without going outside the rules. In the case of the death penalty he made it clear that his views were consistent with those of the Church. But he went on to say that it wouldn't matter if they were or weren't because it was not "dogma," that body of theology, created by the church and which cannot be strayed from.

"There are some basic beliefs that you can not reject and still be a Roman Catholic, a member of an organized religion. For example, you obviously must believe in a God. You must believe in a God of justice and mercy. You must believe in a responsibility to that God. These beliefs are fundamental."

But, says Cuomo, dogma has its limits. He says that there are other things that the church teaches which are not fundamental, and would not lead, if violated, to being thrown out of the Church. "There are a whole variety of other things that are required of you in order to profit from the rules of the church, in order to play on this course. If you want to be a member of this golf club there are things you have to do and have to believe in. For example, you have to accept the fact that women cannot be priests."

Here is Cuomo at his best, testing the ground and challenging the Catholic hierarchy to come out and play. He knows quite well that many Catholic clergy in the United States are deeply troubled about excluding women from the clergy. So he explains that "...there is nothing dogmatic about that, in the sense that, as a matter of conscience, you have to believe that there is a permanent bar to women being priests. I don't. It's simply a church law, made up by the church, to which you have to live up to be a member of the club. You don't have to believe it in your heart and mind to be true to the faith."

At one point the governor and I were talking about the issue of marriage and the clergy. Cuomo mentioned that he was asked about "celibacy and women priests and I said that I don't believe that there is any dogmatic prohibition, nothing so essential to Catholic faith that requires celibacy. Remember that in the past we have had married priests."

"What I said," explained Cuomo, "was that it was possible for the Church to change its teaching, change its tradition, have married priests and women as priests?"

There was no shilly-shallying here. Said the governor, "I believe that it would be a very good thing and I would applaud the result. But," said the governor, "it is not for me to change. We don't get to vote on it and in our church lay people do not make the rules. Rules are made by the College of Cardinals and the Pope and what I said was it would be a good thing if they did it, and if they didn't it's their problem."

In other words, said Cuomo, I choose to remain in the Church but I don't believe everything that they teach. That should be very familiar to many Catholics who remain in the Church but who practice birth control. So, naturally, I asked him, "What about birth control?"

You could hear him rise to the question. "Birth control is very, very tricky. The church teaches now that you must believe that every method of birth control is wrong except for rhythm, if you want to call that birth control. Now there are a lot of Catholics who differ with that but that is teaching of the Church and as a matter of fact, that's the point I made at Notre Dame. If the Roman Catholic Church teaches that it violates the natural law to use contraceptives, why aren't they as vigorous about ordering their people not to do this as they are ordering them not to do abortion? They will tell you, 'Well, one is a matter of

life and death and one is not.'" But then he went on to examine
the church's answer, "Yes, but both are violations of the natural
law, by your own statements. So, as you can see, it can get
extremely intellectual, and difficult to follow. But the Roman
Catholic theology, I think, is misunderstood by many of us." By
saying many of us I think Cuomo suggests that it is misunderstood because it is not logical and he throws himself into the same
pot as everyone else when he says "us." Reflecting on his statement, it seems possible that he is hinting that the Church is hypocritical. If they are tough on abortion why aren't they as tough
on birth control? One can almost touch the excitement as Cuomo
challenges the clergy to explain its inconsistencies. Perhaps he is
suggesting that if they can be inconsistent, "So can I." Perhaps
every time he speaks this way, he sends them a message that the
moment they chastise him for his inconsistent views, he will feel
free to answer in kind. But from long experience I know that just
when it appears he is willing to do full battle with the clergy, he
will throw in a kicker or a sinker and state that he never intended
to suggest any such thing.

Nor are Cuomo's lectures on religious hypocrisy reserved only
for the Catholic Church. He goes out of his way to preach understanding and the importance of living together. There are those
times that he has pummeled those who would use religion to exac-
erbate tensions. He is a man who understands the concept of religious toleration but he insists that all religions, including
Catholicism, be treated with respect.

Cuomo suggests that there are great gulfs that exist between
the "people who call themselves 'right to life people' and people
who call themselves 'pro-choice' people." But he suggests that
there are many things that can be agreed on like "too many unin-
tended pregnancies." Even here, Cuomo flirts with danger with
his own church that does not agree with the use of birth control
devices. Cuomo talked that day of the six million pregnancies in
the country of which 1.5 million "result in abortions." Cuomo cites
"abstention" as a possibility. Cuomo cites the attitude of some

young people that "as soon as they get to puberty they ought to be having intercourse. That's not right.

"Now as a realistic assumption maybe a lot of them do. But should we really forfeit the right to say to our young people, especially in an age where even heterosexual activity can produce AIDS that 'Hey look, nothing wrong with abstention, waiting for a better time, waiting for a more suitable time.'"

But having agreed with his church on that one he takes on the difficult problem of sex education opposed by so many church leaders. "Shouldn't we be giving sex education in our schools? And if you're a parent who doesn't like that, O.K. you should have the option, I think, to say that your child will not receive the sex education that way. You'll take care of the education. I think that's appropriate. For some of us, the use of contraceptives is forbidden by our religious beliefs. And this is a country where you have the right not to use contraceptives or to do abortions or whatever. On the other hand, for all those people who do believe that it is appropriate to use contraceptives, oughtn't we, as a government, encourage them to use contraceptives? Couldn't we agree on these things whether you call yourself 'right to life' or 'pro-choice?'

"Now in this state, Alan, you ought to know that we spend as much and more, as a matter of fact, on women who choose to have the child than on women who choose to have abortions.

"Isn't it an ugly kind of irony," Cuomo asked pointedly, "that some of us can argue ferociously over whether or not an abortion should occur, but once the child is born we lose our commitment to the living child in the world outside the womb?

"Now, the Cardinal agrees that that commitment should be made. The Cardinal is a leader on that issue. There are orthodox rabbis who don't believe that abortion is right and go along on this point. I don't know anybody who would disagree with it. That is where we must put more emphasis. Of course, we will have our differences. But we must do better at recognizing our agreements."

These are words from Cuomo the conciliator, who believes that there are always points of agreement and that he as a leader has a responsibility to point them out. Cuomo honors religion, all religion, whenever he gets a chance.

Once a group of Jewish leaders were angered when Bishop Desmond Tutu was visiting the United States where he was to appear at the inauguration of New York City Mayor-elect David Dinkins. Tutu had spoken out on the need to establish a Palestinian homeland alongside Israel. I asked the governor about it and what I got was a long answer about the need for religious leaders to express themselves on political subjects.

He started by naming a list of religious leaders who had so spoken out. Cuomo said that all the great religious leaders of the world, "...whether they're Bishop Tutu, the Pope, Rabbi Schneerson, the Lubovitcher Rabbi, their mission is life and the world and love and improving the conditions of things. It's increasingly difficult in a world that is so interconnected and interdependent to draw perfect lines that separate religious from civic or civil considerations. Look at the problems we have in this country making that adjustment. Fundamentalists, the orthodox Jews, Roman Catholics speak on subjects that are not exclusively religious. Most of the religious people who condemn abortion will tell you that it is not exclusively a religious precept. They see it as a matter of fundamental morality.

"The bishops of my own Roman Catholic Church will speak on the economy and the fairness of things. They speak on war. I don't think it is illegal, certainly there's no rule against it, certainly we guarantee free speech to anybody. And therefore as a matter of pure legal right, it's appropriate. But even politically, even by a looser standard, I think it is not inappropriate for world leaders to offer people their opinions. You're free to reject them. I'm not troubled by too many opinions. I think I would be more troubled by not enough opinions."

Cuomo, who has been criticized for speaking out on theological subjects, makes it clear that he believes that the clergy has the same right in his sphere.

Still another example of Cuomo's sense of tolerance can be seen in his reaction to the fundamentalist preacher Jerry Falwell and his now disbanded Moral Majority. In 1989 when Falwell announced that the Moral Majority was folding its national organization, I asked Cuomo about it.

"Jerry Falwell announced he's closing up the Moral Majority, Governor."

To which the usually loquacious governor responded "Good. Good."

I wasn't about to accept that brief commentary so I asked him, "Why is it so good? He says he's accomplished what he set out to do."

But Cuomo said that it wasn't Falwell who had made the decision but the American people. "I think the people are back from the extremism of that period. I think the people of the United States of America are very analytical but very fair and objective. I think we're capable of strong opinions and we should be. And we have strong ideas of what's right. And your idea of what's right is clearly different from mine. Take the death penalty, for example. For Chartock to suggest that Cuomo is evil because he doesn't believe in death by incineration, or for Cuomo to insist that Chartock is stupid, perverse and that God doesn't love him because he wants to kill criminals, both of those situations are not just absurd and unfair, they are very, very dangerous and damaging. They tear the fabric of society instead of strengthening it. And I don't like it. I don't like condemnation.

"There are times, I guess, when you have no choice. There is certain conduct that ought to be condemned. It is very rare, however, that you can show me a person who ought to be condemned. Because to condemn a person I have to be able to read her mind, his mind. It's difficult for human beings to do. Maybe even impossible."

Again and again Cuomo pleads for tolerance. When Congressman Barney Frank was being roundly criticized for hiring a homosexual prostitute who was apparently turning tricks in the Congressman's apartment, I asked the governor about it.

"I am not comfortable in criticizing other people for their moral conduct, and calling them sinners. I know some of that, I guess, is essential in government. I'm not comfortable doing it. Where it affects other people in the community in a tangential way, well, then it is a matter of concern for all public officials. If you admit to violating the law, then that is a legitimate basis for being chastised or punished. As for purely private conduct, I don't like being involved, that is not for me. It is your judgment to make. I am sufficiently occupied with my own judgments on my own behavior. So I don't need to get involved with yours. Where your conduct, however, crosses the lines and has implications that affect the larger community then they become relevant. If you are violating a law, of course that is relevant. If you are mis-using money of course that is relevant. Always the test has to be whether or not the act involved is more than just personal conduct. I don't inquire about your behavior at home with your spouse, how you choose to express your affection, the exotic devices you might think up; that is for you. When it gets beyond your bedroom, beyond your home, beyond your private conduct and affects the rest of us, then there is a legitimate matter of interest for the public. So, if I had to make a judgment, my inquiries would have to be: Did you violate any laws? Was this conduct purely private?"

Once again, Cuomo prefers to leave matters of behavior up to those who have to make the choice. He tries to cut enough slack so that he is not being prescriptive even when it puts him at odds with his church.

Cuomo cites his hero, Teilhard D'Jardin, the Catholic religious philosopher, who suggests that man is good and is capable of enjoying the here and now. You get more than a little clue of that in a conversation I had with him shortly after the actor Jimmy Cagney died. The conversation also suggests that Cuomo sees religion as a force which is uplifting and positive, rather than dark and foreboding.

AC: Yesterday you were at the funeral for James Cagney. Do you have any thoughts on that?

MC: I did not volunteer to go to the funeral because I was told that Willie Cagney [Mrs. James Cagney] wanted a private event. I did not have the privilege of knowing James Cagney while he was alive, although I had the same affection and respect for him that I guess most Americans had. The family reached out to us through Mrs. Zimmerman, who is a confidante, or was to Jimmy, and still is to Mrs. Cagney. She said that she would like both Mayor Koch, who was in a movie with Jimmy Cagney, and I to be there, but no other politicians. We were the only politicians there and I felt very privileged to have been invited. I was there really for seventeen and a half million Americans whom we call New Yorkers.

The Cagneys were offered, or Mrs. Cagney was offered, Saint Patrick's Cathedral and said no and chose instead a small church that would fit in one small corner of Saint Patrick's, called Saint Francis DeSales which happens to be the upper Manhattan parish where Jimmy Cagney was confirmed.

Mrs. Cagney arranged to invite people from the community. The ones who received Holy Communion, I would say, were mostly blue collar, working-type people from the community, mostly elderly, who remembered the Cagney family. It was a very, very touching thing.

The homily was by a priest who was a Christopher. That's an aggressive, social action group of Catholic priests whose motto is to "light one little candle." Jimmy Cagney was an important part of the Christopher movement. The priest delivered a beautiful little part of the sermon, that said in effect that Jimmy Cagney was not pious, but he was spiritual; that he played the ruffian, and even the killer, but he was a man of love and generosity. It was a lovely little sermon that Mrs. Cagney enjoyed, and I was pleased I was there. As I say, privileged to be there.

When the coffin was carried out of the church, to be seen for the last time now, something extraordinary happened, which I've never seen before. Ralph Bellamy, Mikhail Baryshnikov, Floyd Patterson, and some others carried the coffin down the steps of Saint Francis DeSales Church and the thousand, or two thousand people lined up behind the barricades across the street from the funeral procession, began applauding the coffin. I've never seen such a thing; what they did tells you something about the consensus of intelligence and instinct of the people in this country—and we've talked about this before—I think they are like a wonderful jury, and when you let the people of our state, the people of our country speak, they can speak some beautiful things. In their inherent, consensus intelligence, they understood this was the way Jimmy Cagney would hear their respect and affection.

It was the mode that was perfectly designed for Cagney, applause. That's the way you tell a great performer what you think of him. You applaud him. It was a wonderful moment, a wonderful moment.

AC: Governor, do you have a favorite Cagney film?

MC: You know, I guess I was ten years old when he made the George M. Cohan film, *Yankee Doodle Dandy*, and no one who ever saw that...did you see it, Alan?

AC: Oh, I've seen it about twenty times and I love it more every time I see it.

MC: You could not but love him, Cohan, and America—incidentally the song we sang at the funeral was "America the Beautiful," which was his favorite song. That was another magnificent moment. At the end of the religious ceremony, a religious ceremony, incidentally, in white—white vestments—twenty years ago, thirty years ago it would have been in black vestments. Thirty years ago the Church, the Roman Catholic Church in this country celebrated death as a sadness. Now they celebrate death as a moment of joy and new beginning, and so with white instead of black. At the end of the religious ceremony, with the liturgy and the prayers and the candles, everyone concludes by singing a patriotic song, "America the Beautiful." That was another lovely moment.

AC: I can't believe there's anyone in America—no matter how much you know they're trying to do it to you in this film by Cohan—who doesn't get a tear in their eye... when he walks out—remember the White House steps—and goes out—and remember the soldiers are marching and he joins them.

MC: Well, that was my favorite. That was also his favorite. What we learned yesterday was that he didn't enjoy movies like *White Heat* where he was a killer. He didn't enjoy depicting hate and sadism and brutality. In his heart, he was a song and dance man. He was filled with joy. I read about him yesterday, "A wink and a smile." He didn't want to be a killer, and at one point he went to the producers and said, "I don't want to do anymore of this."

Well, either Mrs. Zimmerman or Mrs. Cagney was brilliant, I thought, and probably very sincere in the way they put that funeral cortege together, the way they actually carried the coffin, a potpourri of black, and white, and Russian and Jewish, it was extraordinary. It was Mrs. Zimmerman, but also it was sincere. Remember, they could have selected from all of Hollywood—I mean they could have brought airliners filled with stars who would have come at just the simplest urging by Mrs. Cagney. They could have had anybody. I was told yesterday that they had Baryshnikov because he did two or three specials with Jimmy Cagney, and was a great admirer and Cagney loved him. Floyd Patterson—someone told me he know him from the area, from Dutchess County. Ralph Bellamy goes way, way back with Jimmy Cagney and was a friend of his. They did some films together, but more than that, Bellamy said that they were friends. Milos Forman was there. Director, or producer, whatever, these were all people who did indeed know Cagney, and it wasn't just some symbolic presence of Hollywood. These were friends.

You know, we should move on, I guess, but one final thing about him. They told me yesterday that no one taught him acting. That he was in New York. He grew up in the streets of New York. He saw things around him. He saw people around him. He saw life. He lived life. He had sadness in his own life. He had some joy. He had instinct. He had impulse. He liked to sing. He liked to dance. He liked to laugh. He liked to make people happy, and that's what he did in the films. He was Jimmy Cagney, they never had to teach him anything. He was a natural athlete. Just watching him dance would prove that, and everything came very easily to him. When he performed the bad guy role he was just a great mimic. These are pictures he had in his mind of bad guys and he just did them perfectly. But they said it all came very effortlessly to him. It was just a job, it was nine to five, and he didn't have to learn it. He did it. He just did his thing. A great art conceals itself.

If one reads Cuomo's remarks about Jimmy Cagney and thinks about the theme of simplicity, priests dressed in white instead of black and of the value of having tribute paid in parish church rather than Saint Patrick's Cathedral, one gets close to the religious beliefs of Mario Cuomo.

Time and again, religious references entered into our conversations. No matter what the subject, it is clear to me that Cuomo uses religion as a baseline against which he can measure each phenomenon he faces. Take the time I was talking with him about whether there were ever times it was appropriate not to tell the truth.

Said the gov, "There are often little things which we say are not true. Take your little girl, who may not be really beautiful; she might even have a funny nose. You say, 'You are the most beautiful girl in the whole world.' That is not a sin but a virtue."

Kiddingly, I tried to support his point by suggesting that his point was interesting but misguided "because my daughter *is* the most beautiful girl in the world."

MC: It's going to be difficult, because I have the three most beautiful girls in the world and this, I can see, is going to be a contest unless there are three or four worlds; one of yours and three others.

Well, naturally, the governor's reference to other worlds made me think of Superman comics in which there were always "alternative worlds" running parallel to our own. So I asked him about it.

AC: It's like from the Superman comics—competing worlds, different dimensions, all the time.
MC: What is Superman? A God substitute, a God expression.

That got me to thinking about other "God expressions" or metaphors and I told the governor that when WAMC was raising money from listeners, we often said things like, "We are with you in the morning and we are with you in the night and we are with you all the time, we comfort you, etc. etc. Then I say, wait a second—we are not God, we are a radio station."

"Well, I like Superman and I like Batman and I like the Green Hornet. I liked all the comic characters and the Shadow." That remark prompted me to mention that the Shadow was "another Godlike character."

To which the governor responded that these comic book characters "were an expression of virtue." Backing off from the God metaphor, the governor said that the comic heroes "...don't need to be Godlike to be an expression of virtue but they were hero figures for generations to come who were simplistic, perhaps, and unremittingly tempted. They resisted."

The superheroes had moved from godlike figures to human figures faced with temptation who had resisted. It was not hard to imagine the governor making an identification with each of them.

But I wasn't satisfied. I asked Cuomo whether there wasn't some revisionism in our approach to superheroes. For example, I said, the last Batman picture had our hero making love to a woman in Bruce Wayne's mansion. So the governor said that he "did not see the movie." Cuomo said, however, that we have interpreted our superheroes in different ways in the thirties, forties and fifties. "And nowhere is there a kind of cynicism about these characters." But now, says the governor "you have to be like the real world and in the real world there is cynicism and you sin 'seven times seven' times a day."

Maybe it was my upbringing as a Jewish kid on the west side of Manhattan, but I felt compelled to ask him what sin and his seven times seven quotation meant.

"Well, that is what the Bible would say and it's true. I think we have lost a lot in our aspirations and that I don't think it was necessarily unrealistic to suggest to young people that you can be perfect and but that you aspire like Superman to use all of your power to help people." What's more, said Cuomo, "it is important to point out to young people that you can fight crime and that crime is wrong and fighting it is right; that there are white horses and white hats, black horses and black hats and the guy with the white horse and the mask."

And, says Cuomo, the white hat, "comes and saves you—does it selflessly and he does not ask for any reward while he goes galloping off, leaving dust and never stays behind for your embrace or your kind word and even your gift."

Not all of Cuomo's views are quite this simple. I asked him once whether he ever felt hate. "I hope not," he said.

"Even in the passion of the moment?" I wanted to know.

The governor replied, "Ever since Adam and Eve bit the apple, we have all been subject to concupiscence, vulnerability, fragility. We all think thoughts we regret later on. I am sure that we all feel anger at moments. For all those of us who are Christian, we try to embody virtues that lasted in a single individual on this earth.

"And," said Cuomo defining his view of Christ, "we look to that life for exemplars, for instruction. And in the course of that lifetime, as a concession to humanity and as the admission that He was human, He flung a money changer down the steps of the temple because it was a religious place and it was being desecrated by commercial exploitation. And in so doing, he demonstrated for Christians that hate was a human frailty. We recognize anger as real—wrong, but nevertheless real."

I knew that I was in over my head because I understood so little of what he was saying. I asked him what he meant by concupiscence. "I forgot what that is, Governor."

"For old fashioned people, it is the inordinate desire for something that produces a transgression. Concupiscence is avidity, the willingness to desire things, to seek them even though we shouldn't." Weakness, he said, is "the human condition."

"Are you tormented after you have felt this passion?" I asked him.

"Are you, Alan?"

"Yes, but I am not as apologetic as you are."

Cuomo fired back, "Who has apologized? Have I apologized?"

Trying to understand, I explained, "You seem to think that it is a sin. I think it might be a political mistake, or maybe self-defeating behavior, but I don't see it sin."

The governor thought about that for a split second and decided that the word "sin" needed definition. He said that "sin" was a "violation of the moral." To him, sin is in the mind of the beholder.

"Only you can determine that. Only the listener can determine what he or she can regard as a transgression of the rule that should guide their conscience. That is all I mean by sin. You can substitute the word 'wrong' or the word 'regrettable.'" That, said the governor, was what he felt when he felt anger.

How bad is it? Well, Cuomo left it up to each of us to draw our own definitions. He said that hate is a wish "to do harm to another human being."

Whether dealing with politics, with racial relations or with religious bigotry, I often saw how the governor's strong religious foundation defined his philosophy. In stark contrast to today's climate of "hate talk radio," Cuomo spoke of the need to find common ground, to celebrate the ways in which we are similar, rather than use our differences to divide us. His affirmation of the human condition was an underlying theme throughout our many conversations.

He once read me a poem from that same dogeared book of poetry he read to his children. He dedicated it to one of our mythical two listeners, Harvey and Ethel.

"This is for Ethel," he said. "This is one of my favorites and it's one that you like to share with people that you love very much." The poem, by Louise Driscoll, was entitled "Hold Fast Your Dreams"

> Hold fast your dreams!
> Within your heart
> Keep one still, secret spot
> Where dreams may go,
> And, sheltered so,
> May thrive and grow
> Where doubt and fear are not.
> O keep a place apart,
> Within your heart,
> For little dreams to go!
>
> Think still of lovely things that are not true.
> Let wish and magic work at will in you.
> Be sometimes blind to sorrow. Make believe!
> Forget the calm that lies
> In disillusioned eyes.
> Though we all may know that we must die,
> Yet you and I
> May walk like gods and be

Even now at home in immortality.
We see so many ugly things—
Deceits and wrongs and quarrellings;
We know, alas! we know
How quickly fade
The color in the west,
The bloom upon the flower,
The bloom upon the breast
And youth's blind hour.
Yet keep within your heart
A place apart
Where little dreams may go,
May thrive and grow.
Hold fast—hold fast your dreams!

When I asked him about his interpretation of the poem, Cuomo told me. My guess is that when you substitute the word "religion" for "hope" you understand the concept of what Mario Cuomo thinks about religion.

I asked him if he had such a place where he met his dreams.

He answered, "Well we all have it. In our mind, in our heart, quiet corners. Quiet moments."

"You know," he said, "if hope leaves completely then life would have to leave. If you had no hope at all, how would the people go on? The people who faced great acts of terrorism, the Holocaust, who sat there in Vietnam and watched the eyes of their children get blown out of their heads by bombs they didn't understand? How do you continue living as tragedy after tragedy strikes some people? You look around, you seem so lucky yourself. There is always a family somewhere on the block or somewhere in the neighborhood where everything goes wrong and nobody can figure it out. You know, the 'good die young.'

"There is so much confusion about how justice is meted out by fate, not by the courts but by fate that you couldn't make it unless you had hope. All the great religions have been built on that. I mean if you're committed only to hard reality, to the things that you can touch and figure out and know for sure now, you wouldn't have religion."

I asked Cuomo where he had these private moments of hope, where he called them up. Was it in church? Was it when he was exercising?

No, he said, it wasn't in a place. He called on hope, he said, in situations, in places where only religion or hope could be used to explain what was happening.

"When somebody that you love very much dies and you don't understand it because they were younger than you are, deserved more than you did. I had a very good friend named John Gerrity who was a good friend of mine for many years, forty years. Totally blind from the age of six. Magnificent guy. I went through college with him. Law school with him. He was an inspiration to everybody. He overcame every kind of obstacle yet had all sorts of bad luck. Not just his blindness but a disease that struck his hip. He went lame after a while. At his job and in his home life there were these problems constantly mounting. He died just as his son was coming to manhood. A new phase, perhaps was about to begin in his life and he was gone. All of us who went to the wake felt the same way—those of us who had known him for a long time. The guy was so good he seemed to deserve so much more. At moments like that you might find yourself alone—you think for a minute, and you conclude that if you linger for too long on the apparent injustice of it all, it will stop you. You won't be able to function. So those are moments when you turn to hope and dreams. The aspirations for something better.

"Or when you'd done something terribly wrong. When you'd been up all night wondering what horrible price you'd be made to pay for your mistake, and then discover that people didn't notice it or something fortunate happened where it wasn't uncovered. You got away with it. And then say, 'My God how lucky I am. Look at how it turned around. I'll have to remember it the next time.'"

Anyone who had ever experienced a sleepless night of the kind that the governor was describing could hardly not recognize the torment that the governor was speaking of. But I wanted to see what he meant by the words "terribly wrong." So I asked him whether he meant that he had done something terribly wrong or whether he meant that he had made a mistake.

"We all do things that are terribly wrong. We all miss the opportunity to say something nice when it's badly needed. We all, sooner or later, often or not so often, say things that hurt people, even inadvertently. We don't need to hurt them. You know we all have this instinct. I think, if pushed to its extreme, it's the instinct that forces you when you are on a subway platform and the train is coming in and somebody shouts 'Fire,' you run for the stairs, not terribly careful about knocking other people off the platform into the oncoming train. You do it to save your life. It's called survival."

I remember the time that Cardinal John O'Connor spoke out on the question of rock and roll. Little did I suspect that the Cardinal's remarks would lead to one of the most interesting expositions of Cuomo on his Church as well as human nature.

Cuomo, responding to a question I posed about man's capacity for good or evil, noted that "Cardinal O'Connor apparently said yesterday in St. Patrick's Cathedral that he thought some rock music assisted the devil in the devil's work. He meant by that, it appealed to the most perverse instincts in us. I think he talked specifically about a song having to do with the subject of suicide. He talked about demonic possession, and I was asked about it.

"I don't know anything about what the Cardinal said, except what I read in the paper, and of course I would not take that as the full version of what he intended."

But then the Governor got serious. First, the assertion that the Cardinal is "absolutely free to say what he feels and I respect that right. And he is a Cardinal of my church.

"This much is clear to me: that if young people and older people have a penchant for self destruction, if they see opportunities to abuse themselves with alcohol, if they seem to be running away from life, then that is a reminder, or should be a reminder to us of how negative this society has become. It is not just the music. We want capital punishment back because it is the best answer we can give to what we perceive is our law and order problem. We want to answer the brutality problem with brutality. I know that we are for and against it, polls indicate that most people are for it. I think we should admit to ourselves that it is significant. We talk about abortion. One group of people says that one way to deal with this unfortunate situation, where women feel it necessary to stop the pregnancy, is to declare that all women who make this choice are murderers. Children are disturbed and take to drugs as an escape."

But then comes Cuomo at his best. "The emphasis, I think, should be on spending more time telling our children about the brighter sides of life, about what is possible." The problem, he said, was that the society as a whole, and I suspect the Bishop in particular, was spending too much time on how to treat the symptoms of sickness and not enough time on "continuous acts of love." Such acts of love, said Cuomo, "that would bring children back from addiction. So, in short, we need more positive, less negative. I think if there are all these negative vibrations and actions in our society it's because that we don't have enough that is affirmative, good and beautiful. If kids are turning toward the ugly things in life it is because we have not given them the beautiful ones."

Cuomo said that in the last twenty years as a politician he had seen "the emptiness, the loneliness, the vacuum, the need for something positive to believe in. Something to embrace."

What were some of those things? Well, he listed them. They were the forces that uplifted the spirit. They were "religion, God, love, whatever it is."

The governor's emphasis on religion as affirmation led me to ask him why so many religions sooner or later turned from "candoism" to "can't-doism."

He answered that in most religions, "in order to enable the individual to realize the potential of life, there must be disciplines and restraints to avoid abuse." That, he says, is because all religions recognize that a person has "a life to lead"; that each person has "a mind that is the greatest gift of all." In most religions, says Cuomo, there is a recognition that it is wrong "to abuse the mind with drugs or with alcohol."

The governor said that there was always room for improvement in each of us and that religion had the potential to provide the map for such improvement. He cited an article in an issue of *Newsweek* talking about aging. The point of the article, he said, was that "no matter how old you get, unless you are diseased with some ailment," the brain can grow stronger and stronger. He says that the parts of the brain can either grow stronger or atrophy depending on what we do with our brain. Those who continue to cultivate their intellectual interests, he said, seem to continue to maintain all their mental facilities which he contrasted with those who "just settle for television." He warns that the person who does not exercise the brain "causes a shrinking of the mental capacity of brain." The brain, he says, "could grow forever" if ... "you used it."

And from there the governor made his transition back to religion. "So there are rules that in order to make the most of your life you need to be contained within certain parameters." In order to maintain life and to make it better, "you have rules and regulations." Everyone puts names on those rules and regulations. For example, he says, one might give in to an impulse to take what does not belong to you. Religion and law protect you against that.

That, says the governor, is the reason for negatives in religion. In some cases, he says, the tilt has been towards the negative. He points not only to religions but to some of the post war European governments, where oppressiveness in the name of discipline "becomes unbearable." That oppressiveness, he says, was in sharp contrast to the "desire for affirmation" and for "freedom." And that desire, be it in church or state, is part of the cyclical nature of the human existence. Sometimes we demand protection from ourselves. Sometimes that protection goes too far and then we have "the desire for freedom, the desire for growth."

It's happened over and over again, says Cuomo, leaving me with the feeling that what is happening in Cuomo's church and world will continually be faced with the same dialectic.

Mario Cuomo understands that religion takes care of the best and the worst in us. He's a man who's very hard on himself but he knows that religion is there as a safety net and as a comfort when he needs it. It would be a mistake to try to figure out Mario Cuomo's world without understanding how important an element religion is in that world.

FAMILY

It happened on our weekly radio show. I had just congratulated the governor on the wedding of his son, Andrew, to Kerry Kennedy, the daughter of Robert F. Kennedy. Some were calling it the marriage of two political dynasties.

He thanked me for my words and noted, "You've not been through it yet, have you?"

And in the playful style of our relationship I assured him that yes, indeed, I've been married.

The gov replied laughingly, "I know that. It's different, though, when you do it yourself and when you're there as a parent."

But I was anxious to explore the thoughts of Mario Cuomo, family man.

"Let me ask you a question. Did you cry? Come on now!"

"I'm not going to answer that question," he said.

Baiting him as best as I could under the circumstances, and remembering my innocent-child mode of argumentation, I taunted him with the rejoinder, "Then that means 'yes.'"

"I'm not going to answer that question," he thundered back in response. "I'm not going to answer that question," he reiterated for effect.

So I tried to tell him that he would say "no" if he hadn't.

But he saw that question coming and cut me as short as he could.

"It's none of your business!" said the governor.

Then the gov pulled his usual trick—he turned the tables and started to question me.

"Well, what does cry mean? Do you mean tears? Oh, do you have to have tears to cry? Can you cry internally? Are you asking me, 'Is there just a little bit of regret when people are married?' Or is it all joy on the part of the parents?

"'This is wonderful, he won't be around as much as he used to be. He won't be there when I call all the time at 6:30 in the morning. I won't see him on the weekends all the time to play basketball. But this is great because now they go on to a new and full life.' Is that what you're asking me?"

If you don't get it, you ought to read that last paragraph again. He's talking about one of the closest father/son relationships and collaborations in political history. His son Andrew had been his campaign manager the first two times he ran for governor and one of his closest confidants when it comes to running the government. His son Christopher made the key speech at the 1990 nominating convention and the governor kissed him as he mounted the stage to make his acceptance speech.

AC: I saw Christopher introduce you. Now, that was a nice thing.

MC: Wasn't he something?

AC: That was a nice thing. And you kissed him. That is a good thing.

MC: I don't know. Some people think that's too mushy. But he is a great kid and we love him.

AC: That was my favorite part of the convention.

His pride over his daughter's and his wife's accomplishments is evident and sincere to anyone who talks with him. And while he was governor, the family was a big part of Mario Cuomo's political world. We had a brief exchange prior to the 1990 gubernatorial campaign.

AC: Are you going to use your family in the campaign?

MC: No. As a matter of fact, my brother wasn't there, my sister wasn't there, my mother was not there, my mother-in-law was not there, my in-laws were not there, my two sons-in-law were both very very busy, and I told everybody that these are nice things and we would like to have the family but we don't need to put everybody out for every event.

My family has been extremely generous about their support and their time. Andrew runs the show politically. Madeline did most of the work on the convention. Madeline did most of it, with John Marino and his crew and volunteers. They had an army of volunteers. Madeline has always been good at that, good at the organizational work.

AC: What is she doing for her regular work now?

MC: She, of course, passed her bar exam. So she is a lawyer. She will be admitted officially, I guess a little bit, up here at the appellate division. Then she will decide what kind of law to practice. She has indicated to me and to her family and friends that she is interested in practicing the law.

She wants to get the campaign out of the way first. This is the way the kids are, you know. They feel that they have an obligation to help in the campaign. They have no obligation. They have given more than we have a right to ask them. But that is what she wants to do, help us with the campaign. She has already been a huge help, not just the convention. She threw some of the most successful fund- raisers we ever had in the state: Rochester, Syracuse, Albany. She did them all, while she was studying for the bar.

Andrew, while he is getting ready for his own wedding this weekend, he did this whole thing. We have a terrific amount of support. Matilda works harder than I do. She is more popular than I am and deservedly so. This is very much a family effort. I am very proud of them and I love them very much. But Matilda and I are also very reluctant to intrude upon them too much. This is a terrible pain in the neck for them in some ways. They love it and they are happy about it and enjoy it in a lot of ways. But it can also be a burden.

And don't forget about Cuomo's famous mother who became a legend in the first Cuomo campaign.

"My mother would not be regarded as intelligentsia. She never read a book in English, or in Italian, let alone wrote one. She is much smarter than most of the people I ever met who wrote books."

Family counts a whole lot in Mario Cuomo's world.

In the mosaic that makes up Cuomo's operative political philosophy, the theme of family is most pronounced. It was in his family that Mario Cuomo learned his most important lessons and he doesn't mind saying so.

"Our people went through it [racism]—all of us. We all heard stories from our grandparents. They will tell you these stories. I happened to live it first generation. So I am luckier than most because it is very vivid to me. But I will tell my children. Some of my children will not be smart and they will react in bitterness. 'They did it to us, now I am going to do it somebody else.' This is the height of stupidity. Most of my children will be smart. They will learn from their own family experience. So, what is the answer, Alan? Wisdom. Where does wisdom come from? Enduring, listening, observing, there is no other answer."

And if it is family that is invoked there is little question that it is Cuomo, himself, who is the father in the family. He is "take charge," he has vision and he worries a lot about those who depend on him. In other words, he feels about his political family the way that he does about his own family. Those views extended, when he was governor, to his constituents who couldn't take care of themselves and to the state work force which has always been a prime target for newspaper editors and comedians. Unlike his successor, his job as he saw it was to protect those who were under his care and guidance.

Perhaps the most important clue to understanding Cuomo the man is understanding his views on family. And family is a most important theme from a man who refuses to let anyone typecast him as a liberal or a conservative, since "family" is a theme common to both philosophies.

Mario Cuomo *is* a family man. He would rather be with family than with all the high-powered people you could round up for a political cocktail party. But he believes that members of families have responsibilities. He has made it clear to members of his own family that each one has responsibilities to the family unit. On the other hand, he believes that he has a responsibility to them. When he can't protect his political or personal family he is frustrated to the point that he is capable of making mistakes. Nothing seems to wear him down more quickly than not being able to provide protection and comfort to those who depend on him. Incidentally, while he was governor, his political enemies recognized this vulnerability and used it to push Cuomo to make mistakes.

Cuomo has made no bones about the fact that it was his family which made the difference in his life. Back in November of 1988, I asked him about the biggest influences in his life. His answer left no room for doubt. "My mother and father are the biggest possible influences and neither of them were educated and neither of them ever, to the best of my recollection, sat down and delivered a speech to me. I don't ever remember my father saying, 'Sit down Mario, I want to talk to you,' because we had a grocery store, open all the time and just never had an opportunity to sit down. Only rarely did we have family meals together, except on the holidays when we closed the store for an hour or two hours and sat down to have a big meal. So we never talked. But he instructed us just by being there working hard. We knew he was working for us. We knew he was denying himself. We knew my mother, his wife—he would never holler at her with anybody listening and he would never demean her. When she was ill, he would be terribly concerned about her. All these lessons about our youth were never written down. Never heard it from a pulpit or living room platform. Just by his example and her example, they taught us lessons."

One of the hardest lessons Cuomo learned from his family and then had to experience on his own throughout his life was how to deal with anti-Italian discrimination. Cuomo told us, "I tell stories about my own family. We moved from the grocery store in South Jamaica to Hollis, Queens. I will never forget it as long as I live. My father, may he rest in peace, his proudest moment was when he finally had his own house. I can't tell you what that means. A house that was separate from everybody's house with a yard, etc.

"We moved in—my mother was very proud. The first day my mother was there, there were no Italians in the neighborhood. We hadn't thought of that—we didn't know it. Three women came down the hill and said to my mother, who was on the porch of the house, her first day, 'You must be the Eye-talian.' My mother will tell you the story and she will pronounce it Eye-talian. My mother said, 'Yes.' She said, 'Well, you are in the neighborhood now, make sure you keep the cover on your garbage pails.'

"Now, I tell you, to this day my mother will tell you that story, she is eighty-five years old, and you can see tears come to her eyes. It is not rage, it is hurt. She put the cover on the garbage pails every day, I'm sure. Because that is the way she is and didn't react bitterly. But she never forgot that. This insult from these people who said, 'Because you are an Italian, we are going to believe you are less than we are.' That happens always...that is the story of America. One group resisting the one that comes after it. I like to think we are getting more intelligent about that kind of thing."

Getting more intelligent about it means giving others the break his family didn't get. Once I asked him about Matilda's program in which individuals sign on to mentor a child who needs help.

"My family, my mother and my father, my older sister, my older brother were always busy because we had a grocery store that was family operated. I was the youngest and therefore, the most fortunate in the house. And while I took my turn at chores, I was freed of the really hard work by my older brother and sister, who made sacrifices for me, a thing they did almost instinctively in those days, one generation taking care of the next one. They didn't have a whole lot of time to instruct and/or mentor, although they did what they could."

Cuomo had mentors not only in the family but in the schools. He remembers his public school teachers very well. "I remember, I think I've said before, even the scent of Mrs. Mulligan's perfume. Really, I do, that is the impact they had on me, especially in the earlier grades. I remember Mrs. Gubo coming to my father's grocery store, to tell my father, behind the counter, about me in school. At first, we thought she was going to say something terrible and I tell this story about my father slapping me as soon as he found out that my school teacher was coming through the door. He asked my sister, 'Who's that?' My sister, in Italian, she said, 'Mrs. Gubo, Mario's teacher.' He hit me a shot because he figured she would come only for one reason.

"She was actually coming to encourage him to allow me to go into the rapid advance class, as they used to call it. Anyway, these teachers are very much like the mentors we're trying to supply. But they had smaller classes, they had no drugs to deal with, they had no violence in the classroom, they had none of the terrible, terrible problems that some of our school teachers had to face in some of our districts, certainly not all of them. So they were more like mentors to us. They had the time, they certainly had the love and the commitment. Later on I had priests—wonderful, wonderful, Vincentian priests." Then Cuomo went on to name them all.

AC: Was there one of them? Just one of them, if you had to pick one?

MC: Father Caufield, may he rest in peace, Father Caufield, who
      had been back from Chinese mission, and who taught phi-
      losophy and literature. He was a wonderful man who was my
      confessor for a while. He was truly a mentor. He spent a lot
      of time talking to me and trying to explain life to me. Yes,
      I had my mentors, but they came naturally in our neigh-
      borhoods and streets then. Now, we have to create them
      because now they don't come so naturally...there are still
      many of them out there, but the world is more complicated,
      more difficult, the problems larger than anything I ever
      dreamt of when I was a child.

And that view of what teachers could do has never left Cuomo,
who believes that with proper teaching and incentives every student has the potential to make tremendous commitments to the
country. He rejects all the excuses and reasons that our kids can't
make it.

Once, early in his first term, Mario Cuomo made a visit to
Princeton University. When he returned I asked him for his
impressions of the "me generation."

Cuomo said that he was not one of those who believed that
we had a "me generation" on college campuses.

"I never called it a 'me generation.' Many others did and that
was popular. I was not one of those who felt that we went through
a generation of selfishness compared to the previous generation
of altruism." According to Cuomo, our young people want what
young people have always wanted.

"I see on campus an eagerness by the young people particularly, to find a niche for themselves professionally; to build a good
life for themselves and possibly their family, if they choose to have
families. But also to do something more. They're looking for
something real, something uplifting, something ennobling. So they
have two ambitions as I see it. One, they want the practical life,
a secure one, a good one. They don't regard that as inordinate selfishness, nor do I.

"They regard it as the American dream; that's what has lifted generations of people. But they want more than that. They want to feel good about themselves. That's why issues like the environment are very, very strong on the campuses. Even issues like helping the homeless, dealing with the AIDS problem. You find no negatives. They're eager to help out where they can."

That positive view didn't emerge out of thin air for Mario Cuomo. He clings to those images and he won't let go. His father and mother taught him a great deal. In one interesting conversation I had with him about the new books that deal with the dark side of some of our heroes, Abe Lincoln or Thomas More for instance, Cuomo said that his concept of the important figures in his life was more important then whatever the revisionist historians might come up with. He said that he was sticking with his view of his heroes.

"I like the picture of Thomas More I have in my mind. For that matter, I like the picture of my father, my mother I have in my mind. I don't want it to be torn down. What's the good of that? Well, you have to be realistic, you have to see the frailties in all things. I know the frailties, I am the frailty. You don't have to teach me about vulnerability and imperfection. I live it. What's wrong with believing every once in a while that there's something better, and clinging to that? That's what Heaven is. That's what Nirvana is, that's what aspiration is...always hoping for something better."

Mario Cuomo's father was always hoping for something better. The son believes as the father did. His father was a workaholic, providing for his family; and so is the governor.

In his early years in political office, Cuomo was fond of telling stories about his mother and her faith and belief in him. She was incredibly proud of him but never stopped giving him advice, for example her continuous admonitions that he would never be president because he was not for the death penalty.

"I saw my mother cry once and she is one of the strongest people I have met, with the exception of my father. So she has cried once. It did not make her any weaker. Maybe it was evidence of her understanding or compassion or capacity to feel. There is nothing wrong with the capacity to feel."

Once he told a story about how his mother continually called on his brother to help her with the little things in his life. She is "a ruggedly independent woman," he says. One lovely story that people want to hear again and again is how she called the governor's brother Frank to come fix "the sink, the faucet."

"And my brother says," Cuomo recounts, "'Why are you always calling me? Because I am the oldest? Call Mario.' And she says, 'How can I call Mario, he is going to be president.'"

Cuomo always told that story right after a long explanation of why he wasn't going to be president. And that wasn't the only reference to brother Frank.

AC: What does Frank do now?

MC: Frank is a supervisor, I don't know his exact title, but I know his role is to supervise Waldbaum's supermarkets. I don't know how many of them, but I think he has the Long Island area. He has done that for many many years. He is a very committed and loyal member of the Waldbaum family's supermarkets. They've just sold out to, I don't know what the group is, but they've sold out in one of these major transactions.

AC: Do you have to take any garbage when you do something, for example, when you sign a bottle bill which means that Waldbaum's has to take all of those dirty bottles back?

MC: Sure. Frankie was my older brother—a person whom I respect immensely for his strength and for his wisdom and for his kindness to me of many, many years. And that is something that's grown over the years. Another reason you have to love him and respect him is that he would never tell you about incidents like that. He would never call up and say, "Boy they're beating me up because of the bottle bill or this or that." But I am certain that's happened to him more than once, and he handles it very well.

He's a terrific, terrific human being. He's carried the load in my family for a long time. He was in the service at least twice—I think it was emergency action when he was called back for another situation. He did all the work in the store 'cause he was the first in the family. He did all the hard stuff and made it easier for me—I was the youngest in the family. Between my brother and my sister, life was made very, very simple for me as the youngest. I owe him a great deal, and my oldest sister.

AC: And when he comes to Albany to the mansion, how does he feel about all this?

MC: Us, we all laugh. My family's a little bit different from some families. I don't know what it is. My Mama and Papa, my sister, my brother and myself. The grocery store had a very powerful effect on us. It was a marvelous education. Remember seven days a week you're dealing with the whole world.

AC: And a lot of interdependence.

MC: Well, it was a wonderful chemistry that had developed. We didn't have much time for socializing, we didn't even have much time for our own relatives 'cause the store was always open. But we were always dealing with people. The rest of the family more than I because I was the youngest. I was spoiled. I worked too, but nothing like my brother and sister. We don't take too seriously, my family doesn't take too seriously things like the mansion. We love it and my mother's overwhelmed by it, but she's knows it's going to pass. She's seen enough of life not to take seriously all the happiness of the moment, because someday there'll be sadness. While they're delighted and grateful, they are not overwhelmed. They've seen so much of life, the whole family, that they're not apt to be overwhelmed by many things.

Once I threw a question at the governor, asking him what he would do if he won the lottery, which at the time was $28 million dollars. His first thought was about his family. He said that his bet was that there really wasn't much of a difference between the way most Americans would use their winnings.

"What people would really want to do is to take care of the necessities in their own family. They would want to take care of their parents, if they had parents. Take care of their kids, take care of their mortgage—then think beyond.

"The best thing that money can do for you," said the governor, "is to buy your liberty, buy freedom for me as a politician." Then the governor told me about a visit from Dexter Luther King, the son of the late Dr. Martin Luther King. Dexter Luther King, he said, was an investment banker who wanted to make a "contribution to the world." King came to see him "and talked about his own career."

"I had the same advice for him as I had for my son: get economically independent. Why? So that you don't need politics for a living, because if you do then it makes you vulnerable. So if I had the money, what would I do with it? I guess, after taking care of my family and assuring my own independence... there are all kinds of good causes that I would like to contribute to."

With that understood, I asked him whether he wouldn't like to spend some of the money on a yacht. Once again he came right back to his family. He assured me that he was not a yacht person. "I do not want to demean yachts. There are all kinds of persons who build yachts in this state and there are lots of people who cannot live without a boat."

But he said, "I am not a yacht person. I don't enjoy going on the high seas spending weekends fishing." According to Cuomo, "It doesn't take a whole lot to make me comfortable."

In the end, said Cuomo, "I've got to be sure that my kids are alright, sure that my family is taken care of; after that there is not a whole lot I want. I want first of all to be able to do my job. Then, to be able to read, feel productive about my job, spend time with my family, go for walks, that is enough for me."

An understanding about how deeply Mario Cuomo feels about the role of family in American life is illustrated by an early conversation I had with him in 1985 about white collar crime. It was not surprising that he brought it all back to family. The family that sets bad examples for its children should not be surprised when it gets bad results.

"I think when the whole society, even the people who regard themselves as responsible, is detected to be hypocritical about our laws, that makes them harder to enforce. It creates a pervasive disrespect for the law. If you're a parent who regularly runs through red lights, if you're a parent who regularly tells jokes about beating the tax people, if you're a parent who 'cokes up,' your kids get confused when you say to them 'You have to live by the law.'" It always comes down to the love that parents have for their families. This enters into every aspect of Cuomo's life. If people would only treat each other as family, he says, society would be better off.

Take this 1986 example. I was asking him about his eating habits. He went to great lengths to describe how meals were prepared nutritiously at the mansion because of Matilda's supervision. As a result of her watching over things and eating vegetables and healthy meals, Matilda, he said, weighs thirty pounds less than when they were married. That is the good, loving wife watching out for him. But he can never resist showing the love disguised as humor that is part of family life, like the time he discussed finding ways to sneak his favored bagels into the governor's home. That, he said, is because, "...the mansion does not lend itself to bagels." What's more, Cuomo tries to skip lunch because of his continuing battle with his belly. "I make a firm resolution not to eat before dinner when I go home because that is the very worst thing that you can do. "And then," he admits, "every night I eat when I go home." That's a description of behavior most of us can relate to.

One particular conversation on the subject of his parents stands out. I was trying to figure out when in his life he first understood that he was something called a Democrat. The conversation took place a few days before Christmas in 1988, and I think I caught him in a mellow mood.

I asked him, "Governor at what age did you know that you were a Democrat?" I was looking for the influence of family on his political development. I wanted to know what their role was in his adoption of Democratic party values. But he said "no." He said that they were too busy to pay attention to politics. It was the school, he said, that made him into a Democrat. He became a Democrat, "I think when I noticed that there was an unevenness in the world— when I noticed that some people needed help from other people."

Cuomo told me that it was the public schools which gave so many of his friends "a shot," a chance. So he said he became a Democrat "when I came to appreciate the idea of the public school." Cuomo says that the public school "was an extremely powerful experience in my life." Furthermore, said the governor, it "didn't take long" before he recognized that the schools "provided everyone with a chance." It was one place where everybody had equal opportunity, whether you were rich or poor." It was, he said, "a great equalizer."

AC: Were your parents Democrats?
MC: My parents were literally working seven days a week in a grocery store. They didn't understand politics. We had never seen an assemblyman. We had never seen a senator. We had never seen a councilman. Nobody ever came to our neighborhood to win votes. There were no posters on the telephone poles on Rockaway Road. Then it was one of the forgotten areas, so poor that it had no political infrastructure, no organization. Many of the business places did not have unions.

Then the governor told me about how all of that meant an entirely different kind of communication. There was "no television" and "there is no great linkage by communication device."

A large "part of the people couldn't read newspapers and lot of the people did not have time to read the newspapers and a lot of the people didn't want to spend the two cents for the *Daily News* or *Daily Mirror*."

Trying the old trick of "I'll tell you my story if you tell me yours," I told the governor of a time that I came home from the sixth grade and told my mother that we were having a class election and that I was going to vote for Eisenhower against Stevenson. I told him how my mother turned around to me and said, "No, dear, you can't do that, we're Democrats." Then I asked him if that's the way it happened in his house.

But the governor said no, "We came to it by our own devices and we came very slowly." His parents knew little of politics and were too busy working to find out more. As a result, "there were very few of us in the neighborhood who wound up being political."

Cuomo's sensitivity about the media violating the private lives of his children is well known. It's a feeling shared by anyone whose child has suffered at the hands of the media because of a parent's personal position or notoriety. After one such incident, I asked him about these feelings. His anger over a particular episode had dissipated and now he was magnanimous and giving, saying that public service sometimes brought a heavy price with it. One of the most difficult was that families often suffered from rough treatment by the press. But then he went out of his way to defend the First Amendment, as he always did.

Even the family dog, Ginger, to whom Cuomo was incredibly attached, qualified for Cuomo protection. One such example occurred when *The New York Post* ran an exclusive story stating that Ginger had bitten a woman who had come to the mansion at first lady Matilda's invitation. The *Post* had called Ginger (a dog I knew to be a mutt) an "Irish Setter." "First of all," I asked the gov, "is Ginger an Irish setter?"

MC: No.
AC: *The Post* got it wrong, right?

MC: Right.

AC: Now, did the dog bite the girl or not?

MC: You would have to ask Ginger.

AC: The last time I asked Ginger I got into tremendous trouble, you will remember, and now I have great affection for the dog.

MC: You should talk to Ginger, she can bark for herself.

AC: The fact is that this is a matter you may not care to discuss with us. Correct?

MC: Well, Ginger might not choose to bark. She has a constitutional Fifth Amendment right not to bark.

It doesn't matter whether it's a son, a dog or a wife. You only speak positively of them. Once, after Matilda came back from a trip abroad, I asked Cuomo to talk about her.

MC: She's a very bright person.

AC: I know that. And a very nice person.

MC: She is as nice as she is bright. And she has a quality that exceeds even those two: she's tolerant.

AC: Do you think she's tolerant of you, Governor?

MC: Very much so.

AC: What a nice thing for a husband to say. Don't you think it's nice of you to say that?

MC: It's inevitable...if I have any respect for the truth at all.

Matilda is truly seen by the governor as his better half. Listen to this conversation he had with me about my own wife, Roselle.

AC: You saw the Legislative Correspondents Association show last week?

MC: I saw it, yes. I saw you there, I saw your lovely, lovely wife. What is her name again?

AC: Roselle.

MC: Roselle. If you are listening, Roselle, I repeat my question. Why would you marry this guy? She is lovely and bright. I think there is something—I have the same situation at home—I think there is something about a lot of these women. Their one vulnerability is an immense sympathy for people of lesser intellectual stature and good looks. I think they feel sorry for us. I think that is what it comes down to.

AC: You mean less good looks Governor.

MC: Yes. What did I say?

AC: I thought you implied that she might have married me because I was good looking.

MC: No, no, no, no. I am certain that wasn't her motivation.

He continued.

MC: I was at Tulane University recently to make an address. I was at a private dinner at the home of the president. I sat next to this lovely lady, who was struck by my countenance and said, 'You know, you're not as ugly in person as you are on television.' Which I heard before. Seriously, I really have. I shared that comment with the audience and they all roared of course. And I added, 'I heard that before, but this woman happened to be an anthropologist. And from an anthropologist, that really is a heavy indictment.' Well, anyway...

AC: Governor, I can appreciate that experience. We share that small problem in common.

MC: It gets us sympathy.

AC: As a matter of fact, many anthropologists study gorillas. Did you know that?

MC: I'm sure of that. And monkeys. (A reference between us to the fact that Cuomo's children call him a gorilla.)

Cuomo finds himself wanting when he compares himself to Matilda.

There are people around Cuomo whom I don't care for but Matilda is not one of them. She is a wonderful lady. What's more, she has always served as Cuomo's alter ego. He acknowledged constantly on our radio program that Matilda is his better. I once asked the governor about how he met her and he carried on at great length about the old style Italian interview that the Raffa family put him through when he asked for her hand.

MC: That was a whole different era. I was summoned before the men of the Raffa family. Seriously. And they sat as a solemn jury, three of them, my father-in-law and his two eldest sons and asked me penetrating questions about my capacity to make a living.

AC: Sounds like a judicial screening committee.

MC: I did not do well, I must tell you. As a matter of fact, I did not do well with that whole jury. But fortunately I went from there to another room where Mrs. Raffa, my mother-in-law, was very gentle and kind and took a liking to me. And by her own devices was able to turn the men around in the Raffa household.

Then once, when I was interviewing Matilda on a television program, I told her that he had told me the story of his interview before the family. Later, I told him about telling Matilda.

AC: I told Matilda, "The governor told me that when he met you and wanted to marry you he came to your house. And he asked for your hand." You know that you and I have talked about this before. "And the brother and the father interviewed you and Mrs. Raffa had to take her husband into the other room to convince him that you were O.K."

And she looked at me and she said, "He told you that?"

Now I had the governor hooked. He was chuckling and he said, "And then what?"

Now I was laughing so loud that I could hardly get the words out.

MC: Thank God nobody listens. Go ahead, and then...?

AC: And then she said, she said, "You know I had a lot of other suitors."

MC: She did, she had thirty-three. Oh sure, she had Iggy who owned a macaroni factory. She had hordes of guys. She had Iggy and Charlie. They were all lining up to court her. Absolutely.

AC: So those guys, the brother and the father, they thought they were going to make the choice, huh?

MC: It was not unusual, I guess, for them to take a vital interest. They had a kind of paternal and avuncular interest in the situation. They wanted to be sure. This was the first in the family to be married and it was the treasure of the family, their pride and joy and they wanted to be sure that the person who asked for her hand was qualified and worthy. They were quite precise about their questions.

AC: What was the toughest question they asked?

MC: "How are you going to support her?"

So family is at the heart of everything. For example, Cuomo's strongly held views on welfare. Those who believe that Mario Cuomo is an advocate of the welfare state don't understand him. Despite the entreaties of liberal members and leaders of the State Assembly to do more for those on welfare, he constantly held the line and in his final electoral effort he was defeated because many of the very groups who most depended on welfare turned on him for not doing enough. On the other hand, he was infuriated with those who he felt incorrectly said that those on welfare are able-bodied people. Perhaps that's because on one of the radio shows this fiercely proud man disclosed that his own family was, for a time, on welfare for a short period after they immigrated from their native Italy.

Within his own family, Cuomo expected a lot, especially from his children. Matilda told me once that the governor spent almost every dinner hour quizzing his children as he would a law school student, making them defend each proposition and the assumptions behind it. One of the most touching stories that Cuomo ever told me, this one not on the radio show, was of receiving a tape from his son Christopher while at Yale, who thanked him for preparing him so well for college. "They haven't taught me anything here that we didn't talk about at supper," Christopher said.

The governor is fiercely protective of his son Andrew who was so active in assuring Cuomo's political success. He refers to him and to his work affectionately. One December when I was asking him for his New Year's predictions, I asked him about his son Andrew's future. "He will work even harder than he is working now, which is difficult to believe." Of particular pride to Cuomo is his son's decision to devote himself almost entirely to the plight of the homeless. Presently, Andrew Cuomo is serving as Assistant Secretary of Housing and Urban Development. According to Cuomo, his son's effort at building "transitional housing for the homeless, in my opinion, is one of the best things that has ever been done for the homeless. It pulls them out of places like the Martinique (an infamous 'welfare hotel' on the West Side of Manhattan) and puts them into clean, protected environments."

Carefully giving the credit to his son, Cuomo says "people in Los Angeles have called on him to come out there and tell them how he has done it. He is getting volunteers from all over the country." Proud papa says that luminaries such as John F. Kennedy Jr. and Nelson Rockefeller Jr. have either joined the board of Andrew's non-profit corporation or are on their way to joining. "It is something that attracts young people who want to do good things for people. It's also a wonderful thing, isn't it? A terrific idea, and he has implemented it beautifully. I am proud of him. I hope he is happy."

Mario Cuomo also believed that as the father of his political family he had a responsibility to those whom he pledged to protect.

Take, for example, the state work force, a perpetually maligned group of workers who serve as targets for midnight callers to radio talk shows. Often they are favorite punching bags for newspaper editors and columnists.

After a particularly tough article about state workers appeared in a local paper, I asked the governor whether state workers were a convenient punching bag for unhappy people. His answer is very reminiscent of the way he speaks when someone picks on one of his children unfairly.

"I think state workers are picked on and so are politicians. The difference with politicians is that when one takes a job as an elected official, one is asking for criticism. That's the contract one makes. I know I'm going to be criticized. I know that the people are going to scrutinize me and they're going to check my work and some of them are going to reject me and maybe even be abusive. But I know that and I bargain for it and I do it anyway. And so a politician has no right to complain. What are you complaining about? You asked to be scrutinized. I'm not happy when they attack members of my family or embarrass them. But the truth is, and maybe this is part of the unhappiness, that you knew that was inevitable when you took the job. You asked for it in a way.

"That is not true of the person who is changing bedpans in a hospital or of a corrections officer in one of our institutions or of a school teacher. Sure, they are public employees or public servants. But they didn't offer themselves up to be the object of criticism as an excuse for other failings of this society that they have nothing to do with. And I think that's what's happened.

"Can you criticize politicians fairly? Of course you can. Are they perfect? Of course not. Are public servants, the members of the CSEA [Civil Servants Employees Association] and the PEF [Public Employees Federation] perfect? Of course they are not perfect. But I reject utterly the conclusion that they are not at least as competent as the people in the private sector and certainly more competent than the people at the top of this society who over the last few years have introduced new levels of greed; who have introduced a rip off mentality that took down established businesses causing people a loss of work just to have a quick profit; who loaded us down with junk bonds and consumerism and all sorts of false values that now have us more heavily indebted than ever before in our nation's history. And with all that's happened—with all the greed and all the drugs, with all the pain, with all the crime, you're going to spend time taking a shot at a public worker because she wants five minutes more for lunch or because you saw one of them in a state car. Okay. All of that is wrong if it is done, but let's have a little sense of proportion here. And yes, I do think that they've been punching bags."

Like a tough father, Cuomo told me that he had not been afraid to criticize unions when it was appropriate, and told me that "they've not always been happy with me." His fierce arguments and negotiations with them in 1991 are now legendary.

"But, I think in fairness," said the governor, "they deserve more credit than they've gotten." Road workers, teachers, hospital workers, policemen, firemen, were all cited by him as people dedicated to helping improve the quality of life. "How about the people who deal with our retarded children or our elderly people in institutions?

"I was at the Nassau Medical Center yesterday. I talked to doctors and paramedics and nurses and firemen and policemen who saved lives in the Avianca crash because they were there, because they were unconcerned about their own welfare, their own comfort. They worked around the clock. I met some of the victims of the crash. All they could talk about was how magnificent the people of the institution were. These are public servants who work in that public hospital. And I don't think that they're properly appreciated." Once again, Cuomo speaking up for his children, those that were entrusted to him for protection.

On one program I asked him what regrets he had in life. He told me the one thing he regretted was the fact that he hadn't spent as much time with his children as he might have liked. On a subsequent program I asked the governor whether he would compensate for not spending enough time with his children by spending more time with his grandchildren.

He wasn't ready to go that far, he confessed. "Time is a problem," he said. Playfully, he said that it was a tough thing to spend time with "the children of your children," unless, he said "unless you play basketball." He said the time to spend with your children is "when you are young and they are young, extremely young." That, said Cuomo, is the important period because "baby spends a lot of time with the mother and the father." That time is most important because "people now tell us that the first three or four years is our opportunity to create deep and permanent impressions on our children. Children should be surrounded by love and sweetness and good solid firm influences." Here we see Cuomo at his most sensible and perhaps his most bedrock conservative self.

This formative time in a child's life is very important, said Cuomo. It is a time when "there are a lot of opportunities for instructing them by spending time and going for walks and listening to music and reading poetry and teaching them some of the beautiful things." Cuomo cautioned that parents spend a lot of time telling their children what not to do and too little accentuating the beautiful things in life. He counseled parents to look at "the beautiful things and not just the wrong ones."

So teaching one's children by example is most important to Cuomo. Take the hardest physical thing that Mario Cuomo ever had to do, that was to quit smoking. As usual, one of his sons, this time Christopher, figured heavily in his decision.

AC: You smoked, but you knew enough to get away from it, right?
MC: Three packs a day, until April of 1976.

AC: And how did you stop it?

MC: It was Good Friday. Christopher, our youngest, was just then much younger than he is now, thirteen years younger which means he was about six, and he came into my room where I was smoking like a chimney and said "Mommy says you don't love us." And I said, "Your mother said a lot of unkind things about Dad but how could she say that?" He said, "Well, she says smoking could kill you, and if you really love us you wouldn't smoke."

Very effective move by Matilda. Effective enough so that I said to myself, "It's Good Friday. Let me give it up for the weekend. It's traditional for Easter." And I said boldly to Christopher as I put it out in my ashtray, "This is my last cigarette. That's it. Daddy's not smoking anymore."

And then for two days I suffered, and Monday morning after Easter Sunday my lips were swollen, my tongue was swollen, I had headaches, I couldn't wait to get at the cigarettes.

AC: But you didn't have any professional help?

MC: No. Then Christopher came into the room, and says "Mommy says you're going to smoke again because Easter is over. You won't do that, will you Dad?" Well, I was beside myself and so upset, I said "No, no, no I won't." And I went to work, and I was terrible. Tuesday I was worse. Wednesday worse still. Thursday I had hives all over my body, literally. I called a doctor, explained it to him, he said, "That's called withdrawal. You don't understand—you have a nicotine addiction, and it has a very strong hold on you. You people think that only alcohol does it, or the other substances that you might ingest. Nicotine does the same thing to you." That so disgusted and frightened me that I decided to continue to stay off cigarettes. And I have stayed off them ever since.

I will tell you this however. I think I know the secret to giving it up. Because I tried many, many times to give it up before that. And I think that each time that I tried to give up smoking, I said to myself after a while, one week, two weeks, after a while the desire, the yen, will go away and I will no longer miss the cigarettes. And when after a month, the desire did not go away, then you use that as an excuse, saying "Ah ha, the process has cheated me, what was supposed to happen, didn't happen. I may as well go back to smoking." And that's what you do.

The only way to give them up is to understand that the desire never goes away completely. That you always have to wrestle the devil. It will subside a great deal. So that you can live comfortably without them, as I do now, but the desire never goes away. Then there are moments of pressure. When the phone rings and someone says, "That's Alan Chartock and you must do the show, Governor!" That's when the tension comes back and you find yourself reaching across the desk top for your pack of Camels. Which of course is no longer there.

While Cuomo is a public man he is basically private. His family is terribly important to him and I have seen him cancel a whole day's schedule to help his daughter study for an exam or on a Thanksgiving when the family is coming home. And when the family is isn't around the man hurts, as he admitted on one show.

It all began when I asked the governor how he felt when all his children didn't come home because their spouses' families had rights, too. Thinking a bit about the empty nest syndrome I asked him whether he experienced a sense of personal loss when his children were with their in-laws on an important holiday.

I guess the gov was ready for the question. He really concentrated on the issue.

"I think most people do. You have your family, your children, your spouse for better or worse. Mostly, you live together, you suffer together, you fight, you love one another. You want to stay together. When you can't be together on the most important days,

when you reflect on family and life on days like Chanukah, Christmas, Thanksgiving, you, of course, miss them. There is no doubt
about that."

What I wanted to know was whether the feeling of loss, of
the empty nest, actually took him by surprise. In other words, did
he expect the feeling of emptiness?

The governor answered in the present tense. "I am not ready
for it," he said.

I didn't ask him for a prediction. I told him I wanted to know
how he felt when it actually happened, as it did once in the past.
"No, I am not surprised. I am not surprised at all and that does
not make it easier."

Not content to let it drop, I asked him whether it was rougher
on him or Matilda.

"I think is equally rough on both of us and you will experience it some day, Alan."

Then the governor said that he and Matilda consoled themselves when the children didn't come home, saying, "Well, they
are enjoying themselves with other families and that is good and
what we really want is *their* comfort, *their* security, *their* happiness
and if they are happy that is fine. You tell yourself that and at the
same time you feel sorry for yourself."

Mario Cuomo is committed to helping his family but he also
has high expectations from them. Like his expectations of his kids
and his responsibility to them, Cuomo as governor had similar
expectations of those around him in his extended governmental
family.

It is not surprising that he followed the same path with his
administration. He expected excellence from them. But his span
of control was massive. The governor, as father, wanted to know
what was going on in his immediate family. He described his political organization as the spokes of a wheel with himself at the center, rather than as the more traditional chain of command. And,
like a father, he was more than understanding with the weaker links
in his organization. That is, he may have chastised them but he

was unlikely to fire them, thus characterizing himself as one who believed that if someone was not good in one job, there was still another place in his administration for them.

For example, he fired his housing commissioner, Yvonne Scruggs-Leftwich, from her job and put her in charge of a specially created Black Advisory Panel. When his drug commissioner, Julio Martinez came under intense criticism for awarding contracts to friends Cuomo transferred him out of that job and announced that he was putting him into a position in the Department of Corrections where he could use his talents under more intense supervision. Cuomo took a lot of heat for that move.

Cuomo was saddled with a reputation of not recruiting top people to his administration. His detractors faulted him for his recruiting policies, suggesting that some of his appointments were weak while his strongest appointments were holdovers from the previous Carey administration, a charge offered early in the administration by the former governor himself. It seems increasingly clear that Cuomo wanted to run the show and selected agents who were capable of following through on his orders. He had little time or patience to waste, negotiating with inflated egoists who insisted on resisting his orders through passive aggressive techniques.

His favorites within his team of workers seemed to be those who were obedient to a fault; those who had no competing ambition with that of the governor. That does not necessarily mean that he *respected* these people more than those who gave him a hard time. Included in this favorite list were his trusted retainer, Fabian Palomino, who utterly dedicated himself to the governor. Palomino may look and speak like Don Quixote's Sancho Panza but he was built to mythic proportions by the governor who frequently referred to Palomino as "the most brilliant lawyer I know." There is no one Cuomo seems to hold in identical standing as his friend Fabian.

Another example of favorites was Cuomo's long time agent Henry (Hank) Williams, the former Commissioner of Environmental Conservation, who over and over described himself as a good soldier for the governor. Unlike former state conservation commissioners Ogden Reed and Peter A.A. Berle, who gave their governors tough times, Williams chose not to challenge Cuomo but, instead, carried out his commands and never flinched at taking criticism.

As father of the family, Cuomo understands that there is a time when the children will rebel. My guess is that he sees it as a positive and understands it. He is a very demanding and tough father. But when the going gets tough he is there for those who depend on him.

It is essential when looking for an understanding of Cuomo that one recognize that the man was as serious about his responsibilities to the state as he was to the family. That is all covered with an appropriate layer of self-doubt which keeps the man incredibly honest. He saw his father work himself to the bone and he has replicated that pattern. If he isn't working he isn't happy. His kids seem to have inherited the same way of doing things. Those working through both the Cuomo and early Pataki times couldn't get over how much less was demanded under Pataki.

Cuomo is not happy when those who have been entrusted to him suffer. He is practical; he knows that there are limits to his capacity to produce. But like all sensitive human beings, he agonizes over his inability to protect others.

That's what being the father in an extended family meant to Mario Cuomo.

5

A SENSE OF HUMOR

Mario Cuomo once told me, "I think laughter is great. I think humor is important. I think God made the world for everyone to enjoy." Which is the best way to start this chapter devoted to the Cuomo sense of humor.

I began one *Capitol Connection* by simply asking, "Governor, how are you?"

He answered, "Um, ontologically I exist therefore I am good, I guess. I'll settle for that at the moment."

You never know how he's going to begin.

Let's face it, the guy is probably the best political debater in America and he's tough to fight. One of the reasons is because he's so funny. He uses humor to communicate and to make contact with people. Every once in a while I close my eyes and I think I'm hearing Mel Brooks do his classic rendition of "The Two Thousand Year Old Man."

Once we had a long debate during which I could hardly hold up my end. The guy was just too fast for me. Finally, thank goodness, he felt I had had enough. But he couldn't resist one last punch. As usual he referred to the fact that I'm a bit shorter and much lighter than he is, a source of constant gubernatorial comment.

"You know I wouldn't be surprised that a person who is so slightly built as you are, Chartock, should make such a loud splash when your body hits the deck."

Even my marriage has not been exempt from comment. The dialogue went something like this.

AC: What time do you go to sleep, Governor?

MC: Normally? Usually quite late.

AC: Really? And you get up quite early?

MC: Oh, sure.

AC: Well, you're good...

MC: I'm not good. I'm lucky. Lucky to have a job that I love, lucky to be in a situation in which I prefer not to sleep.

AC: I don't like to sleep either, but I find that if I'm not asleep by 9 or 9:30, I can't get up at 4 o'clock in the morning.

MC: You can go to sleep at 9 or 9:30?"

AC: Yes, sir.

MC: Are you kidding? What, do you have your graham crackers and milk and then you tuck yourself in? At 9, 9:30?"

AC: Milk has cholesterol in it...

MC: So you have graham crackers and skim milk or graham crackers and distilled water, whatever...

AC: You know I haven't seen my wife in many years because she goes to bed after I do and I get up before she does.

MC: I was wondering what kept your marriage intact...

But not only does Cuomo pick on my looks and build and marriage, he also deals with his own. Listen to this:

"People feel so sorry for me when they see my face on television. I have gotten letters from wonderful grandmothers, suggesting I should use tea bags; tannic acids in the tea bags, they tell me, will make the bags under my eyes go down. I've had doctors from San Diego write me letters offering to perform operations on the west coast to 'debagify' me. 'It would take nothing at all.

Slit it open. It is not just bad for your looks, it is bad for your health. So we can get those bags our from under your eyes.' So, I don't know. Maybe my homeliness gets me some sympathy, might even be helping me in the polls."

For years, people have been calling me and saying that I should be tougher on the guy. What they don't know is that I'm as tough as I can be. He's a very good talker. But he doesn't like to be reminded about that. Once I made the fatal mistake of saying that he could beat me because he was a better talker than I am.

It was July of 1988 and I was telling him that George Bush was going to be president. He was giving me a loquacious, intelligent and well organized set of arguments which he felt conclusively proved that Michael Dukakis would win. But when I said that Bush would make it he put his tongue way back in his mouth and let me have it.

"Now, that is a truly cheap shot, for a guy that makes all his living by talking, without respect for what he says. Just by glibness you have gotten yourself on television. Nobody knows what you're talking about, but you look quite assured, you seem to have the facts, you have glasses, you have everything going for you. You have the title of professor, but you really do nothing. You don't build chairs, you never made a road or a bridge, you can't put a nut on a screw [he should have said "bolt," a mistake for which he was chastised in the following week], you have no talent, you produce nothing except words. And you talk to me about being a talker? You're a talker and not a doer. Just for that, I'm not gonna talk anymore. You'll see what happens to this program..." He then hummed for a few moments, but began to talk again after the gag began to pall.

For years he claimed that we were all alone on the radio, that there was only one mythical listener out there. Then we were besieged by hundreds of letters claiming that *they* were the long lost third listener. So then the governor changed his tune. Then he said we had *two* listeners and their names were Harvey and

Ethel. But then he would indicate that Harvey and Ethel were dis-illusioned with the show.

"Ethel dropped out, I met her. She didn't like it. I met her in Oswego. This is true. I met her. She says, 'I'm Ethel.'

"I said, 'Ethel, how are you, what do you think of the show?' She says, 'I don't listen any more.'

"I said, 'Why?'

"She said, 'Two borers in a row did it to me.' Now she's listening to a program they pipe in from China or something."

Following along the same line was a conversation I had with the governor about his barber.

AC: Governor, who cuts your hair?

MC: Occasionally I do. You can tell when I do it. If you look at both sides, almost always they're not even. We have a $1.98 razor comb. Have you ever seen them, Alan?

AC: Yes, I know them.

MC: And if you do it, if you have a really light touch, and you have as little hair as I do, you can survive with a razor comb for long periods of time. For when I have butchered, hatch-eted, gouged out obvious chunks, and need to get it smoothed a bit, I go down the block to a guy by the name of Paul, who works diagonally across from the Capitol. I usu-ally go early in the morning, and I'm usually there alone, and Paul straightens out my head. And then I go to work.

AC: Well then, who's Jean Claude?

MC: No, you mean Jean Paul.

AC: Oh, Jean Paul! Now my sources tell me that there's a major leak here. What if somebody in the Capitol found out about this guy and started asking him questions about him and the governor.

MC: Poor Jean Paul.

AC: I'm told that if we had asked him the day before you made your announcement about not running for president, that everybody would have had it a day earlier.

MC: Not true, not true. But I think I know the source of the leak. This barber cuts Peg Breen's hair.

AC: Oh, Peg Breen from Inside Albany. Used to be on Inside Albany, now works for the Commission On Investigation in New York City. That right? Governor, with all due respect, a lot of people never heard of Inside Albany or public television for that matter.

MC: So can I tell you something? What it comes down to, Alan, is that we are our own audience here. I don't know, maybe once in a while, a member of your family will send you a note with some made up signature like "Ethel Baxter from Whalen," you know? But the truth is, Alan, it's you and I.

Mario Cuomo's hair came up again, several years later, after Berk Breathed had featured Cuomo in the backdrop of one of his cartoon strips. Cuomo grabbed the opportunity to conjecture why the cartoonist had inserted his picture on the wall in the back of the strip.

AC: Governor, here's the first question and it's on almost everybody's mind. It gets further than anything else we can discuss because people are coming up to me on the street; they want to know about it, everybody wants to know about Bloom County.

MC: I don't understand Bloom County.

AC: It's the wildest thing I ever saw.

MC: I don't understand what the message was. I am flattered to death that I made Bloom County. I have received congratulations from everybody in the "Yuppie" category. They say, "You have made Bloom County. That's it, you might just as well retire."

AC: But nobody understands what it was. For those who don't know about it, it's a comic strip that runs in newspapers all over the country. And on the wall, I don't even remember what else was going on, some cat was talking to some dog or something. On the wall was this picture of Mario Cuomo in each frame. In the last one his hair is standing up on his head.

MC: I think that was the token of respect, the hair. Let me explain this to you as I see it. Let me tell you what the flattery was in it. I'm not saying I deserve this compliment. This is a yuppie strip, it appeals to the yuppies. They put a picture on the wall of Mario Cuomo looking like Rudolph Valentino with a hangover. Okay? Hair slicked down on his head, baggy eyes, the hair is the key. The first three boxes, they have the hair slicked down on my head. Then they come in with a hair dryer a la Jack Kemp, a la a generation of yuppies.

AC: The $35 haircut crowd.

MC: Yup, and they came with a hair dryer and they gave me the hair dryer treatment which allowed my hair to stick up straight. Okay? That's introduction, initiation, acceptance into "Yuppiedom." Now, there's this interesting little character at the bottom of the fourth piece, a bird, or a goose, or a duck, whatever; and he or she, it's hard to tell, is lamenting. See, this hair dryer facing him is blowing him practically out of this strip, and he says, "See, they don't do this for people of lesser stature." That, too, I take as a compliment, suggesting that I am of higher stature. Now, this may not be true, any of it. It may be that it was a rank insult. It may be that they were making fun of my hair. I choose to feel flattered. It makes me feel better.

Once I told him that I wanted to "throw" him a few key words and asked him to respond to them.

"You're going to throw me words? Are they going to be straight words, knuckle words, curve words? I don't mind high hard ones but I don't like those little dinky curves."

Of course, he can see trouble coming a mile away and that's when he can be at his funniest.

Once I heard that he had stood some people up at a big dinner because of an emergency at the dentist.

AC: That must be extraordinary for a dentist to sit there with his hand in the mouth of the governor.

MC: Especially when you do it for more than four hours or so.

AC: Is that right? Can you imagine, for example, I mean there's no analogy here, but can you imagine having your hand in Stalin's mouth for four hours?

MC: I'd like to think you could've thought of a better analogy...

AC: I said there's no analogy. I said that.

MC: Then why did you even bring it up?

AC: Because I just started to free associate.

MC: Well, fortunately you didn't say Mussolini. It really would've hit a nerve.

AC: So to speak.

Or there is his constant reminder that I am a foreigner, a citizen of Massachusetts, which he never lets me forget. He brought it up once when I got on him about his coffee drinking.

I told him that I had read in the paper that he drank "not one, not two, not three, not four, not five, but six cups of coffee before nine o'clock in the morning." In a voice filled with mock concern I told him, "We have discussed this before and I have tried to give my best advice on this coffee. I have told you not to do it and yet you persist."

I expected that he would defend his imbibing of the stuff but instead he stopped all discussion cold by saying, quite disingenuously and mockingly "...I won't do it any more and ..."

But before he could carry it any further I interrupted and reminded him that the only reason I was commenting on this was "...because I am only thinking of you."

To which the governor said simply but devastatingly "Thank you." I replied, again in mock concern, "You are the only governor I have." To which the governor responded, "No, you have two governors. One where you live and the second in the state where you make all your money. You live this interesting double life where you have your home in Massachusetts and you slip furtively across the line once a day or so to come here to harvest and carry back the goodies. Our state university gives you money, our public radio gives you money, commercial TV gives you money and you put it in your little sack pocket in your vest and go back over the state line in the night."

Months later I said that I'd heard he was to deliver an important speech in Springfield, Massachusetts. "I have a special place in my heart for Massachusetts, you know that," I said to him.

His response had not changed. "I know that you live there and pay your taxes there and regard yourself as loyal first to Massachusetts and then to the places that make you rich like New York."

Similarly, the stories of his childhood are often loving and humorous. Once I asked him about pigeons. I was trying to trap him into saying whether he would execute pigeons who were becoming a public health nuisance in some areas of the country. I was going to ask him why, if he could execute pigeons, would he be unwilling to execute human beings. Naturally he saw it coming. As usual, diversion became the name of the game.

"Pigeons," he said. "Pigeons were a large part of my youth. Pigeon cooping was an institution in an old polyglot neighborhood like the one where I was born and bred."

I asked him whether he had bred pigeons on his roof.

"My brother owned pigeons in the years before they were licensed. My brother had homing pigeons." His brother's homing pigeons, he said, lived "on a tar covered roof. And when I whistled I saw his pigeons sweeping in great waves over the neighborhood." The governor poignantly reached back into his past to say that his brother's pigeons were superior as they engaged in competition with other flocks reminding us that the name of the game was to capture other people's pigeons with your flock. Concluded the governor, "We had great pigeons. We had chubby pigeons, a temptation to a hungry community."

And speaking of family, Cuomo told me that his family, not Chartock this time, had decided that he was drinking too much caffeine and had put him on a caffeine free diet including an inviolable regime of decaffeinated coffee. And then in mock tones he told me and the non-existent radio audience that wife Matilda didn't know something. He told me that in order to beat the no coffee regime he had purchased a coffee maker. "I lock it in a closet in the library. Matilda does not know about it. Meanwhile," said the governor, "they keep bringing me pots of decaffeinated coffee which I pour in the sink."

His problem, admitted the governor, was that he was afraid he'd get caught because "sometimes the whole place smells and I open the windows." The result said Cuomo to the few thousand people who were hearing his admission about how he cheated, was that he drank his caffeinated coffee which gave him "good nerves" early in the morning.

Once I asked him whether he had sworn off coffee as a New Year's resolution. "Well, I've given up cigarettes, I've given up almost every other pleasurable indulgence in life. Coffee stands between me and total sterility, as I see it. I see it as an alternative to worse vices."

There are some subjects that politicians have learned to stay away from, ever since Jimmy Carter admitted that he had lust in his heart. The lesson learned there is that it is proper to ignore such questions. I, of course, have tried constantly to get him into trouble, like the time I asked him whether he noticed that hem lines were going up according to the gurus of fashion. "Does this trouble you at all?" I asked him. He said, straight as an arrow, "I hadn't even noticed that."

Simply not believing such a thing could be possible I asked him, "Is it true that you don't look at such things?"

To which he replied, very safely, "No, of course, I have three daughters."

So I asked him, "Are you made of ice?"

To which the governor answered: "Of course I look and I am constantly observing and I watch television. Not as much as others but I hadn't noticed that."

Well, I just couldn't let it lie. I asked him whether he thought there was something insidious about the fact that the fashion designers were shortening skirts all at once?

The governor was ready to land and land he did. "Alan, I'm surprised even that it occupies any space in your mind as a question. And I don't know what is on your mind that attracts you to this subject and I don't know what it is about a skirt an inch or two shorter than last year that would intrigue you. People wear bathing suits. Some of them are well above the knee the last time I noticed and I don't know why the skirt that varies one inch or two or three should be provocative and I really don't think that it deserves a lot of attention."

The ice man cometh.

Often he will turn what was a serious subject into a not so serious subject just because he doesn't want to talk about it.

There was that time when he announced, to the consternation of many political pundits, including me, that he would not be a candidate for president. He did not do it on our show, *The Capitol Connection*, but on a call-in show on commercial radio, WCBS, in New York City. I asked him about it and I got a rough time for having suggested in print that he would be running for the top office. In the conversation I referred to his admission that he had his secretary prepare two speeches, one saying that he was running, one that he was not. But he got back at me:

MC: I read one of the most extravagant apologias for bad judgment I've ever seen, written by Alan Chartock. Your description of how come you were wrong about my running for

president was one of the most agonized, one of the most artificial constructs to justify your ignorance and error that I've
ever read anywhere.

AC: Wait a second here...

MC: It was incredible. While instead of just saying, "I was wrong,"
you...are you...is your credibility so fragile in your opinion?
Is your image so weak that you are intimidated by the
prospect of admitting to all of your admiring listeners and
leaders that maybe you were just wrong? Why not admit it?

AC: I said I was wrong. Right in the first sentence.

MC: No, you didn't.

AC: I said a lot of people were wrong...

MC: No, you said "however, here's all the evidence that justified
our conclusion."

AC: Wait a second, Governor, let's be fair about this.

MC: Why should we be fair? Why? Do you want to play by a different rule when it's your turn?

AC: Let's be fair about this for a second. You said in your press
conference, you went out there and you said "I had my secretary write it both ways—that I was running and that I was
not running. And I brought those two to the radio station
and no one knew which way." Now, Governor...

MC: Not important.

AC: What do you mean, that's not important. First of all, here's
the Governor of New York picking on a puny little professor, this absolute nothing Chartock...

MC: Tell the truth here. You're 6-foot-1, 215 pounds.

AC: Okay. [I'm 5'6" and weigh 142 pounds.]

MC: You're playing with this little vulnerable image, you think
it will get you sympathy. Six-foot-one, 215 pounds, is what
I'm told.

AC: Governor, it seems to me that there's an old adage about
smoke and fire.

MC: What is the adage?

AC: Where there's smoke, there's fire. Now here's the deal. It seems to me that even if you don't mean to run, and you're not running, and everybody is insisting that you are running, and planting these stories and writing these stories. And you yourself, it wasn't only Chartock really, as you put it so many times so well, I'm sort of a peanut in the bottom of the barrel.

MC: You're right. Where there is smoke, there is fire. Smoke is that which is produced by fire. But where what looks like smoke is the breath of hot air from the media. It looks like smoke—that doesn't relate to fire. What you're talking about is a breath of hot air. That smoke looks like smoke, but it's not really smoke. And in that case, the adage doesn't apply. We have to think of a new adage for "Where there is a breath of hot air, there's apt to be an overzealous media person trying to create a fire."

AC: Except that media people tend to understand that their audience works with their quarters. They buy their papers or they turn things on, so that there are some things that stories seem to mean more about. I know that's inarticulate.

MC: Yeah, I don't know what you're talking about. Not only is it inarticulate, I don't know what you're saying.

AC: Well, what I'm saying is an editor knows...

MC: Let's try it again.

AC: A governor knows...a governor...a reporter knows...

MC: Let's slow down. Alan, did you have proper sleep last night?

AC: No I didn't, Governor. I was worried about facing you as always.

MC: That's all right.

AC: A reporter knows a good story, an editor knows a good story. Mario Cuomo...

MC: You're very combative. You're super-competitive. Were you denied the marbles when you were young in your house?

AC: Well, it's tough to be a twin, Governor.

MC: Did you get the leftover milk? I mean, what did they do to you? My God, you're always scratching, trying to get the advantage. Everything is a war and complicated. Can't we recite poetry or hum a lot?

AC: [hums] Governor, why is it that everyone seems to want you to run for president?

MC: Because I'm not running.

AC: You think that that's the only reason?"

MC: Don't you remember the girl who wouldn't dance? Everybody wanted to dance with her. And as soon as she danced and proved she was a clod, nobody wanted to dance with her. I could end this wonderful thing by running and doing it poorly. That's what I did in 1977. But as long as I don't want to run, they'll want me to run.

Pretty funny. Once I asked him about why Ed Koch was doing so badly in the 1989 mayoral primary. I told him that "Ed Koch seems to be very unpopular."

The governor who was walking a tightrope in that campaign was being very careful on that occasion. To obfuscate, he adopted his tongue in cheek and give-them-Jabberwocky stance that would make Casey Stengel or Yogi Berra into an admirer: "I don't think so. I think it shows that he is at 28 or 30 percent [in the polls]. He'll need only 40 percent to win the primary so that means that he is 12 percent sure to win the primary."

It made no sense but undaunted, I pushed on. "But you would concede that is a very bad showing?" He answered: "No! I won't concede anything."

"Why not? Why don't you concede anything?"

"I am not a political analyst; you are. I don't get paid for political analysis. You do!"

"Why don't you concede? If you concede it means you are human."

"O.K. I will concede something."

"What?"

"I will concede that you are not as smart as I thought you were."

Another time I asked him whether he thought that the a decision in the Court of Appeals that negated some very tough anti-smoking regulations was as bad as I thought it was. He may have been a bit sensitive, since he appointed all of the judges on the state's high court and since I suggested that six out of the seven were "acting irresponsibly."

The gov did not shilly shally around for a second. You could just see the smile on his face as he let me have it.

"What you are saying is that when you disagree with someone you believe that they are irresponsible for not agreeing with Chartock. That requires a megalomaniac egocentricity, an ultimate arrogance that even most politicians are not able to develop. I congratulate you, Alan. With so little justification you have developed that kind of incredible self-confidence."

Like the aforementioned Casey Stengel, when Cuomo doesn't want to answer a question seriously he doesn't mind moving to humor as a way out.

Then there was the time we were talking about an environmental bond issue that he had proposed. I confess that we did get around to talking about the wisdom of the bond issue but not before we had a particularly interesting exchange about the pronunciation of the word "environment."

I told the gov on our show that I wanted to talk about the "environmental bond issue."

MC: Talk about the what?
AC: The environmental bond issue.
MC: How do you spell "environment"?
AC: I know how to spell environment. E-N-V-I-R-O-N-M-E-N-T.
MC: How come we [meaning you] don't pronounce the "n"?
AC: [struggling] Environnnnment.
MC: EnviRONment. It's too hard to pronounce the "n" so people say envirment. Environnnn mint. It's the environs. The things that surround us.

AC: You know what? You may have come up with a fantastic product. I'm going to give you the idea and then you can go out
and get somebody to market it. How about an Envira Mint?

MC: It's a green tablet that you put in your mouth and it sweet-
ens the breath and it's made of natural mint.

AC: And it's antiseptic.

MC: Great! Chartock and Cuomo, we'll be like the Smith Broth-
ers.

AC: [Trying to get back to the more serious subject] O.K. On
this bill...

MC: [Interrupting] Alan and Mario's...no, strike that, Mario and
Alan's Enviro Mint.

Once I asked him about his predictions for the coming months.
I told him he had to concentrate and that the way to do that was
to place his fingers firmly over his nose over his sinuses and assume
a pose like that of the famous "Thinker" statue.

Cuomo said that he was unwilling to do that. "I need both
hands." A clear self-deprecatory reference to the size of his nose.
I responded that it took just one hand to go into "thinker mode."

He responded, "I need both hands for *my* nose. You do yours
and I'll do mine."

I told him that all that was necessary was that he "just think
and concentrate, now are you ready?" The governor responded,
"No, I'm finding it impossible to breathe."

Spelling is one of the governor's favorite diversionary activities when in intense debate or discussion with me.

I once tried to trap him in the following manner. I had gotten on the case of the New York State Legislature's ethics. I had
suggested to the governor that legislators' private businesses thrive
as a result of their positions and that interest groups have found
ways to put money into legislators' firms.

The governor was not buying into my argument, although
he has indicated on several occasions that he has reservations about
the legislators' ethical standards.

MC: Now you might here or there find a corrupt radio announcer, a corrupt talk show host, a corrupt priest, a corrupt rabbi, a corrupt actor, and therefore a corrupt politician. But, you know the difference between politicians and most of these others is the politician deliberately says to the public, in effect, "Scrutinize me." I entered this profession...

AC: They do not!

MC: Sure they do. The very fact that you enter public service means that you're saying to people, "Scrutinize me."

AC: How about their [secret] caucuses? The public can't tell how they're voting or what they're doing...

MC: You are straining at gnats.

AC: Not at all.

MC: How do you spell gnats?

AC: K-N-A-T-S.

MC: [after both laugh] Do we have any English programs on public radio? You can't spell gnats, well, just a minute...

AC: I know how to spell gnats.

MC: You are going to presume to criticize these legislators, to criticize lawyers, to criticize professionals. You can't spell, you're such a beautiful piece of work.

AC: You know, here we are, talking about something really important and you pick on a poor guy's weakness. You divert the entire conversation away from the...

MC: God forbid.

AC: ...illicit relationships of politicians and the interest groups. And now we're talking about my spelling?

MC: Alan, I'm not making fun of you. That would be wrong. Illiteracy is a problem in this society, it's one we have to deal with...

AC: G-N-A-T-S! There!

MC: Oh really, you looked through a window. Of all the cheap shots, this man had to have the word spelled for him by somebody who works with him.

 AC: That's a lie! Not so. Anyway, let's just move on.
 MC: Try talking with your hands...

Then there was the time I asked him about then Vice President
Quayle and he responded that Quayle would do a lot better than
anyone expected him to since the original expectations were so low.
"He could not be worse or even as bad."

One week I asked the governor what he had experienced in
the preceding week that was "particularly difficult."

"The prospect of doing the show with you this week, Alan."

But I asked him to bear down and to concentrate. Was there
"something that really hit you in the face last week?"

The governor returned to his ontology. Again he announced
that, "I am an ontologist." He said that if he sweats (as an ontologist) "that is good." But, said the governor, now fully launched
into his routine, "If we wake up in a sweat that is twice as good.
We try very, very hard to make something good of everything."
But such an approach, said the governor, "is a difficult state of mind
to keep intact. I guess we are all frail and vulnerable so we give
into needs. And we also have desires. Just existing is virtuous and
good fun, so I prefer not to think of what was hard last week. I
think of all of it being beautiful."

So then I tried to figure out another stratagem. I asked him
if in someone else's approach to life it might be said that someone had thrown him a particularly difficult "hard ball."

But the governor could easily handle the metaphor of the
hard ball.

He responded, "You could see it [the hard ball] as a chance
to hit a home run."

Then the conversation shifted from humor to something a
bit more philosophical. Or was it?

"For something difficult to be something you want to enjoy
it has to be something enjoyable in the doing. To despise it has
to be something you fear." And then the governor went on to suggest that to be tested in life you had to risk failure. "If you had no

chance to fail, you never enjoy what you are doing because you would not know where you were going."

I asked him whether he was afraid of failure.

"No, I'm not afraid of failure, which is why I like success. That's is the whole point."

Not since John F. Kennedy jousted with the reporter May Craig back in the early sixties have we seen an extemporaneous speaker able to spar with reporters and emerge the winner each time. Cuomo's brilliance as an attorney combined with his humor makes for a devastating performance. No matter how wrong I have seen him on an issue, I have never seen him lose an argument. If all else fails there is always humor. He is sarcastic, he hyperbolizes, he is sardonic. His tongue is often way out in his cheek.

He can, of course, smell a trap. Once I really thought I had him. He had said of his *Diaries of Mario Cuomo* that he had not anticipated that people would ever get to see them when he was writing them. I decided to lay a trap for him and ask if the continuation, which he was clearly writing, was also not to be seen by the public but would miraculously end up in print.

I started out by suggesting that he indicated that "those remarks were never intended for publication." But before I could spring the trap he saw the inconsistency and said quickly, "That was true in both cases [his *Forest Hills Diary* and his actual *Diaries of Mario M. Cuomo*]. What I am writing now I intend to get money for and to sell. However, this book will not be as believable as the first two." [Presumably because he knew people would be reading it.]

Laughingly I said, knowing by now that I was vanquished again, "That was the question."

But Cuomo couldn't let the diary subject die an early death. He said that the then Speaker Stanley Fink once came into a meeting with him and said, "Never believe a guy who uses a looseleaf book for a diary." Cuomo admitted that Fink's reference was to "the possible insertion and deletion of pages, of course."

Mike Oreskes of the *Times* then followed up and asked him if he actually did that. "No, but it makes a good joke," said the governor.

My career with Mario Cuomo is illustrative of Cuomo's ability to fight with you but not to offend. There are lots of examples.

There was the time, for instance, that a bill on public nudity was being debated. I asked him straight out why anyone should really be offended by public nudity.

"I would suggest that anyone who has gotten even the quickest glimpse of yourself, Alan Chartock, even fully robed, would begin to understand what would be wrong with a law that would allow people like you to disrobe."

Once he was talking about the fact that the Republicans would raise $25 million to defeat him in the next election.

MC: The one opponent I'm most afraid of is whatever opponent has twenty-five million dollars. It could be somebody from New Hampshire, who just moved in. It could even be someone...well no, it couldn't be Chartock. Almost anybody with twenty-five million dollars would be a threat. You, Chartock, with the treasury, would not be a threat.

AC: When I win the lottery I'll show you, Governor.

MC: When you win the lottery, other winners will give back their money.

Our conversations have often discussed lifestyles. I have been adamant, for example, about coffee, an evil which I know he indulges in.

"I see that you have a cup of coffee in front of you, and I'm worried about you, sir, because I have a little piece of paper in front of me that says that 'caffeine is a drug known to produce peculiar and rapid heart beats, insomnia, high acid levels in the blood, high blood glucose levels in diabetics, increased gastric acid secretion and high blood pressure.'"

Naturally he tried to interrupt but I was determined, "just let me finish, Governor."

"Yeah, sure, please."

"Also the raising of blood lipids is expected to be a factor in arteriosclerosis. I was wondering, in view of all this, how you can continue to take another sip of that coffee, sir."

"Well, let me say this about coffee, Alan [he took a very loud slurp of the liquid]. Having heard that litany of implications and effects of caffeine I would suggest that you try it. Almost all of those things are an improvement on your present condition."

He always managed to turn around my lack of New York State residency. Even when I vacationed outside New York he would have the long knife out. "I would say that having vacationed outside the state of New York you've come back looking paler, weaker, more diminished than ever before and I think that you would be best advised next time when you wish to refurbish yourself to do it here in the great Empire State. If not the governor, maybe God was trying to tell you something about vacations outside our borders. But you do look pretty bad, Alan."

Of course the governor, despite his constant badgering me about my appearance, knows that I run, walk and work out. So does he. So once I asked him whether he considered running to be a metaphysical exercise. "I think, Alan, that at one point you have to stop. When you find that you are wearing your legs to the point where you become as short as you are then it's a good time to stop running."

The insults never seemed to stop, once they started livening the show. One of the earliest came when Walter Mondale was running for president. At that time I assured the governor during one taping that Mondale was the sure loser and that Reagan was the inevitable winner. "Governor, I don't agree with that, I think that...."

The governor interrupts, "Who cares what you think? I mean how is it relevant...."

So I told him that I thought that Jackson would erode Mondale's support but I got little further than that as the inevitable diversion began. "Excuse me, Alan. What are you teaching next semester?"

I answered that I was teaching a course called "Acquisition and Maintenance of Political Power."

"Yeah," said Cuomo, "you ought to give back the salary."

On still another occasion the governor and I were discussing Mondale again. "You just said something that I really don't think is right, sir, you said that Ronald Reagan is going to lose and that Mondale is going to win."

Naturally Cuomo interrupted, "No I said that Mondale is going to win."

Confused, I continued, "I don't think that you are right, sir, I think that..." The governor interrupted again, "What do you know, Chartock? You were wrong about me, you were wrong about everybody. You picked Ed Koch, you picked Perry Duryea, you picked Howard Samuels and Malcolm Wilson [a long list of New York State political losers]. You haven't been right since you were eleven and that was a school election which I am told was rigged."

Then there was the question of Cuomo's so called "long memory."

AC: There are people who say that you have a long memory.
MC: I do have a long memory, and I remember every time you ever insulted, abused, disdained me, Alan, on this show.
AC: Every once in a while you have reminded me, for example, that I was "with Koch."
MC: You were with Koch.
AC: Not true...
MC: You were not only with Koch, you said that the other man has no competence, has no record, how could you trust him, Koch has run a big city, Koch is the clear choice.
AC: Not true.

MC: Which is another measure of your brilliant political savvy.

AC: But where...

MC: You will not lead anybody, Alan, as long as they don't bet the mortgage money on your predictions. As long as nobody who works hard for a living listens to you and gets conned into losing anything of value, you'll be okay.

Another time when I disagreed with him he simply said, "Alan, I chalk your opinion up to adversity or naivete."

Cuomo, a former semi-professional ball player, takes his baseball, particularly those games against the Legislative Correspondents Association, very seriously.

I asked him whether he ever felt guilty for beating the LCA in their classic softball rivalry. But the governor only responded by publicly taunting the hapless reporters in our very public forum. "I'll feel happier this Saturday if the LCA shows up for our softball game and frankly, I will understand if they don't show up because the last two times they showed up they were humiliated. But if they show up then I will be absolutely delighted at the end of that game to have won another victory. I may pitch myself, because I might want to retire unbeaten by the LCA." So I asked him, "Let's say that you really beat them quite badly."

"Oh we will, we will, no question."

"Now governor, I think I know a little something about you. I know that you are going to go home to the mansion, you're going to pet Ginger on the head and you are going to feel very, very, badly, about having vanquished the LCA."

Naturally, the governor interrupted. "I'll tell you what I'm looking forward to, Chartock. I'm looking forward to beating them very badly and then feeling very badly about it...for a whole day."

Cuomo, many people know, played minor league baseball under a number of fictitious names. Perhaps he didn't want to embarrass his family or mix his law plans with baseball but he just didn't want to use the name Mario Cuomo. So he used names like "Glendy La Duke," "Lava Libretti," "Matt Dente," "Connie Cutts."

AC: A lot of people have said to me, how can this guy who has such a bad back go around playing baseball all the time?

MC: With a wide belt, and reconciling myself to maybe two weeks of pain and distortion in the way I walk, sit, and sleep. You pay a terrible price for the game, but at those moments in my life when I'm not doing well, especially up here when I'm being pounded by legislature and media alike, when even the people at home are less than totally committed to my point of view, when I need a shot, when I need something to bolster a sagging ego, something to remind me that I'm capable of success. At those moments, we schedule games with the reporters. And we go out and we tape ourselves, bandage ourselves, and wrap ourselves with sashes and belts, play these stiffs and beat them. And for a moment, there's a rush of youth that returns, there's a sense that we can do it all, anything that we choose to do. That's what the LCA does for me.

AC: So, Governor, I hear the strange rumblings of baseball fever. I hear that Glendy La Duke, alias Lava Libretti, showed up just the other day out in Lincoln Park to take on and mysteriously pitch to the Legislative Correspondents Association. I hear, Governor, that he's overweight. I don't know if he can come back anymore.

MC: You heard that Lava Labretti was overweight? Glendy La Duke was overweight?

AC: They're one and the same. They both have the same pseudonyms, both old pitchers from the minor leagues, Governor. Are you in a position to confirm or deny this rumor?

MC: I'll tell you what it sounds like to me. The LCA has played against Glendy La Duke's team for five years, never having won a single of the many contests that were completed. It's not unusual for a psychic reaction to set in, which requires them to seize every possible slim thread of a possible hope, even to the point of imagining that Glendy La Duke—star of the team that beats them every year—might possibly be losing his stuff. Not so. I know Glendy, I know Glendy intimately. He's as hard and as tough and as ready to go as I've ever seen him.

AC: Now, Governor, I don't want to bother you with this kind of trivia, but you know somebody will write a Ph.D. thesis years from now in which they will say that Lava Libretti, Glendy La Duke, and Mario Cuomo were all one and the same. You know they do that to Shakespeare now, Sir Francis Bacon and all the rest of it. What do you think about that?

MC: Well, I'm flattered that I could be the subject of that kind of idle and silly speculation. But there's nothing to it. A.J. Parkinson incidentally wrote an essay on the subject.

AC: I know he did. I remember it very well. It's called "The Sports Charisma As It Relates To The Innermost Psyche." Governor, it's really quite a wonderful piece.

MC: With versions to and references to Carl Jung, no less.

AC: That's right.

Cuomo, ever interested in sports, is an avid fan of college football. He has a fantastic sense of ethnic humor which on occasion shows itself through the sports metaphor.

Take the time he began to explain the success of the Fighting Irish. Said Cuomo, "The Fighting Irish, the Gold and Green, they're very important to us subway alumni in New York City. All over New York State, New Yorkers watch the games. I think of all the Fighting Irish of the past, the names come reverberating back. Nick Buoniconti, Nick Petrasanti, Angelo Bertelli, Jumping Joe Savoldi, Ed and Frank Carideo. Think of them. Who could forget Ralph Gugliemi? John Mello, how about John Petranelli? I think he was an All American." The Fighting Irish had miraculously been turned into the Fighting Italians.

Perhaps our most memorable exchange involved his beloved dog Ginger. I wrote a lengthy column about the dog. In a post-show conversation the week before, Cuomo had ascribed magical powers to Ginger, his most faithful friend, telling us that Ginger was his secret weapon.

Sitting around with reporters after the program, Cuomo told us that Ginger had been brought home on that dark rainy day in 1977 when he had lost the mayor's race in New York City to Ed Koch. It was the worst day of his life, until his son Christopher walked in with a huge black mongrel dog and asked the future governor if he could keep him. "Out," ordered Cuomo but when Christopher got a tear in his eye his father relented and the dog was allowed to stay.

The next day, said Cuomo, the dog had nine puppies and his luck turned around. He found out, he told us, that the dog had ESP and that he was really George Patton reincarnated. Virtually nothing, he told us, had gone wrong since he had found the dog. Sensing a good story, I wrote this in my weekly newspaper column. I showed up to do the radio show a week after the column appeared, Cuomo was ready for me.

"I wish you'd tell your listeners about your column on my dog Ginger and ESP," he said.

So I started to reiterate, "Governor, last week you were sitting here with us after the show and you started to tell us about your dog Ginger; what a wonderful dog she was, how Christopher had brought her home after the mayoral campaign on that black day when you had lost and you had said..."

"Yeah, but you said some unkind things about Ginger. You said something about her attacking anybody who played a basketball game against me. And I want you to know that I read the column to Ginger and she thinks of you as a fire hydrant with a tie." By now everyone in the room was either in shock or laughing as hard as they could. Stammering, I asked him, "Do you think anybody would agree with that, Governor?" The governor didn't miss a beat, responding, "Ginger and every dog on the block agrees with it." The dog stories did not stop there.

Once Mayor Koch, Cuomo's early nemesis, lost his dog Archie. So I said to the governor: "The Mayor's dog Archie has been missing." The governor interrupted and in mock horror he intoned, "Archie is missing?" I answered in the affirmative.

MC: Oh.

AC: We have heard that Ginger and Archie may have a thing. We're wondering whether or not that rumor is true and whether or not those two have run away together.

The governor responded that "Unless Ginger gets an annulment from the ASPCA she is not going to be running around with Archie or with anybody else. Ginger was once married."

Years later I had still another chance to ask the gov about Ginger:

AC: Last question, how's Ginger the dog?

MC: Wonderful, she goes on and on. You know, Ginger now must be...12 times 7...84 years old.

AC: Eighty-four years young. Well, will you give her my love, Governor?

MC: I will give her your love and I will ask her to give you nothing.

And that wasn't the only animal story. There was the time that we handled the bats.

"Governor," I led off, tongue in cheek, "I have an important letter from somebody in Hadley, New York who writes, 'Could you divert a session with the governor to some small problems that plague citizens more immediate, pressing and ongoing like the infestation of BATS [sic]; she claims that her area in upstate New York...."

The Governor interrupted, "Are the bats infesting or are the bats infested?"

"I think the bats are infesting..."

The governor interrupts, "Well, no, because you said 'the infestation of bats.'

"Is it infestation by bats, or the infestation of bats. Because if bats are being infested I think we ought to go to the ASPCA and find out who's doing it to the bats. If the bats are doing the infesting, then we have to be concerned about taking on the bats. That could really drive you literally,...bats."

But I explained to the governor, barely able to contain myself, that the woman had said that there were "hundreds of holes in the house and around there..."

Governor interrupting, "Hundreds of holes in her house...."

"Yeah, and people have had to put on new roofs and things like that in order to get rid of the bats."

So the governor gave me my orders. "Tell her that if she gets a whole lot of holes in the house and she finds it no longer habitable she ought to start up a newspaper, come to the Capitol where there's free space [a crack at the newspapers who do not pay the government for their desk space in the Capitol]. She can move in with the LCA [Legislative Correspondents Association] because they don't pay rent."

Then the governor told of the time he was "attacked by bats in the lieutenant governor's office." He assured me that the tale was recounted in his *Diaries*, "That is if you read my *Diaries*, Chartock, which obviously you did not, that is the *Diaries of Mario Cuomo*, $19.95 Random House, or you can get it, at discount, for $3.12 in Brooklyn.

"There's a whole story about being attacked by bats in the lieutenant governor's office. The bats attacked me while I was dictating, and I flailed away at them with my jacket and the jacket had the same effect as a toreador's cape does."

So I told the governor that he was doing it the wrong way that there were two ways to kill bats that I had employed successfully and those were death by tennis racket or throwing paperback books from your library shelf at them.

Said the governor, "Little paperback books—it takes extraordinary aim." He concluded, "That lady wrote to the right person."

Cuomo once said that he didn't believe in certain types of humor, humor of the kind which made fun of, or ridiculed other people. But Mario Cuomo ridicules people all the time. He ridiculed his 1982 opponent Lew Lehrman with drug store jokes. When Republican State Senator Roy Goodman, the Ex-Lax heir, announced that he was exploring a run at the governorship in 1986 and started to criticize Cuomo, the governor quipped that Goodman, "Must be nipping at the Ex-Lax again."

Then, he lumped Goodman, the Ex-Lax heir and Lehrman, the drug store magnate, into one devastating category. Said Cuomo, "I guess I'm doomed to run against guys who sell things over the counter in drugstores."

He had used a similar line with devastating effectiveness when Hugh L. Carey had double-crossed Cuomo, his own lieutenant governor at the time, and endorsed Edward I. Koch for the governorship. Cuomo then responded that Carey must be "nipping at the PCBs again," a reference to one of Carey's worst faux pas, when the former governor had said that PCBs were so safe that he would drink a glass. In each case Cuomo is able to go far enough to be funny but not to insult.

Despite the fact that Cuomo doesn't like to make jokes about anyone (I have never heard him utter an ethnic joke, for example) he has been known to let me provoke him into something that he would best stay out of. Naturally, it just proves he's human, as in the following episode. It happened when I returned home from a short trip to Nantucket, the beautiful island off the coast of Massachusetts. As I remarked earlier, every time I have ever vacationed anywhere outside the Empire State, the governor has seen fit to stick it to me about deserting New York. This was no exception.

MC: I understand that Nantucket's so far out that whale watching is one of the principal activities.

AC: Yes, people watch whales, they go out in a boat and watch whales...and people also sit on the beaches and watch other things.

MC: You can do that at Coney Island, too, whale watching. Occasionally you'll even see one in the water."

AC: Oh, you're gonna get into trouble...

One of the funnier exchanges revolved around *Playgirl* magazine's decision to name the governor one of the 10 sexiest men in America in 1985. I asked the governor about it. Naturally, the governor reverted to his old line suggesting that *Playgirl* wasn't honoring him but rather, the great people of the state of New York. He also claimed that *any* governor of the state would be so honored.

I reminded him that his predecessor, Governor Hugh L. Carey, who was a social gadfly and had dated the likes of Anne Uzielli Ford and even died his hair, still was never named to the *Playgirl* list. Tongue in cheek, Cuomo said that he "knew" Governor Carey was "about to be named to the ten most sexy list" when he decided not to run for re–election and he reiterated that *any* person who was governor would be named to the list, "with the exception of you, Alan Chartock"—his all too familiar logic that I was short and lived in Massachusetts.

Well, the very next morning, unbeknownst to me, the late Bill Duffy, the senior correspondent for WRGB, the Capital District's "News Center Six," called the governor and asked him about the *Playgirl* list. And, with tongue in cheek once again, the governor repeated his comment that anyone who was a governor could be named to the list and that anyone could be governor except for "Alan Chartock, who does political commentary for Channel Six." It must have been a slow news day because Duffy used the story on the 7:30 a.m. broadcast, thereby setting the stage for my appearance on the evening news.

That night, one of the anchors, Liz Bishop, read the story announcing *Playgirl's* list, including Cuomo's assertion that it could happen to anyone and had nothing to do with his physical attributes. The anchor then called on me for my commentary.

This time I was ready. I stated that I knew that the governor was named because he was the governor, but I also suggested that he was named because "to some women, power was an aphrodisiac." I mentioned that Cuomo was very powerful, frequently being mentioned as a potential presidential candidate, but added that perhaps some women were attracted by "guys who were balding, guys who had bags under their eyes, guys with a paunch around their middle."

At this point one of the two anchors repeated the governor's claim that anyone who was a governor could be named to the most sexy list, adding that I was officially excluded by Governor Cuomo. So Liz Bishop, the other anchor, turned to me and asked if I thought I was either sexy and/or powerful.

I responded that I wasn't sexy because I was short and basically ugly. I explained that I had given up trying to be sexy years ago, and that, in fact, I didn't even want to be sexy anymore because being sexy led to temptations of the kind that a married man did not need.

The folks at the station then pulled the coup de grace. The anchor turned to the camera and said, "Well, you've heard both sides. Now is the time for you the viewers to vote." And right then and there they offered the viewers a chance to participate in the Channel Six Telepoll, deciding once and for all the basic question, "Who is sexier, Governor Mario Cuomo or Alan Chartock?"

Of course, I figured that since I am ugly and short, as the governor had pointed out on a number of occasions, I would only gain a few Republican votes. So I went to bed satisfied that if I won only 10% of the votes I would call it a moral victory and retire from contests of this kind. Well, I was fast asleep when the 11 o'clock news came on announcing the results. My wife, the lovely Roselle, woke me up and said, "Uh-oh, here come the results, honey." Then she screamed, "You won, you won!" And indeed I had. I had vanquished the governor 53-47 percent, a virtual landslide in politics.

A week later Fred Dicker was back to ask the governor some questions about the affair. "Governor, last week Channel Six took a poll pitting you against none other than Alan Chartock. That telepoll, admittedly unscientific in its self-selection, nevertheless had Chartock winning 53 percent to 47 percent with 800-plus voters voting. What do you think of that poll?"

Said the gov, "Frankly, I think he ought to be embarrassed although I don't want to make a public display of it here. If he could beat a grandfather 57 to 43, this young athlete who weekly boasts of his achievements, you know jogging and his youthfulness—if he can edge out an over the hill, balding, baggy-eyed governor whose nose is like a hose handle, 57 to 43, that says something. I think we ought to drop the subject. I did not intend to bring up the subject. I did not intend to embarrass him. You have chosen to do that. Maybe you are a little less sensitive than I."

Even worse, the governor said that I had used my state university students who had been on the SUNY phones "all night long at the taxpayer's expense." Talk about low blows, I thought.

But several weeks later I was greeted by "Charlie the Guard," an older man who sat at a desk immediately inside the Legislative Office Building. Said Charlie, "Doc, come over here, I want to ask you a question. Do you know how much your students love you?"

"Not me," I replied to Charlie.

"Well, I'm not supposed to tell you this, but do you know Gracie, your student who works for Senator Levy?"

I acknowledged that I did.

"Well," said Charlie, "Gracie told me that she and her father were on the phone all night long voting for you in your election against Cuomo."

Almost always, on each radio show there was loving, warm humor. Sometime his political enemies misunderstood this and would call asking me if I didn't hate him for what he was doing to me. I would always assure them that it was humor but if you are not someone who enjoys a certain kind of humor, one with a rapier wit, you might misunderstand.

Cuomo is always looking for a reason to further our humorous relationship and will turn anything into a joke or a jibe; a grammatical mistake, spelling, a mistake about my not knowing when I was married and for how long. Once as he was waxing poetic about gun control, I turned the control down on my machine as I listened to him in order that I might get to drink some coffee and not disturb him as he delivered his impassioned plea. Somehow he figured out what I had done and inquired, "Did you go away Alan? Did you go away Alan?"

"Oh, I'm here," I replied turning the control up and laughing at the same time.

"I know you have a different position," he said.

"No, no, no, no," I stammered. "You see these machines are really complicated, Governor. No one ever really taught me how to work them. There's a thing called a pot on this thing and I had it down so that I could sip my coffee; so when you said, 'Did you go away?' the pot wasn't up...."

"And the coffee was in your mouth," said the governor laughing.

One of Cuomo's strengths as a humorist, along with all the great comedians, is the ability to extend a truth into a half truth or to just plain exaggerate. Sometimes, for example, his vocabulary transcends the limits of all known languages. One day he was quoting an old Polish proverb used to answer someone who is asking another to predict the future. The term, often used by Cuomo, sounds like "Son ashanu bob." It means that anything can happen or literally, "Between now and then a new Pope can be born." One day he used it again but this time, the words, "which Alan knows is an old Massachusetts Indian expression meaning that "between now and then a great chief will be born."

So I came back to him saying that his proverbial "great chief" had to be distinguished from the great Indian Princess Mashuganah. (Mashuganah in Yiddish is "crazy.")

Not content to let it go Cuomo suggested that his imaginary philospher-hero A.J. Parkinson "wrote about her, curiously enough. A little pamphlet on the origins of the Iroquois confederacy and the relationship between the natural law and the first legal statements scrawled on parchment by those Indians."

Once I decided to test the governor on his hero, Parkinson. It was in the middle of a heated budget battle and I decided the time had come to introduce a new Parkinson brother, namely Irving, into the debate.

AC: Irving J. Parkinson, who is the younger and lesser known brother of A.J. Parkinson, is supposed to have said that "the members of the Legislature will do nothing until five minutes after they were supposed to."

MC: Let me deal with the Irving thing. You know, I've heard the name before. I'll be honest with you, and I don't want to offend anybody. I think he's an imposter, I really do. I know a lot about Parkinson. Though it may sound boastful, I don't think anybody in this state, and I doubt that anybody in the country knows A.J. Parkinson the way I do.

AC: I would agree with that.

MC: I don't think there was an Irving Parkinson. Now, I don't want to argue with you but if you have material on it I would like you to send me material on it. Because I don't believe there is an Irving Parkinson. There might have been somebody else who took the name Parkinson which is legal, but I don't believe there's an Irving Parkinson. What is he supposed to have said?

AC: Irving Parkinson, Governor, who I believe in as much as I believe in A.J. Parkinson, is supposed to have said, now this is a famous quote of his, "The members of the Legislature will do nothing until five minutes after they needed to."

MC: Irving was wrong.

That led the governor and me into a long discussion of the budget which was not particularly interesting. When the gov was through though, I took up the reputation of Irving Parkinson, once more:

AC: You see, there's Parkinson again. Everything you just said sort of confirms this man's brilliance, inherent brilliance.

MC: Irving?

AC: Irving Parkinson.

MC: Yeah, eh, you know actually it might have been A.J. It might have been A.J. No, no, no A.J. wouldn't have said it.

AC: That's the problem. Irving, all of his life, has been in the shadow of his older brother.

MC: But, A.J. wouldn't have spoken of the Legislature. A.J. spoke of things more global usually.

AC: Philosophical.

MC: He's more generic and conceptual.

AC: That's why Irving is a little more important to me than A.J.

The governor has on occasion used our radio program to offer a movie review. I know how chauvinistic Cuomo can be about subjects having to do with New York State, and Cuomo is fiercely proud of William Kennedy, the novelist and also the author of *The Cotton Club*, one of the memorable movie flops of recent years. So I asked him about it.

"I loved it and so did Matilda, but you see I came at it very naively. I come from the era of movies where the explicit love scene ended with a tree falling in the forest or a great wave breaking on the beach. The big movie going in our time was the double header *Gunga Din* and *King Kong*, plus a dish. You got a dish if you got to the Savoy."

When reporter Fred Dicker asked him whether he wasn't a bit behind the time, Cuomo responded, "No, no, I'm quite up to date. My son Christopher took me to see *Raiders of the Lost Ark*, which I think is a great movie."

But then Cuomo went on to give a really nice review to his friend's movie. "There was a little too much blood in *Cotton Club* but I must tell you that there was one scene in *Cotton Club* that is pure genius and it has a lot to do with Kennedy's words and the acting, the fellow who plays Owney Madden and the guy who plays Frenchie, it is just an incredibly intelligent, poignant scene and it was brilliant. Greg Hines is a wonderful dancer and singer, the music was great, the costumes were good, the story was predictable so maybe a sophisticate who sees movies all the time and makes esoteric critiques of them doesn't like it when the guy gets the girl or vice versa in the end. I like that. When I want something else I go to the opera, where everybody dies. Then you go home and you feel better about life because you've had your catharsis. You've spent all your misery for two hours at an opera."

Concludes the governor, and I know just what he means, "I like movies where they are on the back of the train as it pulls out of the station and it says, "Just married," and the villain is left in a garbage pail."

Of course, Mario Cuomo is best when he is telling stories about his friends and really putting it to them. After his famous trip to Notre Dame where he laid out his position on abortion, Cuomo recounted an airplane ride on the way to Notre Dame that could have been part of Dante's *Inferno*.

"We flew into a terrible storm. That ship got rocketed and bounced around. Matt Monahan [assistant press officer to the governor] left the seat and struck the ceiling of the cabin with his head. Various articles were flung around as though a poltergeist were directing them. People clutched the seat. Tim Russert [then counselor to the governor, now an NBC vice president for news] turned the most dramatic white I have ever seen. People were praying, screaming. It was an awful thing. Then I delivered my speech, and we flew back that night in tranquility, serenity, one of the most flawless flights I have ever been on and that's the truth."

One of Cuomo's favorite techniques is to turn the tables on his questioners and to start to grill them. At one point I said "touché" to him and he turned around and said:

"Explain, Alan what 'touché' means."

So trying to keep up with him (always a mistake) I said:

"Isn't that a part of the physical anatomy?"

"No, no, it's a term from fencing, Alan, which suggests that you're very good at except after the thrust. It's a term in fencing where the person scores a point by touching you and it's described as 'touché'—having touched."

Fred Dicker jumped in and suggested that the term "parry" was another fencing term meaning to ward off the thrust.

"Yes," responded Cuomo, "you could do it with a thrust, only Alan never has."

If Mario Cuomo's show openings are always original, so are his endings. Perhaps his best was his simplest.

I was saying, "Believe it or not, it's over. That's this week's *Capitol Connection* with Governor Mario M. Cuomo. Thanks to producer..."

As he always does, the governor interrupts, "Does that mean that we never have to do it again?"

CHAPTER 6

CUOMO AND THE MEDIA

MC: That is how the politicians feel about the reporters. Some
you trust and some you don't.

Nowhere did Mario Cuomo shine more brightly than in his
relationship with the media. If I had to choose the single
place that exemplified the real Cuomo courage, it would be
in his dealings with the press. He insisted on being treated fairly,
which was a good thing for all those who were not treated fairly
by an often slovenly and unhappy group of people. It offered discipline to a profession whose members were too often more than
willing to hide behind—and all too often abuse—the First Amendment. And, unlike many other politicians who would not risk facing the press in an open forum, Cuomo did it again and again with
no preconditions.

I teach courses in politics and the media on both the graduate and undergraduate levels and I have spent years studying the
imperfections of both the electronic and print press corps.

I have found that the media has a long way to go before it is
immune from the same kinds of criticism concerning hypocrisy
and unethical behavior that it levels at others.

That's where Mario Cuomo comes in. As governor, he fought the press and they hated it because he was so good at it. They were used to fighting with politicians who would not fight back. But Cuomo picked his spots and never undermined the press's right to speak out. Here is something he told me when I asked him about a negative press report.

"Frankly, everybody gets a bad break from the press sometimes. Who's preserved from the harsh criticism of the press? That's one of the press's functions. As a matter of fact, in recent years it seems clear that they find it more suitable to be critical than to be laudatory. There is something that has developed in the psyche of the press and maybe in the American people that they're trying to accommodate, that says they'd rather hear about a tragedy than a minor miracle. And they'd rather hear negatives. There is, as you know, an instinct for the negative in dealing with politicians. They feel embarrassed to write a story that says, 'The politicians did very well today in Albany.'"

In other words, Cuomo always told members of the press that they deserved protection; but he also critized their work and told them when they were doing a lousy job—which was quite often.

Frankly, in our conversations, I was much tougher on the press than Cuomo was. Once when I was particularly unhappy with a scandalous bit of journalistic behavior, I asked him about it.

MC: You seem to be suggesting that you see evidence of a failure by the press to report things objectively.

AC: Yes, I think I have. But not all press people strike me that way. More and more, I see some evidence that the personal predilections of the press and the editors tend to lead them to a particular direction.

MC: I'm not surprised. I think that is only human, especially if you have a press corps that is permanent or relatively long enduring with a specific assignment. You tend to get relationships developing which are personal instead of professional. You tend to find sources easier for you to deal with. You will find that some reporters spend more time with one part of the government than another. All you have to do is go to the restaurants and see who is having dinner with whom.

There is nothing wrong with that. I think after a while it is entirely possible that one will form relationships that perhaps will have a subconscious effect on the reporting; not the accuracy of what you say, but the sources you rely on, the point of view you are most familiar with. Yeah, that can happen. I think overall though, the press does a pretty good job, Alan.

AC: Yes, it does. You expect perfection from the people you hold up as models and when you get something that is less than perfection you have problems, especially since the press has anointed itself watchdog over everybody else. I just wonder sometimes who is to become watchdog over the press?

MC: That is a question at least two hundred years old in this country, since the beginning of the Constitution when the press was given a specific role even above and beyond the right of free speech. The Constitution provides the right of a free press in addition to the right of free speech. There is no question about the exalted position of the press in our hierarchy. Unlike the other branches, where there is a demand that you meet certain qualifications, the press has no qualifications. To be a governor, to be an executive, to be a judge, to be a legislator, you need to be selected or appointed, you need to be of a certain age, you need to pass certain tests. But to be a member of the press, there are no qualifications.

All you need to do is have a press card and you can write anything you want and say anything you want with impunity and sometimes with devastating effect. You can just about do anything you want. If you had to design the system, I would guess that pure intelligence would tell you that, boy, it is dangerous. But the truth is, however, that for over two hundred years it has worked out pretty well. To be honest, it has worked out pretty well.

Make no mistake about it. Cuomo has thought a lot about the press and he was willing to share his critical views, always championing the right of an errant press to do their thing because he believed it was more important for a bad press to be policing the governmental system than no press at all.

Take the case of one-time presidential candidate Gary Hart. Did the press go too far?

AC: Do you think the press treated Gary Hart unfairly?

MC: I have been asked the question as most politicians have very frequently. I don't know how to judge fairness and unfairness. What is the criterion? What is the rule? What is the standard? It is not written down in a book. The editors don't tell us what fairness is. You can ask me my personal view as to whether I think the press, if I were the press, would I have gone after Gary Hart the way some of them did. I think the answer would be "no." I think that I would not have hidden in the bushes. I would not have assigned four or five people to chase Gary Hart to see if he had a girlfriend other than his wife. And then use as an excuse, "Well, Gary said we should follow him."

If it is not a good thing to do, if it is not a useful thing to do, if it is not a tasteful thing to do, it is disingenuous to use his challenge as an excuse for doing it.

AC: Could I take the other side of that for a second?

MC: Sure.

AC: Governor, if a guy is willing, in our society, so to speak, to cheat on his wife—if that person is going to be expected in our society, on a regular basis to, to be our standard, our leader, and we are voting for him or her on the basis of character, don't you think it is important for us to know about that character?

MC: Alan, I think when you say a person cheats on his wife, when a woman cheats on her husband, is that relevant? You would get a lot of Americans who would say "Yes, I want to know that about a person." A lot of Americans would say yes.

But Mario Cuomo thought differently than most Americans. Cuomo said that if the question were asked differently you would get a different answer. "If you say, 'Mr. and Mrs. America, what I am suggesting to you is the press ought to decide what to regard as moral standards and ought to pursue those moral standards.' For example, some considerable percentage of the American population thinks that we have too many children. People who have more than two or three children are really lending to a population explosion. They should use birth control devices. Should you ask a candidate, 'How do you feel about birth control? You and your wife, how do you feel about it?'

"There are Jesuits who taught, and orthodox people who teach that you ought to have no intimacy even with your wife unless it can lead to childbirth. Can you say to a candidate, 'We understand you are orthodox, we understand that you are a strict Catholic, we understand that you regard it as immoral to engage in certain activities with your wife. Because it is relevant to know your character, because your character is determined by your own moral subjective judgments, I therefore ask you, whether you have ever done anything wrong along those lines?' That is absurd. But what is the difference between that and the adultery question?

"Where does it end? Are you going to ask people whether they are homosexual? Are you going to ask them because you believe that's improper? Would you ask heterosexuals, 'Okay, I know that you are heterosexuals, did you ever have a homosexual experience?' There are a lot of people who would tell you that is wrong.

"I am not telling you what is right and what is wrong, it is not my business, I don't think. I will leave that up to God and the courts. I am very comfortable with that. I am very comfortable with my own conscience making judgments for me, your judgments making judgments for you.

"I may be a little extreme on this, I may be an extremist for privacy. I always have been."

On another important aspect of the relations between politics and the press, just listen to him on what the press can do to your family when you run for office. That's the question I put to him on the show one day after the then soon-to-be New York City Mayor David Dinkins's son was being flayed in the press.

AC: What should one tell one's family when you run [for public office] about what to expect?

MC: Expect to be embarrassed. Expect to be spoken ill of. Expect to be misunderstood. Expect if you do something that is unfortunate or wrong, whether you are the candidate or just related to the candidate, that the press believes it has a mission to disclose that. Expect that when your grandfather runs for office, all of the grandchildren on both sides and their first cousins have been deemed to forfeit their right to privacy.

AC: Is that a difficult thing to do when you decide to make a commitment to run for public office and tell some kid that they may in fact have to bear unfair publicity?

MC: Unfair is a conclusary word. I didn't use that word because you can then make an argument about what is fair and what is unfair. I am a great believer in the First Amendment. When you come into public life, you know what is going to happen. So the people on the other side, the press, could argue, "Hey look, you asked for it when you ran. I didn't tell you to run."

AC: The kid [Dinkins's son] didn't ask for it.

MC: Yes, but you impose it on your child and that is the difficult thing from my point of view, a person who was a candidate, and is a public official. I have to live with the knowledge I made my children and friends vulnerable by running and that is a heavy load. Every once in a while it hurts.

AC: ...Is there a way to make it up to a kid?

MC: No. If you are very lucky, the child understands. It doesn't have to be a child, it could be your wife, it could be your mother, it could be your brother, it could be your father. When I said I would not run for the presidency, people speculated about it and I got asked on national television whether or not my father, who was a laborer, a ditch digger, and a grocery storeman, or my father-in-law, who was a carpenter, both now deceased, were in the Mafia. Now, why did you have to have it said on national television when there was absolutely no basis to it, on a Sunday morning show? Because you're in public life. When something like that happens, it bothers you, it hurts. You can not say they are unfair, that they shouldn't have done it.

They'll continue to do it for as long as there is a free press, and there should always be a free press in this country. But, there is no doubt that this is a heavy part of the burden accepted by public officials. And we do accept it and there is no point in complaining about it. I am not complaining about it. I don't like it but every once in a while you get lucky. Every once in a while you get a member of the press who says, "Hey, you know, I have this little bit and I think it is not true. I'm not going to repeat it." But most of the time, they will use whatever they can to get their byline in the paper. They feel it is their mission. They are supposed to get as much news as possible out in the paper. I am not going to argue with them.

And because often there is no right and wrong, just nuances and shades, it took a Cuomo to sensitize the press to what it was doing. Frankly, it was refreshing since it is so rare.

That's why the surest way to get his goat was to ask him to comment on a matter brought to light by "unnamed sources." You know, something like, "Governor, sources tell us that you..." or "Unnamed sources tell us thus and such...."

Once I started out telling him that some of his critics had said something nasty.

MC: But, Alan, will you tell me which critics?
AC: You know...
MC: [interrupting] No, I don't know. That's why I'm asking you, Alan.
AC: It's just people who...
MC: Alan, are you going to give us a name or is this just another one you made up?
AC: No, I didn't make it up but there...
MC: [interrupting] Okay.

The discussion was over. When you mess with the governor you obviously proceed at your own risk.

If the sin of using unnamed sources got his goat, so did the sin of rumor-mongering. Once I asked him about a rumor I'd heard.

In response he gave me a little lesson about how it might feel to be on the other side.

"I heard a rumor, Chartock, that you were leaving the State University to take a job at a girl's college in Connecticut. Is that true?"

So I said, "No, but it's not a bad idea."

Naturally he was not about to let me have my line, so he kept going.

"For practically no pay, and the rumor was that the students who were polled at the University, when asked about Chartock, said the guy's wacky. Is that true, Alan? Do you have a comment to make on that rumor? And incidentally, I heard that from an unnamed aide in the Chartock office."

Several years ago, Cuomo and I went a round or two over the issue. I began by telling the governor that I used to think he was all wrong about the anonymous quote issue but that I had changed my mind. I told him that I had been the subject of an article which had used anonymous quotes and that I was furious over the matter.

As usual, the governor started by seeing it the press's way. He said that not using anonymous sources would seriously limit the "...supply of information for the legitimate press." The governor concluded, "That's not a good thing."

The governor also commented that, from time to time, a Pentagon Papers or Watergate situation would arise that depended on anonymous sources. But then he got down to the potential abuses.

MC: On the other hand, like everything else in life, it's also subject to abuse and it's as good as the people who implement it. I don't think it's unkind to say that reporters are no better than politicians. I mean reporters aren't better than we are. Individual reporters are no better than individual politicians.

AC: Stipulated, we agree. Go ahead.

MC: Which means you're as subject to temptation as I am.

AC: Right.

MC: And you're as subject to making things up. Now, you're very fond, most of you, of saying, "Politicians make things up." You know, "Why should you believe a politician?" Question: Why should we believe a reporter? Why should we believe a reporter when he says "anonymous person?"

AC: But the problem is, of course, that you never know the motivation of the person if they're on the record as opposed to being off the record, and you never know the level of accuracy of the statement. You could say, "A person in the Democratic party said..."

MC: Well, let's say something on this that we've said before and it's very important. First of all, just to keep it clear, I can't judge the New York press against any other press because I don't know any other press well. I don't know the Washington press the way I know New York. I have known the

New York press for years. And I haven't been the subject of their reporting all of that time. I think, it's hard for me to imagine the press being a whole lot better than it is here in New York. So, I think we have a very, very good press. As for me individually, of course every once in a while they'll do something that I don't like. That's human.

Overall, I think I've been treated very fairly. I try frankly to treat them fairly in return. They probably complain occasionally about me but overall I'm very, very pleased with the whole situation, and I hope the press everywhere is as good as it is here. As professional, as honest, etc., and that I want to make clear.

AC: Okay.

MC: Now, a principle. There is a difference between your profession and mine; between your profession and medicine, between your profession and the law. We're talking now about regulating doctors, a legitimate concern. Who will do it? Government will pass a law that will say if you do such and such you can no longer practice. Lawyer, if you do such and such it's a crime if you violate your profession. Politicians, same thing.

With the media, because of the reverence we have for the media, there is no governmental review of what you do, nor should there ever be. In some countries, Chartock can't say whatever he wants to say on [Channel] six or in a column because some government will censor it or say that's bad taste or that's inaccurate, even. We don't want that. We can't tolerate that. We would rather suffer your imperfection than try to correct it by using government coercion against you. That would be much worse.

Okay, now if we agree up to this point, it leaves us with the following: Who, then, reviews the press? Now you can, well, ask the public. The public won't know when Chartock's not giving them the straight scoop. You're not going to get caught if you're good at it. Well, then who reviews the press? Nobody but the press. Since we're down to that, you must do the best job you can amongst yourselves. Regulating yourselves.

But then I told the governor that the press tended to "circle the wagons" and to protect each other.

MC: Well, that's human too. That's what lawyers do, doctors do, politicians do, families do, that's the human instinct. We're going to have to live with that, Alan. There is no alternative. What's the alternative? To have the government set up a review mechanism? God forbid that you should ever review the press.

AC: No.

MC: Of course you must review politicians. The tougher the better. The more you beat us, the better the system gets. Of course we won't like that, those of us who are the politicians. But it's right and it should be that way. It should not be the other way around.

Another example of Cuomo's ability to sensitize the press came way back in December, 1985. There was a tumult due to the governor's objection to the use in the press of the word "Mafia" as synonymous with organized crime. The governor, who, incidentally, has always enjoyed good support from the law enforcement community, was incensed at a newspaper's coverage of the slaying of underworld figure Paul Castellano in December, 1985.

Why didn't the governor like the coverage, which included numerous references to the Mafia?

"Because it's an Italian word and because every time you say it, it suggests to people that organized crime is Italian. And because it's an ugly stereotype that gets used over and over against Italians. Now, the term 'organized crime' is perfectly accurate. This man [Castellano] was apparently involved in organized crime; so are Blacks, so are Russian Jews in Brighton Beach."

At this point, a reporter who was a guest interviewer on the show, retorted, "But there is a particularly Italian group of organized crime. Historically, that's been the case. Just like there was a Murder Incorporated with a bunch of Jews who aligned themselves with the Italians. But, I mean, that's denying something in our history...."

"Then I would suggest that, when the *Post* writes the story, you write it this way: 'This is organized crime, comma, and we all know that a lot of them are Italian.' Why don't you write it that way?"

His use of the radio show was a good example of his tendency to speak frankly and from the heart. By doing so, Cuomo was able to make a lot of news that might not have been possible in other forums. The radio show was his. I asked the questions but for thirty minutes every week, he had his own space to meet the people. By allowing me to participate, Cuomo avoided the pitfalls of a weekly political recorded message as was often the case in the Reagan years or, on the other side, a free-for-all press conference where it is difficult for questioners to get to know the subject's personality, the human being, or to follow a single theme to a satisfactory conclusion.

Since the press was always given tapes of our radio programs, a good deal of material generated on the program made its way into the newspapers.

There was a method to all of this, of course. Because Cuomo did so much radio and television, he allowed people to hear him directly.

"I don't find any fault with the public for not understanding politics. I do find fault with us for not making it clearer, frankly. And that's one of the reasons I spend so much time on radio, television, forums. I do everything I can to explain what's going on, because I remember being out there and not knowing what's going on and having difficulty in having it translated to me. So are they slothful, are the people lazy? I don't think so. Do they pay the kind of attention to politics that I'd like to see? No. But I can't blame the public for that either. I would sooner blame you and me, you the media and me the politician. I think we have to work harder at simplifying and getting the word out."

Frankly, the Albany press corps was no match for him. Cuomo or one of his top staff answered virtually every phone call from the major press groups and individuals. Unlike past years when men like Hugh L. Carey stayed aloof from the press, Cuomo provided access. He would not allow an allegation that he did not believe to be true to go unanswered. That frequently extended to personally answering hostile "letters to the editor," not only in *The New York Times* but in smaller and far less prestigious newspapers like the *Albany Times Union*.

Any hint that Cuomo leaked information to the *Times* was categorically denied. Yet every once in a while I questioned him when some new story showed up looking as if it had been handed to the world's most prestigious newspaper on a platter. Take a time in early January, 1991.

AC: True or false. You guys don't leak anything to anybody?
MC: True.
AC: I called you, one of your press people yesterday, a wonderful young lady. I said, "Listen, make me a hero. I got to go on the radio and television and forecast what is coming up on this state of the state message." She said, "We don't leak." So I opened *The New York Times* this morning and it said ten percent [tax] on gas, whatever it said.
MC: We don't leak. Mark Humbert had that a week ago.
AC: Only to *The New York Times*.
MC: Well, that is not true.
AC: Okay, okay.
MC: You call Mark Humbert of the Associated Press and he will tell you that a week ago he was talking about approximately what was talked about in *The New York Times* today. Many,

many people were speculating exactly as he did. Now, the reality is the following: when you get to two days from the budget you have printed documents over and over, circulated them to hundreds of people, including many outside of the office. There are copies of them lying around in the refuse bins. There are copies that lay on people's desks. There are copies that fall into the hands of the silly people who like to chatter.

So, the chance of your getting information—you don't have to move, all you just have to do is sit there and something is liable to come over your telephone wire from somebody who thinks he or she can be a big person and win a favor from you—which they'll do. They will trade information for favors. So, it is possible that accurate information will get out. It is also possible that a lot of inaccurate stuff gets out and that accurate information is distorted in the transmission.

Do I or my people leak stories? I think for eight years, eight years and a fraction now, we have tried very, very hard to avoid a situation where any part of the media got an advantage over any part of the media, with one exception.

AC: *The New York Times?*

MC: No, 1987. In 1987, I used the radio to make clear my position on the presidency. I thought I had already done it but when I was convinced that I hadn't, I used the radio. But that gave me a chance, in effect, to do it simultaneously to all the media. But I chose radio to do it. In general, let me say that *The New York Times* is a great newspaper, and they have a large staff. I doubt that they get any more advance information than *Newsday* or Mark Humbert, who works very hard and has a strong reputation, or Fred Dicker of *The New York Post*, who has been up here, who is a veteran and who is very, very good—moving around getting information for himself.

All those great newspapers, including the Gannett papers, they are all here working very, very hard. And sure they will pick up stuff that they hear from time to time. And loose-lip people give them material from time to time. But we don't, it wouldn't serve our purpose well to release a story now two days before I have a chance to present it to everybody.

AC: Then I guess I owe you an apology, right.

MC: No, you don't owe me an apology. Some people are born cynical.

The number one nemesis for Cuomo has been the conservative *New York Post*, first under the Australian press lord Rupert Murdoch, then under Peter Kalikow, a wealthy real estate developer in New York City and finally back to Murdoch. The *Post's* state reporter, Fred Dicker, and the governor had a tempestuous relationship. Once when I mentioned to Cuomo that *The New York Times* had picked up on a story that the *Post* had run earlier, Cuomo, in a feigned unbelieving voice, interrupted me and said, "The *Times* borrowed from *The New York Post*?"

"That's what it says," I told the governor.

"Well, then Kalikow, the owner of the *Post*, should declare a holiday."

I remember one conversation in particular about Father Bruce Ritter, a Catholic Priest who founded and directed one of the most successful drug treatment facilities in the country, Covenant House, in Manhattan. In a series of newspaper articles in *The New York Post*, Ritter was accused by a young man under treatment of having set him up in an apartment for the alleged purpose of providing him with sexual favors. When I asked the governor about it he seemed unhappy.

"I don't like it, obviously. I don't believe it and I won't believe it until it's proven. I have that right. I have that right as a practical matter from human experience because this is a man who has given over his life to helping people selflessly for years and years and years. He has earned nothing but congratulations and commendation and respect.

"Now, suddenly, one person whom I don't know, says something in a paper that likes sensational display. We don't know anything about the background of the story. We don't know anything about the facts. Just the accusation. Before you even heard the response, it's a headline. Why should I believe it?" Concluded the governor, "In this particular case, certainly I will presume innocence."

I suggested that tremendous damage had been done.

"Certainly," said the governor, "a lot of damage has been done already. It will cost Covenant House money, etc."

Now the conversation got tricky. Rhetorically, Cuomo asked out loud whether he was criticizing the newspaper. He answered his own question.

MC: No, we have the First Amendment and they can print anything that they want to print.

AC: Let me argue with that for a second.

MC: Sure.

AC: I still think you can criticize the newspaper even though we have the First Amendment. We can't believe for a second that you can't criticize them sometimes when they do something outrageous or despicable, can you?

MC: Sure you can and the way you criticize them is that you don't buy them.

AC: No, the way that you criticize them, I think, is to say that they're wrong...

MC: [interrupting] No, I don't think that the media can be effectively criticized by politicians.

AC: I don't agree with you...

MC: Well, you know, because every time a politician criticizes the media the media then turns around and says, "He's thin skinned, he can't take it, etc. etc." and that's the end of the criticism. Then they've got the public convinced that if a politician criticizes a reporter that there's something wrong with the politician. So I would leave the criticism to the media.

Here's the way I think it should work: the media should criticize the politicians, which they do a good job of. I encourage that. And, number two, the media should criticize the media, and they do a pretty good job of that.

AC: [interrupting] No, no, they don't.

MC: Oh, sure they do. They've got media groups set up and they collect their own...

AC: No, no they do not.

MC: You mean some are worse than ever.

AC: They are so self-serving. In my mind it's the new despotism and I'll tell you, there is a point when all these chickens are going to come home to roost.

MC: I'll give you a good book to read about that. Alan Fotheringham, *Birds of a Feather*. Fotheringham is a great, great Canadian reporter who has worked in Toronto and Washington and all around the globe. And he has written a wonderful book about the media.

Then Cuomo launched into a discussion about Fotheringham and his views on such journalistic question marks as Westbrook Pegler and the great Walter Lippman "and his divorce and marriage and how he handled it personally."

In his typically Cuomoesque way, after he had made all those telling points about the shortcomings of the media, Cuomo announced that, "I will not criticize the media."

Fat chance. I tried once again by saying that politicians, when they found something despicable on the part of the press, had a right to criticize them.

Finally, tiring of the game, Cuomo conceded, "Of course I have the right. It's a question of whether I use that right."

Cuomo's beauty was that he refused to be cowed by the press. He chose to engage them when others would be running in the other direction. Over and over, I heard people say that the Washington press corps would pound Cuomo into submission. I suspected that they couldn't be more wrong. When he appeared with the toughest of them, like Evans and Novak, I never saw any blood dripping from Cuomo. I did see a few open wounds on his would-be tormentors.

But Cuomo knew that they, the press, were tough. He knew that supportive articles did nothing for a reporter's reputation. In fact, he confided to me that even those who really admire what he is doing politically were afraid to write positive things about him because they thought their colleagues would make fun of them. Once in early 1990, Cuomo, at the end of one of our programs, gave me a pretty clear picture of how frustrating it can be to take on the press.

After talking about how politicians had an almost contractual obligation in a free democratic system to accept the flak, he added, "I will say this if I may, that reporters really can't take it when you hit them back. I mean, I notice that reporters are pretty good at criticizing us but as soon as you fire back you start getting described as 'cantankerous,' 'mean,' and 'thin skinned.'"

I agreed with him that reporters were pretty good at dishing it out but were not really able to accept criticism of their own work, even when it was poor.

Said Cuomo, "I mean, 'What's right is right,' we used to say in the old neighborhood and 'What's good for the goose is good for the...'—uh-oh, we'll get in trouble for that one."

Almost every time Mario Cuomo criticized the press he then turned around to make sure that everyone listening understood that he was indeed committed to a free press.

"Well, let me tell you about the press. I have, I think, an interesting position. I am stronger on the importance of a free press than most Americans."

Unlike others, Cuomo made it clear that he did not believe there were appropriate distinctions to be made between the print and the electronic broadcast media when it came to First Amendment protection.

(In fact, one of the subtle distinctions between a free print media and media which uses the airwaves is that our airwaves are regulated by the Federal Communications Commission and other bodies.)

There may be a political as well as a philosophical reason for Cuomo's forceful position on the subject. He was always best able to get his message out when he had immediate access to people without the intervention of print reporters. In other words, when people heard the governor directly, the response was more positive than when the print press reported what he said and, sometimes very subtly, added their own interpretations. There is no secret that the print and electronic media have been locked in battle for years now. Therefore the stronger the electronic media, the better it was for the governor.

During one particular conversation, Cuomo described how he vetoed a bill that would have forced cable TV companies not to drop some services that were part of the package that the consumer signed up for. The problem, said the governor, was that he favored the concept of protecting the consumer.

"On the other hand, I believe that electronic media should have the same protections as print media and I think that the day has passed when you could say of electronic media, especially television, that it was different from the newspapers because it is a monopoly."

He went on. "You know the theory that, well, they use the air waves. And the air waves belong to the people and therefore we should regulate them. Well, newspapers use the streets and the streets belong to the people. And newspapers use the airwaves, you know, by advertising. So why would you draw the distinction? I believe that if the Founding Fathers rewrote the Constitution today it would say not 'free press' in the First Amendment. You know it says free speech and free press. It carved out the press specifically and the press, of course, was then print. But I think now it would have said 'free media.'

"So my position is that reporters should have more access than they normally get and I have tried to give them that. I believe they should have no restrictions, and I have tried to give them that.

"As you know we house them in state property. Nobody ever raised the technical problem of 'Do they pay us rent?' They live on state property. As far as I know I don't believe that anybody has ever charged them anything.

"We give them all the access in the world. We would never try to interfere with them. I offer whistle blower laws as an example. I'm trying to change the law so that someone who leaks information to the press gets all the protection possible.

"We would never, never try to interfere with the press or try to stifle individuals in the press by going over their heads. We wouldn't do that. On the other hand it's not unfair when the press comes at you, to point out *their* deficiencies. I'll tell you, however, if you do, they'll get back at you. If they don't do it right away they'll do it eventually. I know because I've seen it happen. Take my word for it. It's very difficult to criticize the press, without quickly getting a reputation they can nail into your forehead so firmly that you're buried with it."

And again, having reiterated how dirty the press can get with politicians, Cuomo launched into a defense of the work of the press corps. Included in the list: they are underpaid, they don't take bribes.

"Like public servants, there are many times that the press does not get its due."

At one point I told him I thought *The New York Times* was biased in their coverage devoted to the governor. He didn't disagree about the issue but he did respond about his view of taking "incoming" from the press. His words indicated the importance of a free press, even when it was clear that he believed the reporter to be undereducated or downright wrong.

"I do not want government regulating Alan Chartock and public radio or public television or paid television, or newspapers. I want you free to beat up on the politicians. I don't want anything that impedes you, even if it means I have to suffer your bad taste, your bad judgment, even your corruption. I will take all of that because

I'm afraid of oppression by the government, I'm afraid of the kind of oppression that drove people to revolution in this country.

"I'm afraid of what happened in Nazi Germany, I'm afraid of what happened in fascist Italy, I'm afraid of what happens with emperors and kings and potentates, and all of that. And because I'm afraid of that, I will suffer the imperfection of the media to protect from a worse imperfection."

He was even stronger a year earlier when he once again indicted the press for all its terrible weaknesses yet insisted that the protection of the press was of paramount importance.

"You pay a price for protecting the press, for protecting free speech. When you protect the press, for example, you empower them to tell untruths about people. You empower them to hurt people. Ruin lives, ruin careers. They have that power, and they're protected in it.

"That's the price you pay for free speech and the press. And it is worth it. For all of the sadness of the abuse of the right, the right is worth it. The right keeps us from oppression. The right protects us from governments that would run wild. The right is very, very important to us."

Every once in a while, Cuomo would get into a press duel with an individual reporter. Having been challenged myself from time to time, I can only say that it is always an educative, if unpleasant, experience. The nice thing from the public's point of view is that someone with the know-how and wherewithal to fight back, does so.

One occasional critic was Dan Lynch, then the managing editor of the *Albany Times Union*, the single newspaper in the capital city. He once went on television before a group of student interns and told them that I was far too soft on Cuomo. So when I questioned the governor after Lynch's comments I told him that Lynch had gotten on my case and I mentioned that I wasn't going to be "Mr. Nice Guy" when it came to questioning the governor anymore. The governor entered into a dialogue on the issue.

AC: He was on television saying that I was too soft on you, Governor.

MC: Why doesn't he interview me? [My translation, "He hasn't got the guts."]

AC: That's between him and you, I would think, Governor.

MC: Why don't you invite Lynch onto the radio show for ten minutes to ask me the toughest questions he can. [Translation, "Let's see how tough he can be when he gets here."]

AC: Invite him on my radio show?

MC: Why not?"

AC: Are you kidding? Let him go and get his own radio show!

MC: It would prove that you're open minded, you're willing to be educated and so am I.

AC: Well, you maybe, but none of those things are true about me, Governor.

MC: Oh, I see, God forbid that we should perpetrate a lie. Alright, well, now we understand.

While my position was meant to be humorous the interchange gave the governor an opportunity to make his point. He wasn't afraid of anyone and in the case of Lynch he had no reason to be. What he was saying was, why not bring him onto the show. I can handle him. And, of course, he was right.

The press corps was often hostile to the governor. Too often they believed that it was their job to dish it out.

But he gave as well as he took. Once, when I asked him a question he didn't like, he put his tongue way back in his cheek and said, "I think it's a continuous miracle that this state functions as well as it does when people like you, Chartock, are involved in describing our function to the outside world."

So I bit the bullet and asked him why he appeared on the program each week.

"I don't know," he said. "I'm a Catholic and penance is important to us. Purgatory is an important notion to us. The whole idea of suffering as a kind of requiting for our sin is ever present. And this serves very nicely."

But he didn't stop at humor. He extended himself and took chances in ways other major public officials wouldn't have dared. He fielded questions once a month on commercial radio throughout New York State. He did the same thing periodically on television and on cable television. He met a more intellectual audience once a week on public radio on my syndicated *Capitol Connection* radio program.

Not once, but many times, he gave us clues about why he did this. He specifically said that by allowing the listening audience to hear him directly, he avoided the distortion and selectivity of the press. Over and over he complained, often correctly, that the press quoted him out of context. The electronic media seemed to be Cuomo's way out of it.

One terrible moment came for me when *The New York Times* printed an anonymous column purporting to be humorous which had the governor confessing to Matilda that he was voting for Reagan so that the way would be cleared for his own presidential ambitions. The governor's people blamed me and then he kiddingly told me that he knew I was the offender. While the experts maintained that Cuomo risked media overexposure, he seemed to disagree, balancing humor and his love of language and teaching in such a way as to make his reappearance fresh and interesting.

But perhaps his favorite way of dealing with the press was through athletics. He challenged them over and over to team sports and, despite the fact that he had a terrible back and his doctors constantly advised him against running, jumping and ball playing, he forgot all this when it came time to take on the reporters. And with regularity the former minor league ball player beat the pants off them, despite their cries that he brought state police ringers onto his teams.

But no matter what he did to them, he understood that it was through the press that people learned about him and about government in general. He denied that he paid a lot of attention to them, but he did. Over and over again, minor league reporters who wouldn't have had a chance of getting through to any other governor or senior politician were surprised that he got on the phone when they called.

In his years in Albany, senior Republican leader Warren Anderson was almost completely insulated from the press. His successor, Ralph Marino, a gentleman and a very able politician, was equally unapproachable. But the press as an institution is permanent in Albany and Cuomo knew it. In 1988 when I asked for his New Year's prediction about the LCA (Legislative Correspondents Association) he responded, "They will be back."

Our many conversations demonstrated that it is the media which can transmit the political values to people. What's more, in their attempts to sell papers, over the years publishers would always print dubious material including some terribly irresponsible accusations. Those accusations, simply because they were published, had to be answered even though they were what Cuomo called "obvious lies."

Cuomo said that attacks by those who would destabilize government are a good way to test "individuals who happen to occupy important positions at the moment to see how they respond to these provocations. Do they reduce themselves by responding to provocations using the law as an instrument of revenge?"

During the period of the sensational Tawana Brawley case, Cuomo, who was responding to attacks by Brawley advisors Sharpton, Mason and Maddox, answered that the people in his administration and then Attorney General Robert Abrams hadn't used the law to get revenge. Nor had they bothered to respond to the lies put forth by the advisors. He said that Koch or Abrams hadn't responded in kind.

Soon after the word began to leak out that the Brawley story might be a hoax, I spoke to Cuomo about it. It is important to remember that while Cuomo was practicing extreme moderation under great pressure by the media, the Brawley advisors were saying terrible things about Cuomo.

Understanding the potential for a media field day, Cuomo was very careful. But for the first time he began to deal with the possibility that the Tawana Brawley story was a hoax.

"It may be that this was a hoax. In which case the people responsible ought to be made to pay for the terrible price that they've exacted from the people of the state of New York for their cynical game. But that remains to be proven. We have to be even handed about the application of the law. We can't choose to believe what we'd like to believe and require those whose assertions we find discomforting to prove them through the judicial process.

"Everyone should have to prove it through the process. I don't believe in trying these important questions on television—I don't mean cameras in the courtroom, I mean television talk shows and interviews etc. [a clear reference to Reverend Al Sharpton, a Brawley advisor who had been appearing on virtually every talk show one could find on the dial].

"If it is a hoax, well then you've accused a community, you've accused specific individuals. If it is a hoax, you have used the emotions, or abused the emotions, the concern, the sincere concern, of millions of New Yorkers. You have wasted a huge amount of time, money, and the effort of dozens and dozens of officials. No, if it is a hoax, then it is a terrible thing that's been done. *If* it is a hoax..."

It may be that Cuomo was being cautious. And it may be that he didn't like people playing the issue in the press but even in responding the way he had to me on that session of our little radio show, Cuomo had given his answer and had used at least one media outlet to do it.

One of the things that upset Cuomo the most was the use of polls by the media. Over and over he said that he had grave reservations about them, even though he admitted that he used them himself. On one occasion, *The New York Post* printed the results of a secret Republican poll showing that he was vulnerable in a coming election. Cuomo was convinced that the poll was untruthful and said so.

I got into it with him at one point. "More than ever I feel we have overdone the use of polls. Though of course there is a constitutional right involved."

The problem with the press using polls, Cuomo says, is that the electorate is psyched into seeing elections as contests only. By not emphasizing issues and concentrating on the polls, the electorate is cheated because the media doesn't deliver the essential issue information. "What are you teaching them? How is it relevant that Chartock is ahead of Cuomo by four points? If I am trying to make a judgment on Chartock and Cuomo, how does it help me to know that 200 or 300 or 500 people whose names I do not know, whose backgrounds I do not know, whose educational level, whose interest level and other levels I do not know, whose honesty I don't know and who are answering the polls and asked questions by a pollster I do not know, who may or may not have recorded answers accurately, who may or may not have changed their intonations one question to the next, and one person to the next?"

To Cuomo, it all comes down to advertising—"to sell space." The more polls you print, the more people buy the paper or tune in the channel or the station. "I can't think of any reason other than to sell space."

Alright, I asked him, why are people so interested in polls? Why are people so concerned with them? But having said that the newspapers and the media were after the almighty dollar by doing polls, Cuomo refused to acknowledge that people really want them or are concerned about them.

"Who's concerned? Do you really think that if you announce on Channel six that you would never do another poll that you would get a protest?"

"No," I shot back, "but just the same I think that people are interested in polls."

So the governor said that the same interest could be piqued "...if you put a decapitated body on the screen."

Fascinated, I asked him whether politicians who were opposed to the use of polls weren't just angry because the news the polls brought was often bad. He said in response that he didn't like polls, even if they were favorable to him.

"I am not an admirer of polls because they show us ahead." Cuomo said that back in 1986, when he ran for re-election and the polls showed him ahead, he had the same negative viewpoint about polls that he had in '82. And the polls, in 1982, says Cuomo "had said that I was behind."

"But you *were* behind!" I exclaimed.

"Who said so? How come I won....How come you know I was behind? Maybe I was always ahead. Maybe the polls were wrong." He has a point. He did win despite the fact that almost all the polls had him losing.

But he wouldn't let it rest there. After a protracted argument in which I advanced the thesis that polling was scientific and that you could prove it by the fact that results mirrored the polls, Cuomo advanced the thesis that polls were unscientific. The governor had the last word as he suggested somewhat drily to me that "You must be working your way toward Christianity because Christianity is an act of faith. We believe it's perfectly compatible with the intellect and all that intellect can teach us, but it requires a step beyond and not in contradiction, of intellect." The gov said that he accepted my faith in polls but, he said, "I prefer my own faith, frankly."

Well, he may have said that he preferred his own faith but every once in a while he showed how basically distrustful he was either of himself or the press that wrote about him.

Once I asked him about a book that had been written about him.

AC: Have you read that book?

MC: No.

AC: Is that right? The whole book is about you. How could you have not read it?

MC: That is correct. I tell you why. I have not read the *Time* magazine cover story. I did read portions of the *Newsweek* cover story or one of those in *Esquire*. I normally don't read the long pieces for a couple of reasons. The portions of it that are flattering make me feel guilty. The portions of it that are condemnatory make me feel either, "Gee, I have a fault I have to correct or I didn't have a fault which they describe as a fault which makes me unhappy." So, I see it as a no win proposition. If they say good things, I'm guilty. If they say bad things, I'm disconcerted. Therefore, I don't read these pieces.

Cuomo went on to say that he broke most of the mirrors in his house "except for the little one for shaving." The analogy: "I don't like to look at myself, to be honest with you. I don't mind considering my own thoughts in the morning. I don't like profile pieces. I could do without them all together."

So despite all his protestations that one cannot criticize the press and what it does, the governor has consistently tested them, challenged them and cajoled them into doing better. And my reading of the Albany press corps is that he has, for the most part, won some big victories. The press corps printed negative stories about the governor when they got them, particularly when they got a good bona fide story. But he taught them some lessons. He let them know that they must defend themselves when they did something particularly reprehensible. He called them and made them explain themselves. The next time they thought twice about pulling the same cheap trick. He couldn't control them but he did what he had to in order to protect his contact with the people.

FRIENDS AND ENEMIES

Nowhere is Mario Cuomo's penchant for having fun in politics and his practice of "progressive pragmatism" more evident than in what he does with his political friends and enemies. Our conversations brought out some major, but never specifically stated, operational rules. The first of these is that a good governor doesn't allow himself to get too close to any one individual. That's because such people have a tendency to get you into a lot of trouble.

The second idea is never to get so close to any group that its members think they own you. The idea is to keep everyone guessing all the time.

Finally, at least in public, you keep your cool and you don't allow people to get you so mad that you make a mistake.

Other governors of New York had people who were their alter egos, whose word meant that the deal was signed, sealed and delivered. The Cuomo style precluded such deal makers. There was only one person who was empowered to make deals and that was Cuomo. It drove the big time lobbyists crazy.

As much as possible, Mario Cuomo treated people courteously. Unlike Mayor Ed Koch, who kissed and told in his books to make money, Cuomo wouldn't have thought of it. He'd hit them in the kishkas when he took them on in private or on the phone, but he'd preserve their public image every time. Unless, of course, they were publicly attacking him.

It was all good politics, of course. Cuomo was capable of playing a very tough inside game. He played to win. But he was very aware of his power and of his penchant for playing too rough. On several occasions he told me that he dedicated his later life as governor to compensate for his tougher and meaner earlier days. I am genuinely convinced that he doesn't like to hurt people. When he got mad at me it was clear that he always took pains to meet me halfway in the subsequent rapprochement.

Cuomo didn't like to hurt anyone and even when there may have been subsequent political fallout, he went out of his way to help an employee, friend, or colleague who was in trouble. There were times he took his lumps for doing so. In one case it was his first commissioner of labor, Lillian Roberts, who didn't function well in her job. Cuomo had gone out of his way to recruit qualified women and black administrators into his administration and Roberts was both.

He had inherited her from the Carey administration and it was clear that the public sector labor unions, who had been instrumental in the Cuomo campaign, wanted her in the job for a variety of reasons. Not the least of these included Victor Gotbaum, then head of District Council 82 of the American Federation of State County and Municipal Employees (AFSME). Union insiders told me he didn't want Roberts, a competitor for union power, back in the operation.

Finally, after years of criticism suggesting that the governor could not recruit first rate people, Cuomo switched Roberts to a lesser job in his administration, which she did not accept. On a subsequent show I asked the governor why he had done that and he gave me an answer which I have heard many times since. He said that people had individual talents which could be harnessed in many ways and it was just a problem of finding the right job for particular talents and abilities.

At one point when I didn't have an awful lot to talk to him about, I asked him about Mike Dukakis's troubles in neighboring Massachusetts. I told him that "I was just reviewing my notes and I found that you predicted that Mike Dukakis would come back from the presidential election, take it easy, and become an important voice for the Democratic party. That is almost an exact quote. The question I have for you, sir, are you willing to revise that?"

MC: No.
AC: You know, I have a feeling that you never say anything bad
    about people. You always say the good things about people.
MC: Can I ask you something? Why do you have to say bad things
    about people?
AC: Because sometimes it is important to be critical.
MC: Well, I will leave that job to you.
AC: Thank you.

Then there was the time that I asked him about John Sununu, who had been appointed by incoming President-elect Bush to be chief of staff in the new administration. There had been rumors about scraps between Cuomo and Sununu when the latter had been the governor of New Hampshire. But Cuomo only had good things to say about Sununu.

"Let me tell you about John Sununu. He is, of course, the governor of New Hampshire." Then the Cuomo ability to make love and criticize at the same time showed itself. Just listen to this sentence: "If Sununu called Dukakis a liberal he is a radical conservative, not just a conservative, and proud of it and that is fine. He is extremely intelligent and he has a very fine brain and mind. He is extremely persuasive and very dogged in his advocacy. People have accused him of being harsh. But then they have accused me of being so, too."

By that time, one has the idea about why the two men are poles apart. "I don't think he is personally offensive to anybody but there is no question that he is intellectually combative. I like him—he comes from Queens and he has a beautiful, big family and has been an extremely successful engineer and governor in his state and headed the National Governor's Association as Dukakis did before him."

I knew Sununu had been an advocate of nuclear power and that Cuomo had major reservations on the same subject; he had assured that the Shoreham plant on Long Island would be closed. So I asked the governor, "You fought over the nuclear power, certainly."

The governor responded that he and Sununu had fought over many things, including amending the United States Constitution.

"He wanted to change the Constitution of the United States [to assure a balanced budget] and I did not, so I was more conservative than he in that regard." But despite their philosophical differences Cuomo said that he and Sununu "have a good relationship." Concluded Cuomo, "I think he is going to be a strong chief of staff." But he warns that it is tough to go from being a governor, or your own boss, to being someone else's subordinate. "Whether he will be able to move successfully from the number one position to a subservient position remains to be seen. There is no question that he will be loyal to the president."

Even David Duke, the Klansman turned politician, gave Cuomo a chance to show his fairness. Cuomo had nothing good to say about Duke but he did have an opportunity to suggest that the fact that just because Duke was a Republican, the phenomenon was not unknown to the Democrats. I raised the subject on the program by just speaking the name of this despicable man.

AC: David Duke.

MC: That's the price you pay for democracy. Even bigots can run, even Ku Klux Klanners can run. They say he is an embarrassment to the Republican party—I don't see that. I don't think he is an embarrassment to the Republicans any more than LaRouche was to the Democrats. You will have nutsy, eccentric Democrats, you will have nutsy, eccentric so-called Republicans.

I think it is probably fair to say that some of the harshness in Republican politics of the last eight years, some of what some people think was insensitivity to the race issue, might have encouraged Duke, but I don't think it's a fair charge against Bush, Reagan, and Atwater that they are responsible for Duke.

I believe that Cuomo's parochial school upbringing is partly responsible for the way he treats his enemies. Other politicians get mad and stay mad, destroying relationships. Not Mario Cuomo. Just as the church approaches non- believers, Cuomo believes that all enemies are potential friends. Each of them can be brought into his circle if he just tries hard enough. If he doesn't succeed he seems to believe that he, not the enemy, is responsible. In fact, some have said that he treated his adversaries far better than he treated those who worked for him or were already in his camp.

Mario Cuomo virtually never gave up on an adversary. He called them and debated them. He argued. He flattered. The more they fought, the harder he'd try. He treated Republican Senate Majority Leader Warren Anderson, a former contestant for practical political power, with deference, respect, praise and constant attention. In negotiation, he adopted Anderson's positions and even credited him. In the end Cuomo received the credit anyway, as in the case of the state's mandatory seatbelt law which was a Republican creation but which is known as Cuomo's seatbelt law.

On the other hand, he treated those who pledged loyalty to him far more strictly. They were expected to stay in line and not violate his need for an incredible range of personal control, extending far down into the lower reaches of his administration. He was, according to everyone who worked for him, a very demanding, hands-on manager. His people knew that no matter how hard he made them work, he worked harder.

It was virtually unimaginable for Mario Cuomo to take the type of vacations a George Bush took at Kennebunkport, Maine. For Bush, the glass may have been half full. For Cuomo, it would never, ever be full enough. There was never time to relax. Bush had never known anything but wealth. Cuomo had all the earmarks of one who has known poverty intimately, and who loved, needed and respected the work ethic.

Those whom he saw as potentially harmful or as competitors were most at risk as far as Mario Cuomo was concerned. Most of these people had a tendency to underrate him. By the time they found out differently, they were history. But once Cuomo had vanquished them, once they had shown their necks to him, he would inevitably be gracious in victory. The former attorney general, Robert Abrams, was stopped in his tracks by the governor when they contested, especially in the early years of Cuomo's administration. Then, once the lesson was taught—once it was clear that Abrams would not undercut or second guess Cuomo, the relationship improved.

I remember one particular show when Cuomo was speaking of Abrams and a lawsuit against the major gasoline dealers. Cuomo was trying to get them to give some of the windfall profits raised in the so-called gasoline crisis back to the people in the form of a rebate. He made it clear that Abrams had tried to settle for too little. "The truth here is that, I may be wrong, but I believe that *even* the attorney general recommended a settlement earlier in this case. I'm almost certain that the a.g. in charge recommended it and I said, 'No.' I said, 'If you stay in this lawsuit you'll be able to get more money directly from the company in addition to what they gave the environmental group and I must tell you that was not the popular view at the time. The attorney general's view was that this was a problematical litigation, he wasn't sure if he could win it and he's probably right. They understand this business, they work at it all the time."

Cuomo pressed on, demanding that Abrams do better, and the result, said the governor was "one million five better than the deal they wanted me to settle for."

Stanley Fink, the Brooklyn-ese-speaking tough guy and former Speaker of the State Assembly, and Mel Miller, the Speaker who succeeded him, both tried to embarrass the governor by undercutting his programs. Both were politically dead by the time Cuomo was through with them.

But true to the governor's style, Fink and Cuomo now enjoy a tremendous relationship. Miller never fully learned his lesson although he has said publicly that he has. So we know that Cuomo had political enemies, most of whom ended up as his working partners, if not friends.

Who are Mario Cuomo's best friends?—in politics, at least. I put that to him on a program in the late '80s.

I asked him, "Who are your best friends?" Naturally, being Cuomo, he answered, "Well, how do you define best friend?" "Oh, no!," I thought, "It's going to be one of *those* conversations."

But I did try. "Who do you rely on, who do you find calling and asking for advice?" I wasn't surprised when he told me, "I don't do it that way. I don't have one or two people whom I call, regardless of what the question is." But he did give me some important clues. I've deduced over the years that he did not tend to rely on all subordinates in the same way. For example, a number of commissioners indicated to me at one time that they worked through Hank Dullea, Cuomo's number three guy—his director of operations. But Cuomo kept coming back to his reliance on the late Dr. David Axelrod, his health commissioner. In this particular conversation, circumloquacious as it might have been, Cuomo came first to Axelrod.

"If it's a health problem, health is very much in the news, of course we have Dr. Axelrod, our great commissioner and certainly I talk to him. But there are all sorts of people...."

Cuomo knew his people and had a very special relationship with Axelrod. I once told the governor that I considered Axelrod to be one of the gutsiest people I had ever met. Cuomo's come-back was very instructive. He said that "if he were a gutsy dope I wouldn't think as much of him. He happens to be very courageous but he's also extremely smart, wise and experienced." He added, "He has great integrity."

But my conversation about best friends with the governor was-n't over. I tried still again. "Yes, but I mean as friends, in other words, buddies—people you can rely on, who can remove them-selves from the politics of your position—who can give you the straight answer that you look for as opposed to the fawning answer."

The governor was not being helpful. Perhaps because of his earlier bouts with people who let him down, perhaps because he didn't want to admit that he relied on his son, Andrew, to the degree that he did. Perhaps because he didn't want people to know how to get access to him in one way or another.

He once told me that he would never allow anyone to hand him an envelope directly for fear that there would be an attempt to compromise him. Considering some of the dirty tricks that have been pulled in politics in recent years, one would have to conclude such a move was more prudent than paranoid.

Cuomo went on. He said he had lots of close friends he could rely on in a pinch. "I'm surrounded by people like that. I'm one of the lucky ones who has, first of all, a big family. My kids are all adults now, the youngest of them is going to be nineteen, is in col-lege and is very bright. The oldest of them is thirty-four and a doc-tor. And in between we have lawyers and PR people. So obviously they are friends."

Here's a snippet from an earlier conversation on the subject I had with Cuomo.

"I have a wife that I'll be married to thirty-five years next week. I still have my mother, who's getting sharper and sharper and my mother-in-law, who's also in wonderful shape. I have my in-laws. I'm surrounded by family. I'm surrounded by people that I've practiced law with, practiced politics with for thirty years,

Fabian Palomino, for instance. I have a secretary, Jerry Crotty, who's been with me since the first day I was governor.And there are a lot of people—look around—a lot of people in my government have been there from the very beginning. And these are all people who are close to me, they are all top flight professionals and they are all extremely useful."

The governor, by throwing in everyone including his in- laws, was providing a negative answer to my question. He was saying that no one was really that close, except perhaps his immediate family.

"Let me just try one more time," I said. "Is there anybody, when you really are, as most of us do, feeling... I've got a big problem here. I've got to solve it. Is there anyone who you consider to be a sagacious enough person of whom you'd say, so-and-so is the first person I'd go to. Is it Fabian Palomino?"

At first he went another round with his non-answer but then something happened which I think was closer to the truth than anything he had said before. "I must be candid with you. I think that when you are trying to think things through, the place to start is with yourself. The place to start is in your own mind. You can get help from a lot of sources. You can get help from books. You can get help from philosophers. You can get help from little collections of aphorisms. There's a world of help in the library, frankly. The thought of all of civilization is recorded there. And it would be foolish to think that given enough time and with a little luck you couldn't find answers to most questions, somewhere written on a page. So there's all the wisdom of the world available to us. Even if you're blind and can't read..."

Cuomo was telling us, I think, that he relies on no one so much as himself. Perhaps he was saying that everyone out there has some kind of vested interest. That truth can only be arrived at when an individual figures it out for himself.

"I like very much the notion of spending as much time as possible with yourself, trying to work things through internally." Perhaps that's the truest answer Mario Cuomo could have given, because I have met hundreds of people who have been identified to me as "tight with Cuomo." Some of them were big money raisers, some were politicians, men like State Senator Emmanuel Gold or the late Assembly Ways and Means Chairman and Speaker Saul Weprin. They would tell you how close they were to the governor. But you would never see that closeness demonstrated, by his frank admission, other than with his faithful companion, the Sancho Panza of his administration, Fabian Palomino.

But Cuomo did finally say that after all else has been tried, after you have looked inward and in the library, "Then if you're lucky enough to have someone close to you whose judgment on a particular matter you think is particularly good—it's usually wife or parents or kids—then you go to them."

Here was an early conversation on the matter that gave great credit to his then teenage son, now in law school.

AC: Who have you been talking to lately?

MC: Besides yourself?

AC: Who do you talk to? Who are your favorite people to talk to?

MC: I don't have favorite people.

AC: Come now, Governor.

MC: The truth, you mean if I had a choice, if I had a half hour to sit down and chat with someone? This is going to sound, and I hope you don't misunderstand this, probably I most enjoy talking to my kids. And of the kids, most probably Christopher, who just turned seventeen this weekend. Christopher is very bright. He is very nice. He is a kind of sensitive kid. He is clear minded, in a way a sixteen/seventeen year old can be.

Friends are one thing; a nemesis is another. A major one of these before she was eclipsed from the scene, was Carol Bellamy, the number two New York City official, the city council president.

Bellamy, everyone inside New York politics knows, was a difficult woman to work for. She was demanding, she had tirades and she did what was politically expedient while still maintaining that she was the personification of the non-politician. On one of the shows Cuomo made it clear that Carol Bellamy had some years ago supported Mayor Koch for politically expedient reasons. Bellamy and Koch got along like cats and dogs but if Koch succeeded in becoming governor then Bellamy would have become mayor of New York City.

On one program, the governor described in some detail his relationship with Carol Bellamy. He claimed that the only reason she supported Koch was to become mayor. History has certainly proven him right on that one. Even Bellamy has told me that it was the biggest political mistake of her life.

Sometimes Cuomo has a way of letting those who are close to him know that it really isn't a good idea to do something. Take the time that Harry Belafonte was considering a run for the U.S. Senate. I asked him about that. First, Cuomo told him all that was good about himself, then he advised him to go slow

AC: Okay, Governor, let's talk a little about Harry Belafonte. Here is a major cultural force in this country, somebody who stood for civil rights. He certainly has been a liberal for many years now and he says he is interested in running for the United States Senate. He's reportedly talked with you about that. Can you tell us more?

MC: He's talked to me a couple of times. He's hesitating because he has extraordinary professional commitments. Contracts of various kinds, shows set up he's supposed to be producing. He's trying to figure out whether he can honorably disassociate himself from those commitments, be relieved of them. I'm not sure he can and I like his instinct that says, you know, I have an obligation to these things, I must deal with that obligation. So he's doing that.

Remember he didn't volunteer for this position. People reached out to him. Denny Farrell, a leading black assemblyman from New York and others. Then he called me and sat with Larry Kurlander, the chairperson of the Democratic party. So, he's interested. Would he be good? He is extremely intelligent. I think he needs an opportunity to prove to people how thorough he is on the issues. I think he suffers from what I call the eclipse effect.

You see a star like Harry Belafonte, who is a great performer, and there is an assumption that he can't do anything else. If you saw Bill Bradley on a basketball court at Princeton some years ago and suggested to somebody watching the game, "There's a great senator," there would be a laugh. Watch him playing with the Knicks and say, "That guy would make a great senator" and people would make a joke because the picture of the person as something more than an athlete is obscured by the bright light of celebrity.

I think Harry has to get past that, and could do it at one press conference if he chooses to run. All you'd have to do is to get him ready, prep him a bit, which should be easy, and then let the hard-nosed press question him on the issues. He's so bright, so communicative, so attractive that I think he would establish himself in a press conference. I don't think there's any doubt that he would be a formidable candidate.

Has he worked on these matters? Absolutely. He has been committed to questions of civil rights, hunger, fairness and strong economy. Look, in the Senate you have people like Frank Lautenberg, a senator from New Jersey. What did he do before he was a senator? He was a businessman. Well, Harry Belafonte makes what, $15 million a year? I don't know. He's pretty good at business. He's not just good at singing. He's managed his affairs quite well.

AC: Is it your impression, Governor, that he'd have to move more to the center of the party from his present position?

MC: Center, left, right—what people want is common sense, the truth.

AC: Does he have it?

MC: [Sighs] You know, I don't know him well. I know him well enough to be impressed by his intelligence, his ability. I appointed him chairperson of the Martin Luther King Commission. We took some heat from some black Baptist ministers who said that a minister should be selected. Harry was in touch with me and said that if I felt that I wanted the embarrassment to be relieved he'd step aside. Which is kind of a nice touch. I asked him if he was upset about it and he said, "No, I'll stay" and he stayed. Because I certainly was satisfied that I had made a good choice.

Now, Alan, let me finish this. He was so concerned that he prove his ability to do this job well that he took the time to take a train up to Albany where he was scheduled to address the Black and Puerto Rican Caucus. He wrote his speech on the train, and went over it with me in part before he delivered it.

We were sitting at a table together with his wife, Julie, and I'll tell you, I was extremely impressed with his ability, with his intelligence, with his depth, and anybody who heard him that night was also impressed. Those were his words. Most senators don't read their own words. Most senators read speechwriters' words. He read his own words and they were deep and broad and intelligent. Of course, people will disagree with some of his positions but he holds them with conviction, passion and intelligence. I think he'd make a very good candidate, if he chooses to do it.

AC: Did you urge him to do it?

MC: No, I'll tell you exactly what I said to him. I feel free to do this because he told some reporters in Washington the day before yesterday. I said to him, "Harry," in two different conversations, "I can make the case. I can advocate very strongly for your candidacy. I think it would be a good thing for the party, for the Democrats. It would steal the show, actually— you'd have the camera in the United States here in New York for much of the Senate race.

"I think in fairness to you, in addition to searching out your own commitments and how to deal with them, you should go to people whom you know, who know politics and know your profession, ask them for every negative they can think of. Norman Lear is someone who knows performing and a little about politics. Go to Basil Patterson, with whom you were brought up in Harlem. Go to Bernie Charles who heads up my black advisory group. Go to people who know you. Cleveland Robinson who was with you at Martin Luther King. Ask them to give you a list of all the negatives."

After all that advice, Belafonte chose not to run. I had the feeling that Mario wanted that all along.

Then, too, there is the case of former Speaker Stanley Fink who began his relationship with Cuomo dismissing the future governor as a lightweight. By the time the smoke cleared, Fink had been absolutely outclassed and was out of power, practicing law, with Mario Cuomo saying only good things about him.

In the beginning, Fink seemed determined to teach Cuomo that the governor's office was lesser in power than that of the Speaker, just as he did in the case of Hugh L. Carey. On many of the state's policy issues, Fink upstaged Cuomo. But Cuomo out-maneuvered him at every turn. In the end, Fink left the Legislature to return to practice law. Cuomo characterized him as an extraordinary civil servant and continues to do so.

No one was more of a nemesis to Mario Cuomo than Ed Koch. In the end, "Fast Eddie" was no match for Cuomo. He was the governor's greatest opponent but when Koch was at the nadir of his political existence, the greatest irony of all was that Mario Cuomo was the man who tried to save him as mayor. He couldn't do it.

Ronald Reagan was a tough nut for Cuomo. He realized that the man was beloved by large segments of the American people and was always careful to say that. On the other hand, he did not mind pointing up the inconsistencies in the Reagan record. But always, his criticism was framed in the rhetoric of respect for the president. Just before Reagan left office Cuomo told our audience, "The president will always be popular with the American people." He went on and on suggesting that the reason Americans loved Reagan was that he was a "sincere, committed, gentle, unflappable person who apparently deeply believes what he says to the American people." You will note the use of the word apparently, connoting something less than conviction. But after this homily of good things, Cuomo got down to business. "There may have been times," he told us, "in Irangate where he may not have given us the whole truth. Only God knows that." Then he went on to praise the president's personal courage and "niceness" and "sense of humor."

All of Reagan's good qualities will be remembered, said Cuomo, but there will be negatives also. "The American people will remember that and will know, in the years ahead, the terrible price we pay for the deficit and the trade imbalance; how we have lost ground in the international economy. The middle class is going to figure out before long that in over fifteen years they didn't get a raise, that they are working harder than ever at 30,000 dollars a year."

Cuomo said that the middle class, the key to elections, knows that "this is a tougher and tougher society for a single parent with a kid who needs day care, or even for two parents who will try to raise a child or two children and maybe have an elderly parent to deal with who may need a nursing home."

And, said Cuomo, if the middle class doesn't think about all of that they will think of the problems that haven't been solved. Problems like "drugs, poor education, poverty as sources of social disorientation threatening our twentieth century work force. They will remember all of this but still the people will love President Reagan. I think our next president will be a Democrat."

Still another example came at the point that I was trying to draw Cuomo out on the subject of whether there was any potential conflict of interest in Ronald Reagan's acceptance of a multimillion dollar deal to travel to Japan a year after he had left office. I asked the governor whether there were ethical problems in accepting such a trip. I wanted to know whether public servants wouldn't believe that sweetheart deals would wait for them if they treated a country or a company well during their tenure.

Cuomo started out rather cautiously. First he said that there was no ethical problem. He said that he thought however it was "more a matter of taste. Jimmy Carter," he reminded us by way of contrast, "would not take money for speeches." That was contrasted by the simple Cuomoesque observation that "Jerry Ford opens supermarkets and gets money for it." Cuomo then went into an impassioned defense of Reagan. "If they are talking about President Reagan, I think it is utterly unrealistic to suggest that this man approaching eighty might have, as president, adopted an especially favorable bias with respect to Japan.

"Some people might say it's distasteful but we should not demean ourselves and say that former presidents of the most powerful people in the world would not be able to work for two years after they leave the presidency." Then Cuomo said that overall, "our presidents have been gracious and grateful and great contributors." Having said the good, Cuomo continued, reminding us that "President Nixon was forced to resign in shame and I don't know a whole lot of people who say that in the years since he left office he has been anything but statesman-like and a loyal contributing American."

Of course, Cuomo dealt daily with people who were would-be competitors and who were not Republicans. These were the natural allies, the Democrats, the labor leaders, the other progressives in the society. They could only be described as "friend/enemies." These were the people he needed in order to exist politically but who would have liked to have owned him; who, on occasion, threatened him and tried to push him around. Two in that category would be labor groups, like those which helped to elect him in 1982 and some of the minority groups which have been known to get very tough on him. One such group was led by a top Black politician, who once called him guilty of genocide because of Cuomo's position on the state's budget.

When he had to, Cuomo would fight both labor and minority groups to a standstill. In 1986, for instance, I asked him about criticism coming his way from the Black and Puerto Rican Caucus.

AC: Let's move on to a criticism that has come from some members of the Black and Puerto Rican Caucus toward you, saying that you're not as responsive to them as you might be.

MC: That's not what they told me at our meeting last week.

AC: What did they tell you last week?

MC: They were all joy and happiness, and it was good.

AC: But you did read the press reports that I did?"

MC: No.

AC: Oh. Okay, so the press is not reporting accurately. In other words you're as open to input from minority communities as you are...

MC: [interrupting] This year we have the largest housing program for low income people in the history of the United States. A minor miracle, somebody called it. Biggest housing program for minority people in the United States, thanks to the Legislature. But it was our bill, as you know. We pushed for it for over a year. This year my tax cut becomes effective. My tax cut, the Legislature's tax cut. Five hundred thousand poor people, many of them minorities, come off the tax roll, all together.

This year we've set a new record in money for education in our public school system. Now, who benefits most? Buffalo, New York City, urban areas, heavy if not dominant minority population. I think that if you look at this budget,

Alan, you have to say, never, in the history of the state, has this much been done for the people at the bottom; so much that I am criticized by my Republican friends as having spent too much for the poor; so much that welfare will be used against me in the campaign. I'm being too good to quote, "the lower classes." So that's the fact, that's the record. Now, the politicians will stand up and say you're not doing enough.When has it ever changed?

Cuomo defended his position without ascribing terrible motives to his allies who might criticize him. And because he needed them, Cuomo might look for opportunities to defend them.

One such occasion occurred one Labor Day when I asked him whether the American labor movement hadn't fallen on hard times.

"Hardly," he answered. "If anything, organized labor is stronger than it has been at any time in this decade, certainly."

Then Cuomo, at his best, saw an opportunity to let the Republicans have it and to say some nice things about labor, and some not nice things that may or may not have been true.

"You will recall that with the advent of the Reagan administration and the new conservatism there was a great push on to discredit the unions. The PATCO [air traffic controllers] strike was a symbol of it. There was also a kind of insidious attempt to blame our economic problems on unions, on spoiled unions who inhibited creativity by demanding too much for themselves and their middle class families. I think there was a period when that criticism was effective; when union membership began to fall off; when the public at large turned against unions; when people whose conditions in life as workers had been improved only because of unions—whether they belonged to unions or not—forgot that, took advantage of the good things and used the unions as an excuse for the failure of the whole system.

"All of that," Cuomo said of labor's decline, "I believe, is moving now into the past. It's receding and a new wisdom is taking over. It's clear now that what slowed down the economy was not the working people of this country but the mismanagement of the country by the people who run it. It wasn't the working people who gave Japan an advantage over us. The Japanese seized technology that our people had created and they were the ones to market it."

Using his usual penchant for quoting the other side, Cuomo looked to Walter Wriston, "a well-known Republican banker, and other Republicans will tell you that our productivity, our working people's productivity is among the best in the whole world."

Cuomo pointed to the countries of the Pacific basin which underpaid labor and used that cheap labor to beat us in manufacturing wars. Cuomo said that the answer that the unions were giving was to raise the working conditions of working people in other parts of the world.

Of course, Cuomo is a master at making arguments that others do not make. He suggested in this conversation that the unions in New York State were stronger than ever. Then his argument continued. If the unions are stronger and the state as a whole is stronger that it must be the unions that have made the state stronger.

So I suggested to him that another intervening variable during the same period might have been the presidency of Ronald Reagan. Now comes Cuomo at his most hysterical, which he can be from time to time. Since I asked him whether all the good things that might be happening are attributable to Ronald Reagan, he answers.

"Well, okay. He was the president and then there was the recession of '81-'82 so he gave us the recession. He was the president and the debt went up one trillion dollars, so he's responsible to a trillion dollar debt. It took two hundred years to get a trillion dollar debt before Reagan; and Reagan, to use your logic has given us another." Then he really got hot. "So if you want to say *post hoc ergo propter hoc*, then he's responsible for Nicaragua and he's responsible for Afghanistan. Why did he let the Russians take Afghanistan?" But having said all of that Cuomo then disassociated himself from the very logic that he was arguing. "Of course, that's silly talk. Of course, it's silly to say that the president is responsible for everything that occurs on his watch."

Cuomo then came back to the unions, who historically presented him with a "lose-lose" situation. He needed them and their considerable resources in order to win, but their support often represented the kiss of death with the electorate.

"I say that the good conditions in the state and the success of the labor unions may be coincidental but at least they *are* coincidental, which is to say that there is some evidence that the growth and success of the unions at least hasn't retarded us."

When I asked him about organized crime infiltration into labor unions, he answered the question with another set of questions. Not an unusual gambit for the governor.

"Incidentally," he said, "have you heard of organized crime infiltration into various businesses? Have you heard about criminal infiltration into Wall Street? Have you heard about criminal infiltration into defense contractors who, in an organized way, ripped off the federal government for hundreds of millions of dollars? You've heard of that, I guess?"

Warming to his subject, Cuomo continued, "Have you heard, incidentally, about corruption among politicians? I think I heard a story a few weeks ago about that."

But then the piece de resistance, "There are priests in my Catholic church who are less than perfect, even occasionally a rabbi. Even women sin. What are you telling me? Of course the unions are not perfect. So what?"

But I pushed. I wanted to know what exactly it was "about the unions that is imperfect, that you don't like?"

"Well," he said, "today is Labor Day. Today is the day to celebrate the contributions they make...." But confronted with the inevitable, he does give us the other side.

"Are there unions which have occasionally made unreasonable demands on management—demands which were not accompanied by assurances of productivity increases so that it simply fed inflation? Of course there have been such unions." But even there Cuomo was not willing to leave it alone as he made sure we realized that there were management groups that "unfairly penalized the working people and did not reward them adequately for the importance of labor. Of course there have been."

Summing it up, Cuomo said that "there is no question that organized labor, the union movement, has been one of the most progressive and salutary institutional movements in the history of the United States. If there is any doubt about that, remember where we were before the union movement. Remember," he said, "how women were virtually enslaved in their labor." He added, "Remember how children were allowed to work themselves to death in coal mines. Remember the garment industry fire in which people lost their lives because sweat shop owners cared very little, if anything, for them as human beings. Remember this: that didn't change because a benevolent government changed it without being pushed." He went on to say that this exploitation ended because of labor unions. "It wasn't business that did it. It wasn't the synagogues and the churches that did it. It wasn't the Ford Foundation that it did it. It was the union movement that did it."

Cuomo reminded us that "some of them got killed for doing it." He reminded anyone listening on Labor Day that "it was the union movement that civilized the working conditions of this country.

"Now that they've done their job, in some people's minds; now that they've assured a wage that would allow you to live, assured conditions that would allow you to survive, gave you OSHA, gave you work place rules, gave you regulations against sweat shops, maybe now you can turn and say, well, I've had all the advantage of that. Maybe you can be a reporter for a big newspaper and be snide about the unions because maybe you've forgotten that now, when you work overtime, you get paid it. And the reason that you do is that there was a union once that insisted on it."

Then I asked him a tough one, particularly if you are the governor of New York State. I asked him about closed versus open shops. I asked him about all those people who had to join unions because there was a closed shop rule which stipulated that you didn't work unless you joined a union, even if you didn't want to.

"The objective," he said, "should be to make unions sufficiently desirable so that everybody would want to be in them." But on this holy of holy union principles, Cuomo chose to give credit to the lawmakers rather than himself. "The judgment made by the Legislature of this state is that you are allowed to have a closed shop situation. If the unions are going to be collecting dues from some people and fighting for all the workers in that shop, then the thought of the legislation is that it's not right for some people to avail themselves of the benefits without making a contribution."

However, the governor did concede, "that it's a question you could argue about." Having laid out a classic defense of labor unions, Cuomo offered a prescription for what unions ought to be doing in order to survive.

"I think you're seeing organized labor moving into a new phase in which they are being much more aggressive about working toward enhanced productivity. You saw that in the UAW contract [General Motors] where they made deals that guaranteed them their jobs for a while in return for which they gained concessions from management. If there were to be more money paid out to the unions, it would only be because of increased productivity. Tying their wage enhancements to productivity increase is not something unions want to do because it makes you produce, let's face it.'

The governor talked of money going into building housing projects and public benefit projects like state infrastructure projects. "We have increasingly sophisticated modes of cooperation between business and labor and labor and government.

"Everybody is for the unions politically. The Republicans at least as arduously, strike that—'arduously' is the way that the Republicans fought unions in the Legislature—ardently is the way they express their loyalty to unions."

Cuomo pointed out that the Republicans originally fought the unions but that with 40% of the state unionized, they realized that in order to stay in power it was necessary to cut a deal. In one shot, Cuomo reminded the unions who fought with them and who they owe to. On the other hand, he suggested that union support in politics is a fact of life.

Cuomo, perhaps tongue in cheek, said, "So the Republicans are as supportive of unions as the Democrats are in this state. I say that's wonderful."

Then in classic Cuomoese, the governor said, "I was disappointed that I didn't see any of them march on Labor Day. I'm sure that they're all busy elsewhere."

In September of 1987, Richard Nixon was being quoted as predicting that Cuomo would be the candidate for president. Nixon and Cuomo had been corresponding on a sporadic basis and I couldn't help teasing the perceived liberal, Mario Cuomo, about his friendship with that Republican symbol hated by all Democrats, Richard Nixon.

"Governor," I said, "Richard Nixon, the Republican, predicted that you would be the candidate for president of the United States. My goodness," I chided, "what was that about?"

"I don't know," said Cuomo.

"Well, he's your friend—you talk to him," I vainly suggested, hoping to track the moving target.

"No, no," said Cuomo.

"You write to him. You've been corresponding with him."

"No, no, I wouldn't presume to call him a friend. I would be pleased if he's had some nice things to say, but you know it's obviously just amusing to have him make this comment. Maybe he's confusing me with Al D'Amato. See, I'm not running for president. I really don't know what he has in mind."

It was clear that Cuomo wasn't buying but I tried to quote Nixon to see if I might evoke that famous Cuomo spirit.

"You know what Nixon said?" I asked. "I thought it was fascinating. 'Cuomo is going to be the candidate because the Democrats like to think with their hearts rather than with their brains.'"

Now Cuomo took the bait and dove in. By doing so, he showed his capacity to have fun with the words of others. His paraphrasing of Nixon was hysterical. Here was his interpretation of what Nixon was *really* saying: "He said much more than that. He said that Cuomo was, I blush to repeat this, 'intelligent.' He wasn't suggesting that the Democrats don't think, what he was suggesting, and I think he's wrong, is that the Democrats prefer an approach that is passionate in the sense that it bespeaks a deep commitment to human values, 'yes' to working people, 'yes' to high aspiration, 'yes' to the politics of inclusion. We believe that we can make the circle of opportunity wider. The Republicans believe that we've gone as far as we can. That's the point he's making. We believe in a passionate, aggressive approach to government and the Republicans are less so unless it comes to piling up missiles. He wasn't suggesting that Democrats are any less cerebral. Surely he wasn't suggesting that Paul Simon or Dick Gephardt who knows, apparently, everything or Jesse Jackson...."

AC: Wait a second, nobody knows everything.

MC: No, that was hyperbole. Democrats are also capable of hyperbole. Occasionally even passionate hyperbole.

AC: But, but I have a feeling that he knew what he was talking about when he spoke of you as man of heart, as opposed to....

MC: [interrupting] Forget that. Let's get down to tachles. Did he pick me? Did he say that I would be a favorite?

AC: Yes.

MC: Do you know that this President last year picked the Washington Redskins?

AC: What game is that in, Governor?

MC: For the championship. Do you know how far away from the championship they wound up?

AC: You know what, Governor? Maybe Richard Nixon knows more about politics than he does about football.

MC: Maybe Richard Nixon is a Republican and what Richard Nixon is saying is good for Republicans.

AC: But you said that you wouldn't go to the Soviet Union without speaking to Richard Nixon.

MC: I never said any such thing.

AC: Then how come the press is always so wrong about these things?

MC: Well, if they put it in quotes then at least you'd have some reporter's word against mine, right? Which you don't have here, right?

AC: Right.

MC: Right, again.

In other words, Richard Nixon was, according to Mario Cuomo, praising the Democrats and castigating the Republicans. Obviously, the governor did it all tongue in cheek but ask yourself this question, "How many politicians do you know who would do their jobs and have fun doing it this way at the same time?"

Nixon was easy compared to the fun that Mario Cuomo had with the Legislature. Nothing spoke more about his love of battle than his bouts with the solons in Albany. Cuomo was born to battle the Legislature, patting their heads with one hand, kicking their butts with his foot. I simply cannot remember Cuomo ever saying a personally bad or insulting word about an individual legislator. That would seem to be his code of honor. He brought every conceivable fight to them and every year he seemed to have his way with the Legislature just a little easier than the year before.

It was never clear to me whether Cuomo really wanted an all-Democratic Legislature. The Republican State Senate was always the perfect foil for him. By always having the Republicans as the "meanies," the people who won't let him have his way, Cuomo had the best of both worlds. He was able to follow his conservative instincts and to control the budgetary process, for example, all the while blaming the lack of new spending programs on the conservative Republicans. In 1989, Cuomo gave us a pretty good idea of what legislative bashing was all about as he listed a litany of their failures.

When the Legislature quarreled with him over funding for the State University, portraying him as unfair for not increasing student tuition to fully fund the university's request, he got angry.

"Are you really saying that the only place to get it [money for the university] is tuition? Where did you get the hundred million dollars for member items?"

Member items are the pork (as in pork barrel) that legislators treasure above all. They allow legislators to fund individual lacrosse teams and botanical garden programs. If anything makes legislators as an institution quake in their boots, it's the thought of losing those member items. By raising the issue, Cuomo hit them right where it hurts most.

But then he raised his even more popular program, his mansions tax. That program would have put a tax surcharge on every home in the state worth a million dollars or more. At a time when poor people were being asked to take huge cuts, Cuomo was able to prove that their legislators had said no to such a tax.

Then there are the doctors. At one point they became so furious with Cuomo's favorite, the late Health Commissioner Dr. David Axelrod, that Cuomo agreed to meet with them. In one conversation, I told Cuomo that the doctors were furious about Axelrod's regulation which stipulated that Benzodiazapans like Valium required a three-part form, with one part going to the state government. Cuomo said that the doctors did not say a single word about Valium prescriptions to him. If they didn't say anything to him, the logic went, how could they be angry? "I heard not a word of complaint about this. Not one word of complaint." Cuomo concluded, "So it is very interesting that you should say that they're complaining. And if they should show that Dr. Axelrod is in any way wrong I'll be the first to acknowledge it. They haven't done it yet."

AC: What could be behind their objections [to Axelrod's Valium restrictions]?

MC: I don't know. You're the one who's talking to them. I don't even know them. I don't see their faces. I don't hear them. I don't see what they look like. You'd have to judge that. What do you think is behind it, Alan?

AC: Well, I think it may have a lot to do with money.

MC: [In mock surprise] Ah ha!

AC: That's what I think...

MC: [Interrupting] That's a very harsh judgment.

AC: Well, it is, but on the other hand what would be so wrong with sending a copy to the state?

MC: Well, I'll tell you. Obviously I agree that what we're doing, what Dr. Axelrod is doing, is right but I can think of arguments against it.

So Cuomo showed us a few things. He backed up Axelrod fully, but he warned us that his mind is never closed. "Come convince me," he seemed to say to his adversaries. He also made clear to Axelrod and all the other subordinates that their every action was subject to review and veto. Considering the kind of disappointments every president and governor has had to suffer because of bad decision-making and unethical behavior on the part of subordinates, not a bad idea. Finally, he reserved to himself the right to hear criticism when he wanted to and to some degree when he finds it convenient. The doctors, like the labor unions, couldn't take Mario Cuomo for granted. He could help them, he could hurt them.

The same thing was true with his potential political rivals. He respected them until they stepped on him and then he really let them have it. Republican U.S. Senator Alfonse D'Amato who was a political ally was always well treated except for times where policy differences surfaced. Then, the governor took off the gloves just a bit. His relationship with the Republican Comptroller Edward (Ned) Regan was similar. In these cases he chose not to attack until someone stepped out of line. Then the attack was generally a matter of fine tuning.

In the case of Regan, Cuomo was very kind. Every once in a while, when under pressure from his fellow Republicans to get nasty with Cuomo, Comptroller Regan took off his gloves. At times Regan criticized an agency of government under the governor's control. There were times these shots were fair and others they sounded a bit more political than necessary.

When that happened, Cuomo did not hesitate to send his comptroller a little reminder that things could change. For example, under Cuomo's guidance during one of the big ethics fights, the Legislature passed a law which called for each branch of government to be audited by a major accounting firm of that branch's choosing. In 1989, Cuomo fired off a little reminder to Regan on our show. "That's why I'm so proud of the first audit guideline bill, the first time in two hundred years, and maybe the first time in this country that every branch of the government will have its books reviewed by a private accounting firm. Imagine, they'll come into the governor's office and read the governor's books; into the comptroller's office and read the comptroller's books. The comptroller is supposed to be the one who reads everybody else's books. We're going to have *his* books read by a private accounting firm of total credibility and objectivity." Of course, the governor pointed out that the books of all phases of government would be checked, but if you listen with that extra Cuomo ear, you can hear his little gift for his comptroller or his follow-up comment that "politicians didn't want to disclose, and we don't disclose everything under our new law, but it's better than what we had in the past." Translation: I tried to get them to go further, they didn't and I took what I could get." And finally, said the supreme pragmatist/politician, it didn't come easy. His colleagues had to be forced to go along. "We need that kind of accountability. You've got to force people to prove that they're doing their very best because you don't have money to squander."

But despite Cuomo's ability to take off the gloves and hit hard or take a nip at the heels of someone like the comptroller to warn him not to get out of line, Cuomo still was kind to his adversaries. I always believed, for example, that having Republican Ned Regan around to legitimatize budgets and revenue estimates beat having a Democrat performing that function. The Democrat would be far more suspect than Regan the Republican. As a result, Cuomo tended to protect Regan.

Then there is the case of Rudolph Giuliani, the former U.S. attorney for the Southern District who was running for mayor in 1989. During the campaign a story emerged about Giuliani that was very damaging. It involved Giuliani's men arresting a white collar criminal who was a survivor of Auschwitz. The allegation, never denied, was that to get the man to talk, Giuliani's assistants had written the German translation of "Work Will Make You Free," which was the slogan over the gates of Auschwitz, on the blackboard in the room. When the man, Simon Berger, reported it during the heat of the campaign I asked Cuomo about it on the show.

Cuomo and Giuliani had stayed friendly during Giuliani's tenure as U.S. attorney. On several occasions they had said positive things about one another to the press. But it would not have been helpful to Cuomo to have a Republican in the mayor's chair in New York. After all, Cuomo had an election coming up. So I asked Cuomo about the whole controversy.

I started by telling him that it was *The New York Post* which had broken the story.

MC: I saw Rudy Giuliani for an hour on Thursday morning and it didn't even come up, so he doesn't appear to have been fazed by it.

AC: Well, according to the *Post* he was fazed by it.

MC: Well, I'm only telling you what I observed from Rudy, and he was on television Sunday morning and I understand, although I didn't see it, that he attacked the story very strongly. It can't be good for him. It can't be good for him, especially when you add it to the story of the stockbroker [an unflattering story about an arrest and then vacating of that arrest by Giuliani] and the picture of him and Al D'Amato in flak jackets. [The story of D'Amato and Giuliani dressed in flak jackets making drug buys in Manhattan had been open to question as to whether the two were hotdogging and exploiting a very emotional issue.] You know that whole image I think is probably something that will need explanation by him in the campaign. It's another example of how unexpected events will come up in campaigns.

Then Cuomo spoke of how other candidates got on Giuliani's case over the incident and how Giuliani criticized Dinkins yesterday for not filing his tax returns. Having raised questions about Giuliani, Cuomo then said that he didn't appreciate the politicians' penchant for negativism.

MC: From my point of view as governor, I think that there's entirely too much negativism, not enough positive talk about the real issues. The problem, said Cuomo, is that there is too much that is too personal and not enough substantive issues raised in campaigns. Now to be hearing about your tax return and whom you married and whether you did this naughty thing and whether your uncle has this problem, I guess that is what campaigns have become in recent years— frankly a lot of Republican inspired negativism. The Willie Horton ad, and all that tough stuff that the Republican chairman seems to thrive on, calling all kinds of people names, condemnatory and negative—any jackass can kick down a barn but only a good man or woman can build one. We need to build barns, not to kick them down. So, I am going to be as positive as I can be.

AC: Whom do you support?

MC: None of them.

AC: Why not?

MC: Because it is not seemly for the theoretical leader of the party to come down on the mayoralty and take sides. When I have to work with whomever, I need to be able to work with the winner of the election. I am a Democrat and I am not going to change. Therefore, I will support the Democrats.

The reason he will always support Democrats, said Cuomo, is that Republicans offer the country bad social policy. He cited one of his major victories, when he led the fight against the Reagan administration when they tried to disallow the deductibility of state and local taxes.

"They put the president on television saying that 'this is aimed at high spending states, like New York State. And to punish them for spending so much on their people.' And then Pat Buchanan followed up—he was then the spokesperson—by saying that we were 'neo-socialists.' Remember, he was also the person who said that we ought to keep women in the kitchen, which was about as intelligent a remark as 'neo- socialist.' But anyway, that was Republican policy and I don't see any evidence that it has changed a great deal."

There are many who believe that Cuomo supported David Dinkins in his campaign for mayor of New York. And yet before he became mayor, the governor saw fit to warn Dinkins that there were lines not to be crossed.

I once referred to an article in *The New York Post* which indicated that Dinkins was considering not meeting agreements with the state—agreements which Cuomo and Koch had made to work out difficult financing patterns. And while Cuomo made it clear to me that Dinkins had the legal right not to live up to these agreements, as governor he would have the same option.

"It wouldn't be the best way to govern, I think, to say that nothing the previous mayor did can you count on, because if you want to start from scratch, then you have to start from scratch on everything. And there are a lot of things that we agreed to that are good for the City, that are done on a handshake. But, he's free to walk away from any understanding as a *legal* matter." Any one who knew Mario Cuomo knew when he issuing a warning and he certainly was that day on the show. If Dinkins could walk away from agreements that his predecessor had made with the state, then Cuomo could walk away from the agreements he had made with the city.

Mario Cuomo's views on friends and enemies extended to the international scene as well. His views on Israel were just one example. In fact, the governor came down pretty heavily on his political adversaries, the Republicans, in defending the Israelis.

When I asked the governor about the Israelis and the ways in which the foreign policy bureaucracy in this country was becoming more and more critical about them, he made it clear that our debt was to Israel and not to those who would take our money and betray us. The issue had come up because of the Israeli kidnapping of terrorists tied to the kidnapping of Col. Higgins, the U.S. soldier who had been executed while in captivity in Lebanon.

"The Israelis are surrounded by millions of enemies who want to destroy them. They have been kil'ing Israelis for years. The Israelis are doing things to protect themselves and to protect us in that part of the world."

Cuomo criticized Republicans like U.S. Senator Robert Dole, who claimed that the Israeli hostage-taking might have had something to do with the death of Col. Higgins and compromised our position in the Mideast. "I guess you can make that case in logic," said the governor, but he warned that the Israelis are "protecting us in a portion of the world where we have no other friends and we have no friends as loyal and as committed as they are.

"They are our bastion in the Middle East. In a very real way they protect us, so we invest money in them and their ability to stay alive."

The governor warned that to accuse "them directly or indirectly" of being a threat to us is not a good idea.

Cuomo was profoundly influenced by his friend Benjamin ("Bibi") Netanyahu whom he got to know when he was U.S. ambassador from Israel. When we were talking about the Israeli situation, after the execution of Col. Higgins, I asked Cuomo whether he was still in touch with his friend, then the Israeli deputy foreign minister.

"I don't think it's my place. I know Bibi Netanyahu, you don't have to talk to him. You can read his book. He wrote a book on terrorism and I think it's clear that he feels that you need to respond with force. He thinks the Arabs don't understand anything else."

But the governor left some light between the Netanyahu approach to terrorism and his own by suggesting that "I think you need more than force here." Netanyahu's position, said the governor, is what it is because "it is the only way to respond to these people." And that, said the governor, is to snatch one of theirs and then work out a trade or threaten to kill theirs the way they kill yours. One came away with the feeling that the governor subscribed to his friend's prescription but left enough room to disagree later.

Perhaps Cuomo's greatest contemporary nemesis was the hapless Speaker of the Assembly, Melvin Miller. Miller, unlike all the others, seemed to declare war on Cuomo immediately upon his ascendancy to the seat which many consider to be the second most powerful political post in New York State.

When he was feuding with the Legislature over ethics legislation, Cuomo announced the establishment of the Moreland Act Commission to study ethics in the state. Fearing that it was a witch hunt, the Republicans in the Senate and the Assembly Democratic majority under Miller refused to fund the Commission during the budget negotiations. They actually got Cuomo to agree that the Commission would stick to matters involving the executive agencies of government and would stay away from the Legislature. Ironically, of course, it was the Legislature which needed the most investigating, as almost any casual political observer knows.

They were also able to discourage the governor's choice to head the Commission, super-lawyer Joseph Califano, from accepting the job.

There was a major brouhaha when the Commission asked the legislative leaders to testify on the matter of campaign financing.

Cuomo was asked to testify and did before the Commission. But Senators Marino and Miller resisted.

I asked the governor about the whole thing. Cuomo showed once again how he operates.

MC: I have learned that if you bring public attention to bear on the subject (which I have been fighting for fourteen years) you can get some movement. We have some movement now. We have a five way discussion among the legislative leaders toward a campaign financing bill. I think the movement will be accelerated after the appearance of Ralph Marino and Mel Miller on Friday. They are both appearing voluntarily (after they had initially refused to appear). And I think as you discuss campaign financing, its reasonableness becomes more obvious and I am hopeful that we can deal with campaign financing this year.

AC: I see that Marino and Miller are both appearing before the ethics commission. They originally had great trepidation about doing that. They talked about how the commission was not set up to study the Legislature. I was critical at that time that they didn't do it. Do you think that they have unnecessarily bloodied themselves? Perhaps they should have done it in the first place without kicking up their heels.

MC: I don't think that's important. What's important is that they are now coming in voluntarily and they are going to be heard and they are going to take an oath the way we all did. And I hope that they enjoy it the way I did.

AC: What led to your enjoyment?

MC: I like that format. I liked to share with the people all of our insights. I like the idea of public officials being challenged under oath to tell the truth. The possibility of embarrassment; facing the possibility of accusation. I think that's a good thing. It is good for public officials to do that. I had an advantage when it comes to campaign financing in that I have detached myself from raising campaign funds for years.

Cuomo, with his tongue in cheek, kept referring to the fact that the legislative leaders, Miller and Marino, had to testify under oath. The clear impression I had was that he was emphasizing that they could not dare lie under oath. What's more, Cuomo seized the discomfort of his two rivals as an opportunity to make the point that he had adopted a code of ethical standards, which they had not.

MC: For fourteen years, ever since I have been in this business, I've known we have to raise money. I don't like doing it and I don't like to know how it's done, because I want to know very little about the people who gave us the money.

AC: On the other hand, if people invoked your name improperly, you would be pretty furious wouldn't you?

MC: As a matter of fact, we have a policy. It's written and distributed from time to time and it says that if anybody uses my name, they must let me know, because it is not generally authorized.

AC: But if they are collecting money for the Cuomo campaign they obviously have to use your name.

MC: This is for the Cuomo administration. But if they say, "Alan, Mario told you to give," that's a lie. I don't do that. I don't

give names. I don't point people out. In the fundraisers I
stand up and say that I regret that we have to do this. Some
people don't like that. They say that you take our money and
don't say thank you.

AC: Do you think that most people give money because they
expect something back?

MC: If they do, they will be terribly disappointed.

Mario Cuomo goes out of his way first to compliment and then
to criticize. There were times his comments were so subtle that
the listener had to be fast in order to get what was being said. And
there were times when he hit you over the head with a sledge ham-
mer to make his point.

It is not easy to be either a friend or an enemy of Mario
Cuomo. His friends bear great responsibility to him and can all
too often disappoint the governor. I know—I've been there. In the
end, family is everything. Enemies, on the other hand, present a
real challenge to Cuomo. I have seen him work on them for years,
in an effort to turn them around. He never gives up.

CHAPTER 8

CHARACTER

People vote for political leaders on the basis of character. So who is Mario Cuomo? What are the forces that shaped him? Perhaps most important, Mario Cuomo's personality has been profoundly influenced by his immigrant family. As an elected official, he was a compulsive worker who slept just a few hours a night, preferring to work on governmental problems, his vocation and avocation. He has shown signs of fury at those who excluded him because of his ethnic background. His battling with and sometimes baiting of the banks, the insurance companies, and *The New York Times* are clearly tied to the early rejection of an emerging Mario Cuomo by society's elitist institutions. Once, when I told him that someone had written about me that I was an "overachiever" he looked at me and said, "Chartock, don't let that bother you, they've been saying that about me all my life."

Mario Cuomo fears adulation. Like an animal attracted by fire, he is afraid to get too close to that adulation because he fears it, as Adam should have feared the apple. He is afraid he will be consumed by it. To handle that, during his governorship he created surrogates in the form of his wife, Matilda, and his child,

Andrew, whom he designated to accept the adulation on his behalf. Some said that he was very wary of giving his subordinates any credit. By the same token, he was more than generous about sharing credit with his political opponents.

Cuomo is a self-confident man whose character was profoundly tempered by what he learned about the world. But although some people don't believe it, he is a very humble man. He once told me that he had intended to be a teacher but instead chose the law in order to provide a better living for his family. Cuomo's teachers were role models for him. Much of his success in politics can be attributed to the fact that he is a natural teacher. When he has a political theme he sounds it over and over again so that even the slowest in his class will grasp the message. He spoke constantly of the affection he had for all those important teachers who brought him along when his own parents were busy earning a marginal living. They were among the most profound influences in his life.

AC: What's the greatest thing that was ever invented?
MC: [no hesitation] Love.

On the other hand, once when I was talking to the gov before a show he told me about a person whom he thought had been unfair to him; he put it this way, "I am a gentle, giving person, I have been taught to be that and I am trying to make up for past sins. But, I am not a fool. He has now taken us for a fool and he will regret it."

Cuomo is certainly not a fool, but he is a straight talker who will not underestimate what those around him are capable of doing in the thought department. At least one person I know consistently said during his governorship that Cuomo would never be president because, he, like Adlai Stevenson before him, talks at too "high" a level. But Cuomo believes that everyone is capable of understanding who is sincere and who is not. Knowing that fact is central to understanding the character of Mario Cuomo. Recognizing the influence of his parents, his religion and his sense of mysticism is also important in beginning to know the man. He once told me that accidents can have strange affects on the way in which one's life will progress.

"I think perhaps the one thing that happened to me accidentally, in recent years at least, that's had the biggest impact is Ed Koch's decision to run for governor in 1982. I think probably if Koch had decided not to run, I would not be governor. I think if Koch had not decided to run, there would have been a very large field consisting of people like Carol Bellamy, Bob Abrams, maybe Stanley Fink, maybe Al DelBello. And I think in a large field like that I, as a relative unknown at that time, without any money, would have found it very difficult to win a Democratic primary. When Koch entered the race in 1982, everybody left but me. I was able to make up for the lack of money because the presence of only two candidates required that television give me equal coverage with the mayor after Labor Day. That free coverage, which equaled the mayor's, is what compensated for his superior resources and allowed me to win the primary."

Cuomo knows all about the negatives in life. He had to deal with some of the most awesome problems that we bring on ourselves, from the killing of fellow human beings to our capacity to destroy ourselves through drugs and crime. And yet, this man who can get very angry truly believes that we have the capacity to make ourselves whole by accentuating our goodness. Cuomo believes that we are always capable of doing better. He believes that for himself most of all.

AC: When you look in the mirror and see yourself, are you surprised at what you see?

MC: I think many of us can step outside ourselves and see ourselves as separate creatures. We have a being, an essence, a soul, an identity, a mind. I think it is not impossible for us to step back and look, for example, at yourself, Alan Chartock. Look at yourself objectively, see your faults taking over in your life, your hair falling out, your teeth falling out, the wrinkles forming. I think you can see yourself quite objectively if you tried and if you work at it.

We ought to try looking at ourselves. We ought to try looking at ourselves in a way that allows us to work toward improving ourselves. I think that is one of the things that gives life meaning, the opportunity at every instance to stop the entire process and start it over in a new and better way no matter what happened. You can stop and start all over again, do it differently, do it better, do things you never did before.

As long as you have a free will, you can do anything. You may have powerful emotional impulses, you may have strong drives, but with a mind and a will you can recognize those drives and you can change them. You might think you will die if you don't eat for one day. I must eat a meal during the day. But if you found yourself locked in a room by some evil criminal and locked there for three or four days without food, you would find a way to stay alive. You would not die. A stronger ideal would take over, the will to survive. We ought to think more about using our mind and will. All of history teaches us that this capacity has gone terribly under-appreciated and under utilized in the western world.

I asked him once how he handles the substantial back pain that he lives with every day.

"Reduce pain? I don't work to reduce it, sometimes I even entertain it. I do a lot of exercises in the morning. I think you should make the most out of everything in this world, that's what ontology is all about. You should make the most of pain, you should understand it. Think about it. Appreciate the lack of pain because you've experienced pain. Use it."

Always think positivly.

When we look at ourselves, the governor has said, we must accentuate that part of us which is capable of doing good and downgrade that part which is motivated toward the bad.

"In a nutshell, I think we need more positive and less negative. I think that if there are all these negative vibrations and actions in our society, it is because we do not have enough that is affirmative, good, and beautiful. If kids are turning towards the ugly things in life it is because we haven't been giving them the beautiful ones. It is the one theme that is most prevalent in all of my own personal limited thought over the last twenty years, it is the thing about this society I noticed most, as I move into a role where I have to study it more as a politician—the emptiness, the loneliness, the vacuum, the need for something positive to believe in, something to embrace, something to uplift, religion, God, love, self, whatever it is."

And that inner strength is what Mario Cuomo is all about. It's what makes him different from others. There are those of us who can't handle being criticized and those who take it in stride. Once I asked him whether he felt badly when some Black and Puerto Rican Caucus members took him to task. After he got all through telling me what his government had done to help those groups, I asked him again.

His answer, "Now, do I feel stabbed in the back? Do I feel hurt? I think, Alan, we're all human beings and I think anybody who says that when his kid forgets his birthday, he's not hurt, or when an old friend turns on one, that one is not hurt, you're probably not telling the truth.

"Everybody who's human wants to be treated well and is a little bit disappointed, I guess, when they're not. How you show it is something else. Number one, we're all human. Number two, you had better learn to develop a thick skin if you want to come into this business, and you had better remember if you want to be a governor, a legislator, or a public official, you're not doing it for yourself, unless you're a real hypocrite, you're supposed to be a PUBLIC SERVANT. S-E-R-V-A-N-T.

"That means you're supposed to be serving the public, and so when you come in what you're asking for is for a chance to help people. Not a chance to be loved by people, not a chance to be congratulated by them. So, on the human level, all of us are distressed when people don't love us, and say so. But if you want to be a governor, or a legislator, you had better learn that's not what you're here for. You're here to serve. And if everybody loves you in return, and gives you plaques and re-elects you, that's really nice. But that's not why you came."

Keeping who you are in perspective is very important to Cuomo. Just listen to this little snippet from the show. It occurred when he was advised to strengthen the personal security around him because of threats to his life.

MC: I personally didn't like the idea of believing we needed security. This is difficult to explain. It's not a good feeling to say that my family and I, official representatives of this, the greatest state in the union, need to be protected from our own people. I don't like feeling that when I go out with a crowd. I don't like the state police with me when I go into crowds, parades, etc.

AC: Yes, but consider what's going on. Consider [John F.] Kennedy, and from then on...

MC: I'm no Kennedy, I'm no president, no Martin Luther King. It is not the same. Those people were idols, those people were on pedestals, those people reached the hearts and minds of the public in extra-ordinary ways, they had become symbolic of certain forces. I'm not at that level.

Years ago, Cuomo told us what he and Charlie Brown, the *Peanuts* character, had in common.

"Cartoons are very important, I use them all the time, I use Charlie Brown all the time, Alan." Then he told me how he talked about Charlie Brown with some San Antonio, Texas reporters.

MC: They were asking me how the Democrats felt after '84, the debacle, getting wiped out by President Reagan for the second time in a row, and I said, "Like Charlie Brown." Great cartoon strip. Charlie Brown is sitting on a fence with Linus, and Charlie Brown in the first box says, "We lost 29 to nothing. It's embarrassing." And in the second box Linus says, "Well, you know what they say, Charlie Brown." And in the third box Linus says, "Win some, lose some." And in the fourth box Charlie Brown says, "Wouldn't that be wonderful."

AC: Do you feel the same way, Governor? Are there some weeks you feel you'd just like to win one?"

MC: I am so far ahead of the game of life in the things that really count that it's difficult to get me in a position where I feel sorry for myself. I think when I was younger it was easier because you don't count as accurately, I don't think, or at least I didn't. I won't speak for people generally, but when I was younger I don't think I saw things as clearly as I do now. Oh, you have a political reversal, a governmental reversal, a legislature knocks you on your tush, that's not pleasant, but when you look around at the larger picture, your health, your family, the wonderful experiences you've had. My good luck so outweighs my misfortunes, and I've said this before, I feel guilty about it sometimes. If they're keeping score in the sky I'm afraid of Judgment Day because I'm so far ahead of the game.

The amazing thing about the guy is that each bout with adversaries is soon forgotten. He does not return to get even or criticize. A few years ago, after Martin Luther King Day, he reflected on his feelings about marching in the parade.

MC: I'll tell you what I wrote in my diary, okay?

AC: All right, sure.

MC: This is a quickie. This is Tuesday, January 21. That was yesterday, Tuesday, correct?

AC: Right, I think so, yes.

MC: Ten A.M. I was going down to New York. I felt spiritually nourished by the Martin Luther King Jr. march and ceremony yesterday. Albany turned out more than 2,500 people, most of them white. They marched arm and arm in the rain, singing, chanting, remembering a great black minister. But most of all celebrating an idea.

It seems so plain. People do so desperately want to believe in something. Something they can embrace, make a commitment to, share with, love, fight for, feel good about. That's what Martin Luther King Jr. was, and Kennedy, and the Statue of Liberty, and Lech Walesa, and Mandela, and that's what we're missing today.

Simon and Garfunkel had it just right in the haunting words of 'Mrs. Robinson': 'Where have you gone Joe Dimaggio, a nation turns its lonely heart to pray'... No more Joe Dimaggio, no more Martin Luther King Jr., no more Kennedy, and in their place a genial, even lovable man, who tells us with a smile and a wave, that perhaps the best we can do is let people play the cards that fate has dealt them. For a few hours yesterday I felt better than I had for a long time. That's the end of the diary entry. And I must tell you, that's the way a lot of people felt.

I am quite sure that Mario Cuomo knows that he, like society, has both positive and negative sides. He knows that the way to heal himself is to emphasize the good that is within him. Knowing that is basic to understanding the psychological road map that makes up Cuomo. What's more, Cuomo thinks he knows what motivates people. Listen to him describe what makes others act in a particular way. Then ask whether he isn't also engaged in a little self-analysis.

"What motivates people? Fear, self-interest, love. And the perpetual continuing struggle for the politicians to know is how to get people to do what the politician thinks is the right thing to do. How do I get the legislators and their people to understand that I need a billion dollars in spending cuts right now? How do I get them to do it? In this case, you have to explain to the public and to the Legislature that it is in the public best interest to do this. It is not something that the lawmakers are going to do out of love. It is something that they will have to do because not to do it will produce a worse situation."

Mario Cuomo told me once in 1989, "The one thing that people prize most in a politician is sincerity. Competence is obviously important, reflecting their point of view is relevant, but the thing they prize the most is sincerity."

There are those who believe that Cuomo is not sincere because he is complex, but I think they are wrong. When you see the world in grays instead of black and white, people can be confused. But the smarter you are, the more grays there are. Mario Cuomo is very smart.

He knows that he, like the rest of us, is imperfect. He strives for perfection but he is humbled whenever anyone suggests that he is doing well, almost as if such mouthings are negative magic that will work against him. It comes out in the simplest of ways. Take the time I asked him for a new year's prediction about Mario Cuomo. He thought about it for a second and said, "Hum, hope springs eternal." And once I told him that he was leading in the California polls as a prospective presidential candidate. He replied, "They don't know me." So I asked him whether he was telling me that the reason they said they liked him was because they were projecting; placing their own values into the form of Mario Cuomo. He interrupted me to say that, "In Yugoslavia, I'm doing very well, too." Always game, I tried again, "They attribute values to you because they like your face," I suggested again. Came the reply, "No, no, they don't know. The more they know me, the less they vote for me."

The guy is incredibly introspective, he is very decent and remembers who he is. Most of the time he seems to like himself a lot. That's very important for a politician. People sense the strength that comes from that. What's more, he almost always remembers where he came from. People like that, too. Once I read in a newspaper that Cuomo had taken to driving himself around, foregoing the use of any chauffeur. I asked him whether driving his own car "put other drivers at risk."

"No," he said of himself, "I'm a safe driver, I think, and I certainly try hard to observe the rules and the regulations."

"Well," I said, "do you enjoy driving?"

"Yes, I do enjoy it. It's a different kind of life you lead as governor and it has to be. I enjoy driving. I do enjoy helping myself. I enjoy shining my shoes. It's not an exercise in populism. It's what I prefer to do. I enjoy the idea that on weekends, at least in the mornings, we don't have anybody in the house, except for ourselves. There are no maids, no help on Sunday mornings, so you can make your own coffee, and we kind of enjoy that. Political life is a different kind of life; it's an artificial kind of life in many ways, and unavoidably so. You can't go all the places you'd like to go. You can't avoid all the places you'd like to avoid. You can't dress exactly the way you'd like to all the time. You need those little bits of liberty that you can preserve, like driving, going for a walk alone, walking into a supermarket."

More than any politician I have known, and I have known quite a few quite well, Mario Cuomo suspected the worldly trappings of his office. He didn't take all of his salary from the state. During the 1991 fiscal crisis, he even recommended that the executive mansion be turned into a museum to save money for the state. He refused to drive fancy cars when all the politicians in the state drove only top of the line automobiles. He refused to buy a new airplane. Most of all, while he clearly respected those who had the initiative to make money, he remained fearful of it. That need to keep it simple, not to be corrupted by worldly things is basic to understanding who Mario Cuomo is. Perhaps it's his intellectual debt to Catholic education and to all those priests who taught him so much. Perhaps it's the ultimate Catholic vision of who and what Christ was. But you see it over and over again.

Here's an example from a conversation I had with him one day in June. *Sports Illustrated* had written an article about his early days in organized baseball. I asked him about it and he began to reminisce.

"Last Sunday, it was very warm. I escaped out the back gate of the mansion grounds in my sneakers and jogging pants and a sweatshirt. Went for a walk down to Lincoln Park, and there were five guys hitting a softball, playing around. I went out, borrowed a glove, and for the first time in, let me see, almost thirty-five years, shagged flies.

"I cannot tell you what a wonderful feeling it is to discover that, although with limited speed and not a great deal of agility, I could still turn properly, go back looking over my shoulder, stick up my hand and catch a fly ball on the run. I cannot tell you what an exciting feeling that was.

"It was wonderful. I even enjoyed sweating. Something about playing, about running, about feeling the ability to run from one spot to another, to see that ball bouncing as you run across the outfield, and to be able to time it perfectly, to put your glove out at just the right moment, to close the fingers a little bit just as the ball strikes the palm of the mitt. It's a wonderful feeling, and I enjoyed myself a great deal. And then didn't walk well for two days."

The nice thing about the guy is that he suspects himself. He is always examining his own motives. He is unafraid to tell us that he is just like us.

MC: The following process should take place in your mind. If they say something commendatory, well that is nice, but don't put too much stock in it. If they criticize you, then pay close attention to the criticism: what is it, what did they say, is there any truth to it, are you really arrogant, are you too strong, are you apparently vindictive? If so, and if it is a fault, then do everything you can to correct it.

   If you study the criticism and you find that there is no basis for it, if it is unfair, if it is a misunderstanding, try to correct it, try to correct the perception. If you cannot correct the perception, then the heck with it. Ignore it, that is life. You can't please all the people all the time. Move on. That should be the process. Is there something to the criticism I can correct? Is it a misperception I can clarify? Or is it something I should simply ignore because I can't learn from it and I can't correct it? Let me just suffer it and move on.

AC: Can you give me a single example in recent times of applying those criteria to one problem?

MC: Oh, certainly. I was, in my early days, criticized for not delegating sufficiently and I thought about it. Am I delegating sufficiently or not? I concluded that I was delegating plenty, but that it was not to career-oriented people. I was delegating plenty, but the people to whom I was delegating weren't being identified. I worked very hard to correct that.

It has always been interesting to me to see what motivates Cuomo to look inward all the time. Part of it is clearly his religion. Part of it may the same sort of guilt that we all carry to one degree or another.

   Take the subject of guilt. Here's how we opened one show.

AC: Governor, how are you?

MC: Probably better than I deserve to be. I've felt that way most of my life.

AC: Why do you always say that?

MC: I feel that way. I have been given so many blessings, so much good luck, that after a while you almost feel guilty.

AC: You mean that, don't you?

MC: Sure. I think on a good day, the way you react to that is that you work hard to say, "Thank you." And the only way I think I can work hard to say, "Thank you" is to work hard at my job.

But that wasn't the only clue about guilt. Once I told the governor I thought someone was guilty of the sin of hypocrisy. He made it clear that he wasn't about to throw the first stone.

AC: Why can't you just say the word hypocritical?

MC: Because that is for God. I don't know what is in people's minds and hearts. I am not going to judge them harshly. The reason I am not going to judge them harshly is that I don't want to be judged harshly. The older I get and the closer I get to the celestial chimes, the billowing clouds, and the big role figures with long white beards with those great big books they open with those huge pages to see what was recorded next to your name, I don't want any guy up there who left early and shows up standing in the celestial choir leaning over the scorekeeper saying, "This is the bum who took a shot at me." You understand that.

There was the time a while back, when I started talking to the governor about Mike Tyson's 90-second victory over Leon Spinks. I asked him, "Isn't there something obscene about a guy getting twenty-seven million dollars for something like that?"

Well, as is his style, the governor started slowly, warming to the subject. "It would be obscene if he got up and took it with a gun; if he picked people's pockets to get it. I'm not sure it's obscene, however or even undesirable, when you do it voluntarily, when it is, in fact, an expression of our democracy."

Then the beauty of the man, his subtle use of sarcasm, began to show itself. His major point was that democracy allows us to make bad choices but it leaves the choices up to us.

"This democracy allows you to spend money almost any way you wish to. If you want to go to the most elegant French restaurant, which is really not as good as a neighborhood restaurant...and if you want to spend 250 bucks for a skimpy little piece of veal, good luck to you. In this country, you can do that. You can spend 50 bucks to watch a play, or you can watch a better play on public television for nothing. "Now, I think it is appropriate for us to reflect on how much money stars get and on our tiny minimum wage—and how many people you can hear on C-SPAN call in the middle of the night to ask politicians why they oppose the minimum wage increase. As I heard the other night, 'I have a family of four, I'm trying to raise two children, my wife is disabled and cannot work, I make two hundred dollars a week, I can't do it. I can't do it on this salary.'"

It was at this point that the governor started to turn around his argument. It's alright, he told us, to spend foolishly but what is really obscene is the way the society distributes wealth.

"It's interesting to reflect on a society that can produce 23 million dollars for two fighters, or whatever the amount is, or a million dollars for a basketball player's contract, or 25 million dollars for a corporate executive for one year, and say productivity is low and the workers' wages are too high." And then, having said that, it was back to the original premise, "I think it's appropriate to reflect on that. I'm not sure that I would call it obscene. This kind of erratic distribution is the essence of democracy."

"The difference between democracy and communism and some socialist systems is that they guarantee an equality of distribution, or come closer to guaranteeing it—by force. By not giving you the choice.

"Somewhere in the middle, between the grotesque distortions and the enforced equality is the Utopia that we all strive for."

Cuomo is a man who understands what it's like to be in the middle. He's a man who has taken personal initiative to get ahead in his life but he always remembers where he came from. It is his constant reference to his early life that makes Cuomo different from other politicians. Cuomo is always trying to differentiate himself from those who would capitalize on their positions of public trust. Whenever I was deprecating politicians, on the other hand, he was there to defend them.

"The difference between politicians and doctors and lawyers and everybody else is that the politician's life is voluntarily more visible. If all people were revealed as fully as politicians are, you would find that politicians are no different, no better, no stronger, no wiser, no weaker than the rest of the population."

Perhaps just one more story might explain how Cuomo sees human nature. This one began when I noticed that the governor's voice was somewhat distorted on the other end of the telephone. I asked him whether something was the matter and he answered that nothing was the matter other than the fact that he was speaking on the radio and chewing on a piece of stale whole wheat bread at the same time.

MC: Stale whole wheat bread can be nourishing.

AC: Do you toast it?

MC: No, we just nibble on it just the way it is, reminding ourselves that there are some people who have not even that.

AC: Where'd you get it from?

MC: We always keep a couple of slices of stale whole wheat bread around.

AC: I'd like to think you have lobster back there...

MC: Listen, if you don't have stale bread around, what are you going to throw out the back window to the birds?

AC: Do you do that, Governor?

MC: Of course we do.

AC: That's very amazing. And how do you prevent the squirrels from stealing the bread from the birds?

MC: I wait until I see very quick birds who are quicker than the squirrels, and then I throw the bread.

Mario Cuomo helps those who are prepared to help themselves.

Once when he was talking about his wife, Matilda, I asked him whether he believed that he had "married up." He stopped for a second, thought about it and said without hesitation that she was better than him in every way. A friend who heard the show thought that he might be insincere, but I told her that from everything that I had ever heard the governor say, that was certainly not true.

To my question about "marrying up," the gov responded, "Oh, yes, I married a person who is brighter than I, better than I, that's what I thought at the time and after thirty-five years, I'm absolutely persuaded of it. It's true, I'm not exaggerating. She was in all ways better than I was. She has been a better mother than I have been a father, I've tried hard but I think it's fair to say that she's better at her job than I've been at mine. Yes, I suspected at the time that I was marrying up and now I'm sure I did."

Mario Cuomo gives his parents tremendous credit for helping him. Yet with a father who dug ditches and then ran a grocery store, knowing little English (but who scrimped, sacrificed and managed to save a little) and a mother with great wisdom but little education, Cuomo had to figure out a lot for himself. He had help from his teachers and priests but over and over again, Cuomo preached the doctrine of self- reliance. Much of what he learned he got from books. Once, in one of those very revealing moments that occasionally come along, Cuomo took those of us listening back to the days when a very lonely little boy would run to the library for an escape.

He remembered how he had told Mrs. Jacob Javits a story about how he first "met" her husband, the late senator, in the library when he was doing research for a junior high school project.

"That was way back at the Queens Borough Public Library. On summer days when I wanted to get out of the store and I wasn't playing ball and when there was nobody around and when there was no ball game on the radio, I would run down the block under the bridge, through Kings Park, around the corner to the Queens Borough Public Library where you could browse and read endlessly. I could read Mr. Tutt [adventures of a country lawyer in the

Saturday Evening Post and in book form] and the great authors and got interested in the law."

Cuomo said that he would occasionally wander away from reading but he would always come back. Now those early years and the reading are part of his life. It isn't every kid coming from a poor family who somehow knows that the library is a place to find a better way.

But Mario Cuomo was not a complete saint as a child. He could get angry then, as he can now. I've always believed that's what makes him a good politician. He enjoys a fight, even though he denies it.

Once I asked him about the death of Billy Martin, the tempestuous ex-Yankee baseball player. His answer was instructive. He said all the right things about a great New Yorker. But it was his assessment of Martin's character that was most interesting. The more I listened, the more I became convinced that he might have been thinking more about himself than Billy Martin.

"Tragedy," he said. "I remember him as an aggressive guy, a little bit like Ed Stanky of the Dodgers. A man who was not a person of overwhelming talent but who got every bit out of himself. Who used up all of his potential. And that's a great virtue in life. A colorful guy. A troublesome guy from time to time in life. Well we all are. His troublesome moments received a lot of publicity, but a man who was loyal to what he loved." And what was it that Cuomo really liked about Martin? "He was a man who lived. He is a man who had basic virtues, basic qualities, that were good. He was not perfect. He was human, but so are we all, and what was good about him I admired, a lot more than I regretted what was not so good about him." It was not difficult for Cuomo to admit that, while he might idealize his heros, he must always remember that measuring up to these standards oneself is tough.

"I like the picture of Thomas More that I have in my mind. I don't want it to fade away. What's the good of that? Well, you have to be realistic, you have to see the frailties in all things. I know the frailties. I am the frailties. You don't have to teach me about vulnerability and imperfection. I live it.

"What's wrong with believing every once in a while that there's something better and clinging to that? That's what heaven is. That's what nirvana is. That's what inspiration is... always hoping for something better."

According to Cuomo, his number one imperfection is his quick temper. He has always regretted his own fiery temperament and has identified his anger as the one thing he has to work on. I have seen politicians or newspaper people take terribly unfair shots at the man and watched him explain that getting angry is counterproductive. That can't have been easy, considering his sports mentality and his ability to debate anyone into the ground. As he grew as a politician and a man, I have watched him gradually win that fight against himself. He won it because he is basically a conservative man with "sand." He has a set of values which serves him well as he stakes out his position. His philosophy of life directs him to hold no grudges, no matter how badly he's treated. At the same time, he knows of his capacity to get angry. That puts him at odds with himself.

At the beginning of one show he read me a prayer that he had circulated in his office. "Forgiven the past. Renewed for tomorrow. Let us go forth to a year of great goodness."

Struck by that, I asked him if the words weren't basic to his philosophy... "not to maintain old hatreds and gripes."

He answered, "Well, hatred is a very heavy word. I can't think of an uglier word. I can't think of anything worse. I remember when they were talking about Gary Hart and whether or not his transgression should eliminate him for consideration for public office."

Therein, one might see a projection of Cuomo's golden rule of politics: "No cheap shots when the other guy is in trouble, even when he or she's an adversary." Cuomo was no fan of Gary Hart as the 1988 election grew closer. He had made that clear to me in public and private conversations.

But that didn't mean that the governor would be less than understanding when it came to Hart's predicament after he was caught with a model on his lap on the yacht "Monkey Business."

According to Cuomo, the sin of hate was worse than the sin of adultery.

Referring to Hart, Cuomo said, "I remember being in Iowa. I was giving a speech the day after the story broke, as I recall it. I said to somebody, 'If you are going to start condemning public officials and others for sins, let me offer you one that is maybe even worse than misplaced affection. How about hate? Why don't you ask people if they've ever hated another human being; if they ever truly want to see another human being hurt; if they ever hated their wives; if they ever slapped their children; if they ever said, 'I hope that guy drops dead' and meant it?

"Now can you think of a worse sin than that? Okay, adultery is wrong, we all know that, and certainly no one approves of it. But that, at least, is misplaced affection. "Hate is a bad thing, an evil thing. It is a fundamental contradiction of civility and humanity."

Hate and temper are Cuomo's devils.

From music to religion, Mario Cuomo is a profoundly conservative man. He does not desire fancy foods or fine restaurants and has told all of us that his breakfast food each morning consists of grapefruit sections and "too much coffee." He even doubts whether he should be having the coffee.

Mario Cuomo liked to read poetry to his children. What he read to them could hardly be called avant-garde. It was good, family stuff. He once told me that he had a book that "goes all the way back to 1936, *The Best Loved Poems of the American People*."

One that he particularly liked, he said, was a poem about noses, ["To My Nose" by Alfred A. Forrester] since the governor is well aware that his is humongous. He started to read it to me once before the show.

> Knows he that never took a pinch,
> Nosey, the pleasure thence which flows?
> Knows he the titillating joys
>
> Which my nose knows?

O nose, I am as proud of thee
As any mountain of its snows;
I gaze on thee, and feel that pride

A Roman knows!

So when the tape for the show began to roll, I immediately hit him with his penchant for poetry.

"Governor, my informants tell me that you're into poetry. Is that right? Is this the time of the year when you explore the muse?"

"Well, I have read poetry for a long time. Like most people in this state, I had to study a little bit when I went to high school and I wound up writing a bit and we fooled around the way most people do writing verses, etc."

What kind of poetry does the governor like?

Well, he said, "I am not one for long abstruse poetry. I'm a kind of Walt Whitman guy because he was a New Yorker and I like simple old, old poems."

Cuomo told our radio audience that he liked reading the old poems and "...kind of associating them with the life around me."

I told him that we at public radio had a favorite poem about the pig who came and sat down next to the drunk. The governor was concerned about drunkenness and said that, "Frankly, beautiful as those holidays are, they are also a time of the year when people are inclined to party and we have been very aggressive, as you know, trying to encourage people to be careful about their drinking and if they're drinking, not to drive."

But the governor confessed that he also knew the poem about the drunk and the pig.

He asked, "Would you like to hear it?"

"Oh please," I responded, and so he recited:

One night in late October,
When I was far from sober,

Returning with my load with manly pride,
My feet began to stutter,
So I lay down in the gutter,
And a pig came near and lay down by my side;
As I lay there in the gutter
Thinking thoughts I could not utter
A lady passing by was heard to say:
'You can tell a man who boozes
By the company he chooses,'
And the pig got up and slowly walked away.

I asked the governor whether he could think of any political adversaries from whom the pig would have gotten up and walked away.

Cuomo said something which I think is tremendously important when summing up Mario Cuomo.

"No, I can't think of any political adversaries, frankly, that I respect a whole lot less than I respect myself. Most of the people in this business, you know, we differ and we fight with one another politically—I think they're a pretty good bunch over all. I don't see a lot of lowlives in my business. Not any more than in your business or in business generally."

I was struck by the upbeat nature of his remark and I wanted to know whether it was disingenuous. So I asked him whether he classified himself as an optimist, so positive was his view of his colleagues.

He didn't remember the name of the particular poem but he referred to the piece of poetry about the optimist who fell off the top of the Empire State Building. As he passed each floor, all the way down he shouted to the people inside, "Alright so far."

Soon, the gov started to quote the lines from "Strictly Germ-Proof" the poem about the Antiseptic Baby and the Prophylactic Pup by Arthur Guiterman, whom Cuomo identifies as having been "...very popular when I was growing up."

According to Cuomo, the poem reminded him of two of his commissioners at the time, Health Commissioner David Axelrod and Environmental Commissioner Tom Jorling. Anyone who knows Jorling understands that he is one of the most knowledgeable environmentalists in the United States but is also one of the biggest squares around. In a word, antiseptic. Axelrod had a reputation as a stickler for detail and was the head of a big New York laboratory, one of the most antiseptic places you can find. The poem, quoted by Cuomo on the radio show, ends:

> There's not a Micrococcus in the garden where they
>   play;
> They bathe in pure iodoform a dozen times a day;
> And each imbibes his rations from a Hygienic Cup—
> The Bunny and the Baby and the Prophylactic Pup."

Like the pup, Cuomo is personally fastidious, favoring blue suits, polished shoes, and crisp white shirts. He was tough on his staff when they didn't follow his sartorial lead.

I was always on his case when he got named to a best dressed or a most sexy list. Some years ago, I took note of the fact that, "You've have been named to the best dressed list," to which himself answered, "That's a joke." In response, I told him that I had always thought that it took a lot of money to get so named. "Do you have a secret?" I asked. "Is it Matilda?" I wanted to know.

"I think when you get to be governor..."

What he was trying to say before I interrupted him was that all New York State governors are so honored. So I said to him, "You mean as soon as you are governor they get to..." Well, he wouldn't even let me finish my sentence. He indicated that Matilda was his worst critic and that she regarded him as "one of the worst dressers she has ever met, and I when said, 'Why is that?' she said, 'Because you get your clothes by mail,' which is true. I get suits by mail. I tell them my measurements and they send me a suit. I have never had a fitted suit in my life." Once he told me that in his earlier days he bought suits by mail and had other labels sewn in.

Two of Mario Cuomo's best stories illustrate the man and his values. He may have embellished the stories, in one case he says he likes to think that it *could* have been that way. But both stories underline the America that Mario Cuomo believes in: a benevolent place where hard work pays off. I have told these stories often, and even more people heard them when the governor recounted them for the radio audience during a WAMC fund drive. He read aloud excerpts from his diary which was published back in 1982; and all these years later, those excerpts never fail to bring tears to the eyes of those who hear them.

The first story he shared was the story of Papa and the Spruce Tree. Cuomo's diary entry, dated Friday, October 22, 1982 began, "Tired. Very tired." He was in the midst of one of his toughest campaigns, he told us, and feeling less than hopeful. Rummaging through a desk drawer, he came upon one of his father Andrea's old business cards.

Wondering what Papa would have said if he'd told him he was tired, or worse yet, discouraged, Cuomo recalled how his father had reckoned with all the hard circumstances life had dealt him. Cuomo's memories brought him back to his family's house in Queens—their first home with land around it—and a great blue spruce that stood majestically in the corner of the property.

As Cuomo tells the story, less than a week after they moved in, there was a terrible thunder storm and they awoke to find the great spruce tree torn up by the roots.

City boys, the future governor and his brother, Frankie, knew nothing about trees. They looked sadly down at the fallen spruce when Papa, undaunted by the challenge, announced to his sons in broken English, "Okay, we gonna push him up. He's a-gonna grow again." His pronouncement was met with skepticism, but he remained absolutely certain that the tree would indeed be saved. With shovels and ropes, the man and the boys worked for hours in the rain, restoring the roots to the ground and propping the spruce tree up into its natural position. Their work done, they looked at the spruce made straight by ropes and Papa repeated, "Don't worry...he's a-gonna grow again."

"I looked at the card and wanted to cry. If you were to drive past the house today, in Hollis Wood, you would see that great, straight blue spruce, maybe now, sixty feet tall, pointing straight up to the heavens, pretending it never had its nose in the asphalt. I put Papa's card back into the drawer, I closed it with a vengeance. I couldn't wait to get back into the campaign."

And I couldn't hope to find a better story to demonstrate how the governor's family instilled in him that can-do work ethic which makes anything possible. I get the feeling that Cuomo often looks back at the struggles of his family and recalls how far he has come. With this recollection is an abiding gratitude for his good fortune.

Once when I was, as usual, scared to death to ask him the "P" or presidential question, I told him, "I go on my knees and ask you this question." I told him I didn't want to but that "...people want me to ask you this question." And then, once again, I asked him how it felt, knowing that he might have been president of the United States in 1982, but chose instead, not to run. He said, "I feel extremely fortunate to be the governor. That is more than I had to expect out of this life. It is probably more than I deserve." And he continues, and for what it's worth I believe him, "It is probably more than my family ever anticipated standing on Ellis Island, with my father praying for a job as a ditch digger in New Jersey."

Like so many immigrants and children of immigrants, Cuomo knows what he owes to this country. "I have had fulfillment and more. I want to spend the rest of my days paying it back." Cuomo said that to suggest that he was content as governor would not be accurate. Rather, he said that his holding the governor's chair left him "exuberant." "I am full of joy and fulfillment." But that joy, that honor, said Cuomo, brought with it a responsibility, "And I want to express it by working even harder than I did during my first five years as governor."

Then, said Cuomo, "How could I dare say to God, whatever forces there are—choose your own God—how could I ever say, 'Gee, I have been denied something.' I who have received so much. No, I have not got the slightest regret."

Cuomo, the realist, knows that he came farther than anyone could have expected. But there is part of him which wants everyone to know how proud he is of his parents and what their contribution to the American experience has been.

Near the end of 1982, Cuomo wrote another diary entry, describing an imaginary conversation between his mother and a reporter on Ellis Island. I love this story because it is not only humble, it's a little anti-establishment.

The entry from which Cuomo read had been written after he had won the election, but before his swearing in. In it, he reflected upon the differences between his life in the old neighborhood in South Jamaica, Queens, and the new road that lay ahead, leading to the door of the governor's mansion. "How far is it?" he asked, from King's Park in South Jamaica?" And he recalled his mother's path, which led her from southern Italy to the gateway of the United States, Ellis Island, and an imaginary interview that took place there.

Stepping off the boat, Immacolata Cuomo was greeted by a reporter. She is asked her name.

"Immacolata Cuomo."

"What do you do?"

"What do you mean, what do I do?"

"What do you do for a living?"

"Nothing. I'm going to go meet my husband in New Jersey. I have a baby."

Says the reporter, "What does he do?"

"Nothing. He's looking for work. Now, he's digging ditches in Jersey City. They're making a new church. But that job is going to be over soon."

"What skills does he have?"

"Well, he has no skills. He never went to school and they never taught him how to be a carpenter, how to make wood into furniture. He was never educated."

"Well, do you have any skills?"

"No, I'm not even a seamstress."

The man went on. "Do you have any friends? Any relatives? Any money?"

"No, no friends, no money, just a baby."

"Well, with no friends, no money, what do you expect of this country, Immacolata Cuomo?"

"Not a lot. Only one thing, maybe, before I die. I want to see my son the governor of New York State."

The governor laughed. "They would have locked her up if she'd actually said that. That's how far it is from here back to Ellis Island."

Cuomo is angered when anyone uses the word Mafia, which he considers an ethnic slur.

One of the things he shared with his one time political adversary, Republican Rudolph Giuliani, was his hatred of those who would classify all Italian-Americans as Mafia. As a young man he clearly was taught to fight those bigots who would spread that kind of intolerable nonsense. In his adult life, he was the object of smears by those who would dismiss him because "...he must have relatives in the Mafia somewhere."

Once, when I asked him about it, and mentioned that Giuliani was talking about the same thing, he asked for an opportunity to "...talk about this important subject."

Cuomo said that Giuliani had been one of the most successful organized crime fighters in history. Giuliani, he said, had decided to speak out on the issue.

"He did not say it in the earlier years, but he is saying it now." What Giuliani was saying, said Cuomo, was that people sometimes adopted a "...syndrome which blames Italian-Americans; people tend to believe somehow that they are all part of organized crime." Cuomo said, "I agree with Rudy that such a stereotype does exist and I have said so over and over, especially to Italian-Americans."

Cuomo warned Italian-Americans not to buy into the lie themselves. "You should never believe that you are any different than anybody else regarding this matter. The truth is that every group I am aware of has been discriminated against in one way or the other."

Furthermore, said Cuomo, Blacks, Jews and Hispanics had all been similarly treated.

The way to beat such discrimination, said Cuomo, is to do what Rudy Giuliani had done with his career, "Excel." And, said Cuomo, who obviously had been following his own formula, "We'll do a lot to rebut, to refute" the stereotyping. "And finally," said Cuomo, "I have a challenge for Italian-Americans. If you don't like the memory of being called a dago, a wop, or a guinea, a mafioso, if you don't like the idea that they castigate you that way when you are not around to hear whisperings, the way for you to respond is to fight that syndrome wherever you see it, wherever you hear it."

Cuomo warns Italians that "The worst thing an Italian-American can do is to use words or even think words like nigger or spic. That," says Cuomo, "would be the ugliest, the worst sin of all...to react the way people react that we condemn is to strengthen the hands of those that we condemn.

"If you don't like being discriminated against, I suggest that we lock arms and fight discrimination wherever it appears." To his Italian-American brethren, Cuomo advises that "We should lead the league to a new level of intelligence." And that intelligence says Cuomo, should go hand in glove with "wisdom and love." Cuomo says that that is the "...challenge that Italian-Americans should accept themselves and that's the speech that I make to them, every time I have a chance."

Cuomo, like my own father, learned a lesson that no one group can discriminate against another and then expect to be treated fairly. He understands all too well how prone each group is to that type of behavior. There is one thing in this world that no one ought to do around Mario Cuomo and that is to tell an ethnic joke. He doesn't like them. That's because he has suffered too much from them.

One of his most eloquent testimonials on the subject came when a group of conservative columnists had written articles mentioning the words Cuomo and Mafia at the same time. I took the opportunity to ask Cuomo whether the references hurt. He answered:

"It hurts in a way I can't even explain to you. To hear people say stupid things like 'Shylock,' to hear people tell stupid Polish jokes, to hear them making fun of 'niggers,' to hear them using all these ugly repulsive hating words, sure it hurts. Sure it hurts to remember how stupid we are and how mean we are, when we have a potential for being so beautiful and so good. Yes, it hurts, it's frustrating.

"But I also think it ought to be an occasion for us to resolve to try harder and to do better. The only way to do that is by example. The only way for me to handle, for my children's sake, to handle this question of Mafia and guinea and dago, is never to say polack, and never to say kike, and never even to joke about it. That's the only way to do it, by example."

But the best look into all of this is a story Cuomo once told me about a man named Mark Conrad.

AC: Governor, who's Mark Conrad?
MC: Mark Conrad. There probably are Mark Conrads, it's a common enough name, I would guess. But Mark Conrad when I use it is a reference to a comment I made several months ago in describing to someone my ethnicity and its implications. I was asked if it was true that when I left law school I had done very well, but I couldn't get an interview in a Wall Street firm. And I said yes that was true. I pointed out that the dean, may he rest in peace, said to me at the time that

maybe we should try changing your name. I said to this group which I was addressing, can you imagine me—take a good look at me—can you imagine me as Mark Conrad? Something about it just tickled their funnybone, something about looking at me and thinking of me as Mark Conrad that makes people smile or even laugh.

But despite the fact that Mario Cuomo and his family suffered because of their immigrant status, Cuomo doesn't ever indulge in the "get-even-now-that-we've-made-it" policy that is so common to others. Once, after he returned from a speaking engagement at Princeton, I asked him:

"Okay, Governor, just very quickly and I'll get off the topic of Princeton. You were raised, of course, as a child of immigrants. How does it make you feel to go to a Princeton? Did you have the normal feelings that these guys might be stuck up and...?"

"That's an interesting question, Alan. I think you hear about Princeton, Yale, Harvard, you think that these are the elite, the sons and daughters of the elite, and there are many of them there who are indeed sons and daughters of wealthy people, accomplished people, in the upper levels economically. But, not all of them. Yale, Princeton, Harvard all have an admissions policy that has nothing to do with their wealth. When they accept students they don't know anything about their ability to pay. If the person who has been admitted can't afford to pay, they provide loans, jobs, whatever necessary to put that person through. I know it's true at Princeton, I talked to some people about it yesterday. I know it's true at Yale and I know it's true at Harvard. I can't say it's true at all the other schools. But it's certainly true at those three great ones, and that's a wonderful thing. It means you don't have to be rich to go to Princeton. Now, a lot of them are rich, but not all of them, and you don't have to be, and that's a good thing."

The political scientist, James Barber, has established a series of political typologies for analyzing the character of presidents.

The best among these are the "active positives," the men who invest the most in their presidencies and who, down deep, like themselves. Clearly Mario Cuomo meets the first test and probably the second.

Cuomo is proactive. He picks on others, he uses fights, and he never, never lets anyone take him for granted as each of those Democrats who have run for president have found out when they have attempted to control Cuomo. Cuomo once likened Mondale to that bland Italian food called *polenta*. But when asked to justify his use of the term, the governor maintained that it was a compliment because *polenta* sticks to your ribs and is nutritious.

Reagan, he said was Charlotte Russe, a highly caloric sweet with no nutritional value. But when I asked him about Mike Dukakis I got this answer:

AC: What breakfast cereal is closest to Mike Dukakis?
MC: It would be sugar-free, it would be popular, it would be nourishing, it would be smart. Whatever you can find that's nourishing, sweet, and smart, that's the breakfast cereal you should associate with Mike Dukakis. Bush would be a different breakfast cereal. He would be less nourishing.

Listen to him talk about Ronald Reagan, whom he knew would win but still wasn't afraid to pick on: "If President Reagan wins, and I don't expect him to, I certainly don't expect him to win by any landslide. I would be stunned, frankly, if that were to occur. Whatever success he has is purely personal. His record doesn't justify his popularity. His ability doesn't justify his popularity. He has struck an interesting chord in the American psyche, or in the psyche of many people."

Mario Cuomo is a man who is very much aware of his mortality. Often, he would mention how fleeting life is. But there is mortal death and then there is political death. Once he combined them when I asked whether he was concerned about the possibility that his popularity would go down in the polls.

"There's no question that they will go down, no question that someday I will disappear, there's no question that someday I will die, there's no question that someday people won't be able to spell my name. There's no question that someday your grandchildren, or for all I know my grandchildren, will not remember Mario Cuomo. I'm not concerned about that. I am concerned about the moment. I am concerned about what I can do to put more people to work, what I can do to help more children escape drugs, what I can do right now.

"I am concerned about how we use this God-given and voter-given opportunity to do good things. One thing I would never want to see happen, one thing that would spoil the rest of my life, is to have to look back and say 'I blew it,' 'I didn't pay attention, I didn't take advantage of the moment, I didn't try as hard as I could.' I can live with failure, I can live with not achieving everything I wanted to achieve, I can live with that as long as I know— that I tried as hard as I could. I look at the polls with that kind of disposition."

When the Colombian drug cartel marked certain New Yorkers for rub out, Cuomo's name was supposedly on the list and he had to receive extra protection. And when he fought the new Archbishop of Brooklyn, who came into town with verbal guns blazing in Cuomo's direction, Cuomo took a very forgiving, restrained and soft line, proclaiming that he expected to die in Queens where the new Bishop was to be installed. His constant reference to death underlines his awareness of the short time he has been given on earth.

He had several harrowing airplane rides on the state plane, which was riddled with mechanical problems, but he refused to replace the plane, thinking the voters wouldn't understand. After one such flight, when many of those aboard the plane actually thought that they wouldn't make it, I asked the governor how he felt about the whole thing.

"I think one of the first things you think about when you're confronted by a situation that could be life- threatening is the people who depend upon you. What does it mean to your kids, your wife, the people you leave behind? If you're important in your job, what does it mean to your office, your business, or classroom? For most of us, and certainly this is true of politicians, we needn't be terribly concerned about what it means for the people we serve because the one thing that's clearest about this democracy is that they can do very nicely, thank you, without us. Others could do the same job.

"Much as I don't want to feel it, this state would take time out for the funeral, a couple of hours to put a flower on the coffin, but that's it. Then things move on. So too with public radio or television. I'm afraid, Alan, that if we were to go together this afternoon and hand-in-hand walk into the clouds, I can tell you the ratings wouldn't be affected..."

But death is a complicated matter to Mario Cuomo. Once I asked him about euthanasia and suicide. He answered,

MC: I'm opposed to playing God. I'm opposed to euthanasia.

AC: How about letting people do it to themselves?

MC: As a society, we've said suicide is wrong. We don't let you kill yourself.

AC: Yes, but should we change all that?

MC: I think not. I think we should be affirming life more than negating it. I think we should put more of an emphasis on making life more desirable, rather than driving people to the grim alternative of having to end life. With abortion I think there has been a raging argument since 1973 and before about the circumstances under which a woman can exercise the right to abort a fetus. I think however there is not a great deal of dispute over the proposition that it is a hard judgment for a woman to make, under the best of circumstances.

AC: But, Governor...

MC: And it would be better if the question never had to be answered, which means more careful protection against pregnancy when it's not desired. More education, more discipline. I think women generally agree with that. I think we all agree it would be better if there were fewer occasions when we have to deal with the question.

AC: But, Governor, now we're talking about somebody who's eighty-six years old and incurably ill or a young man dying of AIDS in a hospital bed, being eaten and riddled from inside? He just wants to go peacefully and to make that decision for himself. Why can't such patients be permitted to do that?

MC: Well, to a certain extent sick people are allowed under our law to provide that if their functions end, and they do not want themselves artificially resuscitated, we do not resuscitate—it's called DNR. We would presume that you wish to be resuscitated by artificial means unless you say no. I'm not a theologian and I'm not a philosopher, but there is a general principle held by some people which draws a distinction between ending your life by a positive act and allowing it to end by not intervening with extraordinary life-extending devices.

If you can remember that far back, the question with Karen Anne Quinlan was whether or not to unhook her from the respirator, which as a practical matter would cause her life to end. You did not kill her, say these philosophers. You simply refused to intervene with an artificial device. Some people say that that's not logical, that it may be intellectually sound but it's all wrong. So you have a raging debate over it, and you know that in this state we did do the DNR regulations.

I wasn't happy with his answer and tried once again to get him to tell me whether people had a right to make choices like that for themselves.

MC: Are you saying that at one point, we should give people the option of ending their own lives? How about in the case of a forty-year-old who's distressed? Found mentally sound, but unhappy with life, finds it all vacuous. And would like to go into a hospital, do this with dignity, and on the third day take a cyanide capsule. What do you say about that?

AC: I think it's tough.

MC: But what's your answer, Alan? I'm opposed to that. I'm opposed to it. I'm opposed to allowing people under such circumstances to take their own lives because I'm afraid of where it goes.

We came back to the subject again when we inevitably took a few moments once to discuss the governor's beloved dog, Ginger.

AC: How is Ginger?

MC: Not well, not well. 1977, what is that, 14 years, 1977, she is 14 years old, that is 108 on the human scale. She is...it depends, if you give her medicine and she takes it, if she takes her aspirin and her food, then she can walk around a bit. But there are days when her legs are gone.

It's painful to see and it raises all the difficult questions about pain and how much of it should be tolerated, and life and what it means. And how much life and history are worth. And memories, all these sweet thoughts about loyalty and happy, shared experiences. All the difficult judgments that are your responsibility to your dog. Some people would say, 'She is only a dog.' Well, people get attached to animals because animals are life. And we are getting more and more subtle and more and more sophisticated about life and the planet. People are almost religious about the ecology because that is a form of life. And what has happened over the years, as we have grown older as a civilization, begun to understand more fully the miracle of life all around us, not just in our form, with a shirt and a tie and hair that falls from the head after a while. But all forms of life. The miracle of life.

Certainly, dogs and animals are a very much a part of that.

AC: Did you ever consider at some point, if Ginger became completely incontinent, for example, of putting her down?

MC: I don't even think about it. People face that when they have to face it. It is not the kind of thing one encourages or enjoys thinking about. So I am not thinking about it.

AC: Well, you may have to though.

MC: If I have to, I have to. But as long as I don't have to, I won't think about it. And I hope that is the way they treat me.

While on the theme of animals and nature, there is the matter of Mario the Mayfly. Once when I humorously asked Cuomo what animal (other than human) he would be if he could, he treated the question in a far more serious and philosophical manner than I would have expected. I asked him if he would agree with his children's playful assessment that he was a gorilla. I got a terse "No," to that.

"I think I would want to be whatever animal is the most sentient, most aware. I think whether it's a dolphin or a monkey, whatever animal is closest to awareness and understanding." He wanted to be whatever animal "...comes closest to being able to understand emotions. The things that give joy, the things that give satisfaction, the things that give even pain, but not just physical pain, but the pain of disillusionment and lost expectation, that thrill of succeeding which means so much to us as human beings, that you can't have unless you understand, unless you know. So whatever animal comes closest to knowing and understanding, that's what I'd want to be."

But I pressed, would the governor want to be known as an ocelot, or a leopard? "No," said the governor, "and, if I had to be one of the things that does not understand, then I think I'd rather be a mayfly. I think I'd rather be a mayfly because it lives for only seven hours, or five hours. That's not an animal, it's an insect, but if you would just stretch the category a bit to living things, then I think I probably would want to be a mayfly."

Cuomo said that the Anti-Defamation League of B'nai B'rith had written a short book honoring Jonathan Netanyahu, who had died in the famous Israeli raid to rescue hostages at Entebbe. The story, said the governor, was "wonderful" and about "a very senior mayfly that lived maybe to be nine hours old, talking to young mayflies about how he didn't regret an hour of his wonderful, long life and all the things that had happened to him and all the pain that he had felt. So if I weren't going to understand things fully, I think I would want my life to be as short as possible so I would opt for mayfly. Dolphin or monkey on the one hand, mayfly on the other, is my guess."

It is a safe bet that the governor sees his life as just as fleeting as the short-lived mayfly. But since he had injected the concept of dolphins, I asked him what was so attractive about the dolphin.

"Dolphins," he said, "are as close to sentience and understanding as you can get in the animal kingdom. I don't know a whole lot about it but they seem to understand a great deal." Understanding and feeling are those values that the governor seems to treasure. And yet there is no denying that the governor likes a good intellectual argument above all.

What we have in Mario Cuomo is a man who loves his work, so much so that he worries he may not have paid enough attention to his children or to the type of life he has given his wife in terms of more material things.

I suspect that one of the most telling conversations I ever had with the guy involved the concept of retirement. It came about after the death of Vladimir Horowitz, perhaps the greatest pianist of our age. Cuomo said the right things about the Horowitz, that he was "...a great, great pianist, a real genius." Cuomo was particularly taken with the fact that he had "natural ability" and didn't spend the almost always mandatory hours of practice.

I told him that I was particularly impressed by the fact that, despite being in his eighties, "he had been playing right up to the end, keeping his dignity, keeping at his profession."

The governor seemed very interested in that. He came up with two words, "Katharine Hepburn." Cuomo added that "Last Sunday I just happened to catch the senior football league." Cuomo explained that the men who play sports at that age are "extraordinary." He also said that he was a basketball player "...and I expect to play it for a long time." The former minor leaguer from the Pittsburgh baseball organization quoted himself. "I said once I want to go out either sliding into third base or home plate or when my left hand hook shot hits the cords. Then my heart should stop as the buzzer goes off."

Cuomo told me that "...there is nothing wrong in having the kind of aspiration to be active and vital right until the end, even though the end comes at a relatively advanced age." And, said the workaholic, "I think one of the reasons that you stop functioning is that you think you have to. At a certain age God intervenes and we should make the most of whatever time allowed us."

Anyone who knows Mario Cuomo knows that what you see is what you get. A man of superb rhetoric, a religious man, a conservative man. Trust yourself, like yourself, follow the golden rule. Provide for your family and remember the rules that your parents taught you and you'll win. Repress the urge to fight unnecessarily because it's your worst feature. That's Mario Cuomo.

THE CUOMO DIALECTIC

March 4th, 1986:

AC: Well, that is a good question.

MC: Yes, it is a very good question. Would you mind answering it?

AC: You are so good at this, Governor.

MC: No, no, no. Excuse me, Alan, that is game playing.

AC: No, no, no. I frequently can't answer a question, because as you know, I'm not privy to all of the things that...

MC: Alan, no fair. It is not fair. It is not fair for you to say every time you can't answer a question, "You are good at this, Governor." That puts me in an impossible position. It makes you invulnerable and perfect. Because this way, you don't have an answer, you blame it on my cuteness. That is not nice, Alan.

AC: Who me? I just couldn't answer the question.

I have learned from sometimes painful experience on *The Capitol Connection* that Mario Cuomo loves to engage in dialogue, either up close or at a distance. He appears to have absolute faith in his ability to debate any opponent, even though I have heard him argue that he does not like political debates as they are now structured. Despite that, it is clear that his debating ability is unmatched among contemporary politicians. It is also clear to me that he loves dialectic or debate because he truly learns from it. When Cuomo is debating he is listening, truly listening, to what the other person has to say. If the other guy has a point you can be sure that Mario Cuomo will attempt to utilize that thinking in subsequent activities. That's because Cuomo is convinced that when people talk to each other, truth emerges. This happens, he believes, because in some cases there is no clear right or wrong.

"Our lives are filled with competing values. If there were only good things and bad things, if there were only good choices and bad choices, and plainly so, if every issue was absolutely unambiguous, life would be a lot more simple and a lot more boring. But there are many, many questions that cannot be dealt with in absolutes. Maybe abortion is one of those issues, maybe the death penalty is one of those issues, environment generally...."

But no matter what Mario Cuomo says, when he gets into a debating situation he is good at it. I have seen him reduce experienced debaters like Ed Koch and Evans and Novak to rubble. But despite his ability, Cuomo has always said that there is something about political debates that he hates. He says that they turn into circuses; that they are not designed to bring out truth. Of course, he has been accused of hypocrisy by those who believe that he took advantage of the opportunity to debate Koch all over New York, but that he did not allow the same opportunity to his opponents. But Cuomo denies all of that. This is the way he explained it all to me.

MC: If I had my way, there would be no debates, by me, as a candidate. I don't like them. I have never liked them. I begged for them, I fought for them in 1982, but I was honest about it. I said, "I wanted the debates because I want to get on television." I had no money. Ed Koch had all the money. The only way I could do it was by getting up there with him. I would have done the tarantella with him if that is what it would have taken for me to be on television because, unfortunately, you need television.

AC: How could you say you are opposed to debate? Isn't that the best way to inform the people?

MC: Of course not, of course not. You will be asked about the budget; you will have one minute to answer. Does that make sense to you? One minute to talk about the budget?

AC: Doesn't have to be one minute.

MC: Alright, two minutes about the budget. That is no way to convey information. That is a way to test glibness, to test presence of mind, swiftness of tongue, cleverness, sense of humor, your looks. These are not the things that will make you a great mayor...

AC: It seems to me you would not be governor if you had not debated with Ed Koch... what makes you say this?

MC: That is nonsense. The question is not how I won the campaign, but "How does one govern?" Being a good debater has not made me a good governor.

To be a good governor you have to make an intelligent budget, that takes months and months and months. You have to take the right position on the issues, you don't make that up on the spot. You don't do that by clever repartee. You don't do that with a sense of humor, you don't do that with the swiftness of your mind.

You don't negotiate with Ralph Marino or Mel Miller without notes, with your best red tie on, and with your close shave and make-up. I mean, you don't do it that way. That is not a way a person governs. You govern with thoughts, with help, with deliberation, and with care.

I was asked during a presidential campaign, "What do you think of the debates?" I said, "I am opposed to them." I'd rather see you put George Bush up there with all of his aides and his books. Ask him the important questions, have three inquisitors and give him all the time he wants to answer. Then film the whole thing.

Let him talk to his consultant. Do it the way you actually will govern. Or give him the actual questions in advance and let him prepare the answers the way he will when he governs. Then cross examine him and let him say, "Well, let me now confirm with you. Here is my view," or "I will get back to you with my view in two days."

Then have it all filmed, put it on paper. Have the true answers well delivered after careful study so you will know what he is really about. Don't have the kind of debate where if the man is clever enough to say, "There you go again, Jimmy" the world loves the charm of it, the style of it, the timing of it. The other guy sounds like he has pebbles in his mouth if that is the case with the candidate.

But no matter what he says, there are many who thought that with Cuomo's oratorical and debating gifts he might have won the 1988 election had he, and not Mike Dukakis, been the candidate. Dukakis was clearly floundering during the summer of that year, having blown a twenty point lead. I asked Cuomo what advice he had for the Duke. Here's what he advised Dukakis to say:

"I, Michael Dukakis, acknowledge that we need to do better, after I acknowledge my gratitude for all of the good things we've done in my state and elsewhere. But I am committed to doing better. Child care, health care, education costs, housing costs, the environment, the debt, the work force of the twenty-first century. And the difference between me and George Bush, frankly, is that he does not acknowledge we have to do anything more.

"He says, in effect, leave it where it is. He says the economy is good enough, we gave you millions of jobs—he never mentions two trillion dollars in debt. Is he telling you that over the next eight years he'll give you another two trillion in debt?

"If I were Mike Dukakis, I would say to the media right away: 'Look, forget about the National Guard, forget about all those less important issues, I want to talk to you about change and how I'm going to do it. So give me your four toughest inquisitors in the media, put me on the stage anywhere without notes, and let's talk to the American people. If Bush doesn't want to join us, that's up to him, I'm not gonna argue. And I don't want any empty chair or any cuteness. I simply want to talk to the American people.'"

Of course, Cuomo could have followed his own advice. Dukakis couldn't have. One was an orator, the other didn't have a clue about how to perform, despite the strength of his commitment.

But no matter what Cuomo says about debating, he is the best there is at it. In fact the tougher the challenge, the better he is. Cuomo loves to argue, he loves to contest. And this ability extends far beyond the actual dialogue. It has to do with campaigns, setting a strategy, and sticking with it.

It means being so sharp that you can anticipate what your enemy or adversary is trying to do to you and sticking him before he can stick you. But most of all, Mario Cuomo's ability to debate is greatest when he is speaking about something that matters deeply to him. Something like racial prejudice.

"The best speech I ever made, I made in 1982, I think. Near the end of the campaign I went out to Belmont, the Italian neighborhood in the Bronx where they speak Italian. Where just because my name is Mario Cuomo, all you have to do is say 'Bravo Italiani' and the place goes crazy. I made my speech about Mom and Pop at Ellis Island; I am Italian and I could get to be governor. They were very proud. I said, 'Wouldn't it be a terrible sin if now that we are making it as Italian-Americans, we felt toward the Blacks and Hispanics the kind of discrimination they used to feel towards us?'

"Remember they called us 'dagos,' 'guinea,' 'wop.' Remember how you felt? The worst thing we can do is start calling people 'niggers' and 'spics.' Wouldn't that be terrible? These Italians cheered,

'You're right, you're right.' Once that lesson gets across, that 'when you insult me, you insult everybody. That when somebody insults the Jew, then you are just begging the Jew to insult the person who comes after her or him.' That is a lesson in intelligence."

Cuomo was master of the technique of dialectic. When he thought I was about to make a fool of myself, he would allow me to come ahead. But if he suspected I had something, he'd interrupt. Of course, there were times when he'd interrupt just for the fun of it.

We had this conversation, for example:

AC: You look terrible, sir. You look like you have been up all night. You look something like Bluto in...

MC: [interrupts] Thank God for radio, Alan.

AC: You look something like Bluto in Popeye.

MC: Can I tell you something?

AC: What?

MC: You're right, Alan. It is your function as a relentlessly objective reporter to point that out. It is my function as a politician sometimes to disguise facts. For example, you always look that way, Alan. Even when you haven't been without sleep for two days. I'm not going to make a point of that because...

AC: ...It wouldn't be right.

MC: I am a politician.

AC: Governor, you had your cake and ate it. I think you are right, Governor. You have pointed out that I always look that way, and at the same time that you are not going to say it. Okay, now look.

MC: To say what?

AC: To say I look terrible.

MC: Yes, now that is three times.

Mario Cuomo needs a dialectic in order to make sense out of things. He says that he doesn't like acrimony, and that may be true, but he does treasure true intellectual discourse. I believe that's because he thinks the truth can be discovered by listening to what a lot of people are saying and then finding certain common denominators.

I always marvel at how much he likes the negotiation process. In the middle of one of those late budget, up-all-night debating situations, we talked over his ability to function under that kind of pressure.

AC: Some of us, like me, love getting into trouble and being argumentative; but I don't like it when I'm there, Governor. You, on the other hand, seem to like it when you're there.

MC: No, no, no. I don't like it at all.

AC: When you say "exhilarating"—I mean you're handling this problem. It's a very tough problem, and yet you use the word "exhilarating."

MC: Look, what is life, Alan? What is life? Life is meeting the exigencies of the moment, enjoying what there is to be enjoyed, life is functioning. Part of functioning is meeting problems and trying to overcome them. And whatever force put it all together, call it God, whatever force it is, it seems to me it had to be a rational, infinitely intelligent source. What they have said to us is, "Look, make the most of this world that you can't figure out. The one thing you can be sure of is that you can function with everything that happens. If they visit pain on you, live through it. If they give you an opportunity to paint, paint. Enjoy it and let people share your joy. If they give you a problem to solve, solve it. But do. Don't run, don't hide, don't cover your eyes, don't roll the stone in front of the cave so that nobody can find you. We give you a limited time to function—use every bit of it. And if it happens that most of your time is spent dealing with problems, well then that's your lot and make the most of it."

The more you get a chance to live, it doesn't have to be that you're riding on a ship around the world, it doesn't have to be that kind of life. It could be that you're struggling with a child who's in trouble. It could be dealing with a marriage that's troubled. It can be dealing with disappointment. Or it can be feeling the great feeling of somebody putting a crown on your head; but it's all part of life. We are privileged to be able to participate in it.

Despite the fact that Cuomo time and again called Ronald Reagan the great communicator, it is clear to me that his use of dialectic, often in the form of debate, was central to the way he communicated with his political constituency.

In debating, Cuomo applies some time honored concepts used successfully in debate and teaching. Once he has what he considers a successful theme, he seems to understand that repetition is the key to effective message sending. He will use each opportunity to return to his central theme. Each time that people questioned the fact that he was collecting a lot of money for his campaigns, Cuomo would say that he had to do it to keep up with the massive amounts of money collected by the Republicans. He hammered that home to the point that it was used with the same regularity as grace before a meal in a religious family.

Almost always, Cuomo could anticipate trouble before it actually occurred. I found him to have an incredible "anticipatory antenna." He could smell trouble when it was still miles off. Anyone who can do that can structure debate to avoid potential problems.

One example of the governor's ability to anticipate trouble from a questioner occurred once just before Christmas when a governor usually announced his or her clemency decisions. Many people were applying heat on the governor to pardon Jean Harris, the convicted killer of Dr. Herman Tarnower, the Scarsdale diet doctor.

As usual, I started slowly on the general topic, hoping to get Cuomo to talk about Jean Harris. "Perhaps you could explain a little bit about the clemency process?" I asked.

Of course, if I thought for a second that I was going to get one over on this guy I had another think coming. He obviously saw what was coming a mile away. The best way he could deal with the thing was to move it out of his venue and into the federal jurisdiction, the land of Gerald Ford giving Richard Nixon a pardon.

This was Cuomo at his best as he announced that, "We have a number of clemency processes." Included among these, said the governor, was the constitutional power "to pardon people the way the president could pardon Oliver North and Poindexter or Ford pardoned Richard Nixon." Now Cuomo had firmly established some horrendous examples of actual or potential pardons committed by Republicans. This gave him slack in dealing with his own difficult choice. But he stayed with the presidential model longer in explaining what a pardon was. "To pardon is to say that even though you were convicted or even though you might be convicted, I the president, in my discretion alone, on the phone, without going to the Congress, without having a public hearing, I say you are free. You need not go to jail for whatever reason.

"The president, he has that power, our Constitution gives it to him. It also gives it to every governor in the United States." Then he went on to explain *why* both the federal and state constitutions allow presidents and governors to pardon. The reason, he told us, is that sometimes laws are not enough; there are reasons why some people should not be in jail. "Sometimes you can't prepare for every eventuality in your laws." And to make the point even stronger he took us back to the old George Raft, James Cagney, and Humphrey Bogart films, when in all the old prison movies, in the last moments, the governor makes the phone call: "Don't pull that switch; we have evidence that Charlie Rafferty didn't commit the murder." The reason for pardons, said Cuomo, was the belief of the American people that "there ought to be a power resident in the chief executive to pardon without a trial." That power, said Cuomo, had never been used by him. He had established, after setting the whole thing up, that he had been very,

very judicious when it came to using his power to let criminals go; he was not going to allow anyone to paint him into a corner as a soft-on-crime Democrat. He had already had his share of that kind of heat when he extended clemency to convicted cop-killer Gary McGivern, whom he had championed when he was both Secretary of State and Lieutenant Governor.

Cuomo said that there is still another power, the power to commute—or what we in New York State usually refer to as "clemency." And clemency, said the governor, is a means to reduce the effect of the sentence, "...to accelerate the way it usually comes up in this state." Continuing the lesson, the governor explained, "In this state you have to serve a certain period of time before you go to the parole board to be freed." The parole board has to be "given evidence of good conduct." The parole board, said the governor, has to determine that the prisoner seeking clemency is not a threat to society. "The kinds of clemency that we [governors] are asked to give is to reduce the years or period of years served before going to the parole board. My clemency doesn't free anybody." Cuomo made it clear that he doesn't let criminals out of jail easily. He told me that day on the radio, "I have given fewer [commutations] than any other governor in modern history. The reason for that," he said, "may be that I have more respect for the legal system than some others.

"I don't mean it in any disparaging way," he explained. "I have and have had great respect for the legal system." "It works," he said. What's more, Cuomo always insisted that, "I don't like putting myself above the law any way." So Cuomo, who knew that Mike Dukakis may have lost an election by giving Willie Horton a prison furlough, tried to avoid being labelled in the same way. "My clemencies have been really a matter of saying, 'This person can go to the parole board now.'"

In the case of convicted felony murderer Gary McGivern, Cuomo made the point that all he did was to allow McGivern to go to the parole board and ask for release. "So there is no guarantee of freedom by clemency. Jean Harris is asking for clemency.

All that means is not that I would free her, but that I would allow her to go to the parole board before her time." In McGivern's case, the parole board said no and later said yes. By that time the heat was off Cuomo. In Jean Harris's case, Cuomo finally granted clemency although I believe that he correctly concluded that her notoriety was no reason for jumping her ahead of other prisoners with just as strong claims for release as Harris.

In McGivern's case, according to the governor, he concluded that there was not enough evidence to grant a full pardon but enough to go before the parole board and to try to convince them. When I suggested that he could have given McGivern a pardon instead of clemency, the governor said that was true, that he could have given such a pardon if he had concluded "that he was innocent and the trial was wrong and he should have never been convicted, but I did not conclude that. I concluded, given all the facts, that, yes, he deserved a chance to talk to the parole board and he got that." Finally I asked Cuomo whether, in a case like Jean Harris's or Gary McGivern's, legislators and other big shots were recommending clemency. Here, too, he was willing to share the responsibility or the blame. "I think it is reasonable to assume that whatever a legislator says to me I will consider and weigh." But, said Cuomo, and anyone who knows him knows how true this is, *how much* he listens "depends on what the legislator says" and not on whether they are Republicans or Democrats. "I am completely oblivious to their party registrations."

But party registration does count in the Cuomo dialectic in other places.

Here's an example of a fight he once picked with me. He started it by asking me what I thought of the Republicans and the budget. "Uh-oh," I said to myself, "this could be trouble."

So I told him it was an interesting question and I had every intention of asking him about it. But instead, he said to me, the interviewer, "Let's debate it."

I started to tell him that I didn't think it was appropriate for *me* to debate the issue with him, but no sooner had I said the words, "I don't think..." than he interrupted. His problem now was that he had to get me to behave like a Republican. To do that he used the fact that I agree with the Republicans on such issues as the death penalty.

MC: You are a Republican in your heart. Let's talk about it.

AC: Governor! Will you please? You know very well that I am a registered Independent. That I can vote for both Democrats and Republicans with ease.

MC: I never said anything about how you are registered I talked about what's in your heart.

AC: You can't look in my heart, Governor. You are the one who always says that I can't look in your heart.

MC: You are correct. I take it back.

AC: I am a little bit more conservative than you...

MC: [interrupting] Excuse me, on what subject?

AC: Death penalty.

MC: What makes that conservative?

AC: What do you mean "what makes that?"

MC: What makes that...? What is your definition of conservative?

AC: Well, I think that if you choose an independent sample of 500 people and asked them to rank...

MC: I did not ask that. I hate to interrupt. You are an academician and an intellectual at heart. Tell me how and what your definition of conservative is.

AC: I think somebody's whose values tend to see... Let's see how can we put this... more in a tradition of coming down harder on criminal justice.

MC: I see. Then the Soviet Union is more conservative because, like you, they believe in the death penalty.

AC: Conservative in the wrong direction, sir. There are good conservatives and bad conservatives.

MC: But they are conservatives. Are you serious?

AC: Of course I am serious.

MC: Well, then you are saying that the people of the Soviet Union are conservatives.

AC: Who said that?

MC: I thought the death penalty makes you conservative. I am asking you. You said that you were more conservative and I asked, "How," and you said it is was because you believed in the death penalty. Show me how that believing in the death penalty makes you a conservative.

AC: Well, it's because we assign certain values to certain words. It seems to me that there is a general agreement in this population that believing in the death penalty might be seen as being more conservative than liberal.

MC: WHY?!!

AC: Because most people, if asked, would say liberals tend to be more against the death penalty.

MC: You are still not answering my question. The Soviet Union is conservative if they are for the death penalty. South Africa is conservative because they are for the death penalty. Ireland is conservative because they are for the death penalty, and you are conservative. That's pretty good company you are keeping, Alan.

AC: But how about all the states in the United States? They are all conservative too, right?

MC: Well, by your definition.

AC: I understand. Yes, by my definition.

MC: By my definition a conservative is one who believes in less government. That is, less government intrusion in business, less government intrusion in all sectors. Not less government intrusion to help people unless it's a bank procedure or a loan to Chrysler. I am not at all sure that people who call themselves conservatives today are real conservatives.

AC: Well, again, you have to have your baseline about what you consider conservative.

MC: You are included. You just called yourself conservative because you want the death penalty, the ultimate in government action. That is deciding whose life is to be taken, while understanding, though, that you might be making a mistake.

AC: That's the one that troubles me.

MC: Is the Supreme Court conservative?

AC: Is this Supreme Court more conservative than the Warren Court? You bet!

MC: Is that why they said you can burn your flag, which I disagree with? I don't think you should be able to burn your flag.

Then the governor switched the topic once again. He asked me about abortion. Now he really laid the trap. Why was the Rehnquist Court more conservative than the Warren Court if it called for more intrusion into the private rights of its citizens?

When I responded that there was a developing conservative coalition in this country that included the anti-abortion conservatives, he grew impatient. I told him that I thought the conservative coalition in the court paid attention to the election of Ronald Reagan and the election returns.

"Do you think it is conservative to say government ought to make judgments for women about whether or not they should have abortions?" Concluded the governor, "Someone is going to have to define 'conservative' for me."

So I admitted to the governor, after his lesson in humility, that someone was going to have to define the word for me, too.

"Well, you are the one who used the word."

I was always trying to get the governor into some trouble during our conversations and he almost always caught me at it. On several occasions I tried to get him to endorse one New York team over another. A few times he made it plain that the only all-New York team is the Buffalo Bills franchise, since the Jets and the Giants both play in New Jersey.

AC: We see that the Giants won the Super Bowl by only one point. What do you make of that? The New Jersey Giants, I mean the New York Giants who play in New Jersey beat your team, the Buffalo Bills.

MC: Beat our team I think. New York State has one home team, and that is Buffalo. I think this was an extraordinary athletic event and sports event in that you had a great winner. In my telegram to the Giants, I said, "There were two great teams who played a great game and you were the deserving champion. And I congratulate all of you." And that is true. The Giants were magnificent. But there were no losers in that game as far as I could tell.

AC: I thought the Giants lost.

MC: No, the Giants won.

AC: No, I mean I thought the Bills lost. You said there were no losers.

MC: I believe there is a larger sense of the word. They didn't lose. They didn't lose prestige. I said yesterday in Buffalo, that they demonstrated more class, more style, more character in coming up one point short than many teams had demonstrated in victory.

AC: Sounds like you went to a progressive high school, which I know you didn't.

MC: I don't know. What do you mean by progressive high school?

AC: Progressive, when they say there are no losers. You know, when they say, "There are no losers, everybody wins."

MC: Well, sometimes that is true. Sometimes everybody loses. Sometimes the winner loses by the way the winner behaves. Sometimes the loser wins by the way the loser behaves. I think all of that is true. I think there is some metaphor in sports—I think that is one of the reasons it has such a hold on the psyche of the American people. We're very good at being wedded to metaphors that we enjoy. The whole struggle of life is represented on that field. Why do you think yesterday in Buffalo, twenty-five thousand people, reported by CNN, twenty-five thousand people shouted for one player before all the others at the outset of the victory ceremony yesterday?

Scott Norwood. They shouted for Scott Norwood, the kicker who missed the kick that cost them victory. And they said, "We want Scott" and he didn't want to go up. And finally they pushed him up. His chin down and a tear running down his cheek. They screamed for him and he put up his hand to silence them and said, "I am having difficulties speaking" and they cheered again, twenty-five thousand people, and then finally he put up his hand and stopped them, and with the tears now running down both cheeks, he said, "Last night I was discouraged and was dejected. But at this moment I feel like I have never been so loved in my whole life." Twenty-five thousand Buffalonians stood in the cold of Buffalo and cheered and roared their approval of a man who missed the kick. Now that is class.

An interesting story coming from a man who, at the time he told it, was in the middle of one of the biggest budget shortfall messes that New York has ever seen. I couldn't help but think he saw himself as Scott Norwood at that moment.

Or take the time, one of many, that he decided he would discredit me because of one of my many flaws, in this case, spelling. If memory serves, the governor had mentioned Harry Belafonte's name. I said, "Governor, you just said something that piqued our interest." Well, I think the governor did not particularly want to talk to me about Harry Belafonte, so he decided that the subject would become my inadequate spelling preparation. So he said, "How do you spell piqued?"

AC: I am not going to go into that now.
MC: Can you spell it, really? You are a professor.
AC: Of course I can spell it.
MC: You get paid by my state to teach.
AC: Of course I can spell it.
MC: How do you spell it?

AC: I am not going to go into that with you, Governor. That is irrelevant. Now you are just trying to change the subject. I am on to something good.

MC: I want the whole world that is listening to you...

AC: I am on to something good here.

MC: ...to note that you didn't accept that challenge.

AC: Alright, Governor, here it is. P-E-A-K-E-D. Peaked.

MC: No.

AC: Oh yes. The right kind of peaked. If you were on top of the mountain, wouldn't that be peaked?

MC: I hope that every listener with any sense of integrity or respect for the English language will look up that word "pique."

AC: I know how to spell it.

MC: Look up the French.

AC: I peeked in the closet.

MC: No, no. You said "pique" in the sense of titillate. And that is not P-E-A-K-E-D.

AC: Of course not.

MC: And you take money from the State University to teach students.

AC: Not enough. Okay, Governor.

MC: Okay.

A short while later I was back trying to trap Cuomo by throwing him a tough spelling problem.

AC: It is very tough, Governor, running an eleemosynary institution, don't you think?

MC: Well, I have come very close to running them. I have been on the board of eleemosynary institutions: The Industrial Home for the Blind, The Unincorporated Hospitals of Brooklyn and Queens. So, I've worked for eleemosynary institutions for a long time. Yes.

AC: Governor, I have so much admiration for you, sir. I hope you understand that this comes just purely from the heart. Would you care to spell "eleemosynary" for us?

MC: This, Chartock, is another of your dirty tricks. But that is alright. I want to remind the listening audience that a week ago you embarrassed yourself, humiliated yourself, revealed yourself to the students by misspelling the word "piqued" in the most obvious fashion.

AC: I didn't misspell it.

MC: Now you wish to embarrass, not your governor—your governor is Governor Dukakis—by spelling eleemosynary. Can you spell it, Alan, to know if I'm correct?

AC: I'll know if you are correct.

MC: Do you know if its derivation is French or Greek or Latin?

AC: Yes.

MC: Which is it?

AC: I know.

MC: Which is it?

AC: What? Wait a second now. This is traditional. I asked you to spell it and now you are asking me.

MC: Well, that is easy. Spelling it is very easy.

AC: I bet you never—I bet this, Governor—I bet you'll never get around to spelling that word on this show.

MC: What would you like to wager?

AC: I bet there are thirteen assistants looking this up in a book right now.

MC: E-L-E-E-M-O-S-Y-N-A-R-Y, and it is French.

AC: Uh, no. Well, you got it right.

MC: You have to understand that lawyers study the law of eleemosynary institutions and trusts, charitable trusts. Eleemosynary is a well known word to lawyers. How could you forget a word which has three e's in the first four letters?

AC: Okay. Now look, Governor, congratulations, you got that right. Now the other thing.

MC: Thank you very much. Don't be piqued.

AC: There will be others. P-I-Q-U-E.

But spelling is not Cuomo's strongest suit. I believe that honor goes to his ability to make the best out of a difficult situation. Whether it is the announcement of a huge budget deficit or the resignation of a trusted aide, Cuomo is at his best under fire.

When, some years ago, the governor's own Commission on Government Integrity came down hard on substance abuse commissioner Julio Martinez for the way he ran his agency, Cuomo forced Martinez to resign. In so doing, he told Martinez that he would be offered an assistant commissionership at the same salary in the Department of Corrections, in charge of the prison system's drug addiction program. Cuomo took real heat on that one, trying to explain how you could fire a guy from one job and hire him in another. If he was bad, the press wanted to know, why not fire him outright?

The press was very aware that Martinez, as a top ranking Hispanic member of the administration, had the backing of powerful forces in the state. Cuomo had to make the best of a bad situation and he did when I spoke to him about it. My experience with other politicians was that they would have conceded a lot and sounded foolish. Cuomo did not. He took credit for having established the Commission that found Martinez wanting and for unleashing State Inspector General Joe Spinelli, a former FBI man, to find those who were not doing their jobs properly. He pointed out that he was the one who had put these watch dogs in place and that he deserved credit for doing so. He pointed out that when his top operative, during the time he was lieutenant governor, had stolen money from that office, it had been he, Cuomo, who had made the discovery and put the guy in jail.

Then Cuomo said that Martinez had been accused of being a bad bureaucrat, not a bad man. "Julio was accused of not being a good bureaucrat. Of not watching, of not managing well, of not applying the system. Nobody ever accused him of dishonesty himself, not knowing the subject, not being a great, great advocate against drugs. Not being one of the most knowledgeable people in the state and maybe in the country, not being one of the most effective spokespeople. Nobody is faulting him for that."

Cuomo cited a *New York Times* interpretive piece which noted that no one had accused Martinez of doing anything dishonest, only of being a bad administrator. Cuomo said that Martinez had not been accused of venality or of lacking the ability to help addicts. So, in making his plan to reassign Martinez, he said, "I'm trying to get him out of a position where he can make a mistake, and still use what he has to offer."

In placing Martinez in the new job, Cuomo said that "it wouldn't be his bureaucracy. He wouldn't be managing the bureaucracy. It's already in place. The people, the systems, the procedures are already there. Everything is done by the people in the Corrections Department, one of the best run agencies in the state for sure." In putting the best possible face on the whole thing, Cuomo said that Martinez "would be able to go and supervise and visit and give his advice, but he wouldn't have to manage and he wouldn't have to deal with outside providers which is what got him into difficulty here."

During his debates with Mayor Ed Koch during the famous 1982 primary, Cuomo demonstrated that he could beat one of the nation's best talkers in a head-to-head confrontation. His list of techniques is enough to make a debate coach bow her head in respect. If an opponent has a point and is going to make it, Cuomo cuts him off at the pass with a joke, an aside, a request for evidence. Almost as if he has an internal radar system, Cuomo knows when an opponent is going to make a fool out of himself, and he lets the hapless soul continue until he decides to pull the trap.

Cuomo also likes long range philosophical battles. The press will focus on them, keeping his name before the people while he continues to handle some of the more mundane day-to-day, and often unpopular, chores of government. Perhaps the most celebrated example of his long term fights were those with Archbishop

O'Connor concerning theological subjects. Others were his incredibly funny exchanges with potential presidential candidate, Representative Jack Kemp, the ex-football star to whom the governor had affixed a number of hilarious nicknames.

One of the best tricks in the Cuomo arsenal is to take the strongest argument of the would-be opponent and make it backfire. One of his adversaries was the columnist and conservative Republican, Pat Buchanan. Once Buchanan wrote a column chastising Cuomo on his approach to combating racism. I couldn't wait to ask Cuomo about it.

I began by asking Cuomo to characterize the Buchanan column for me.

Cuomo started by saying that Buchanan had said, "...if you read the article, that crime is somewhat a black syndrome. That most of it is committed by blacks. And he even compared it, at one point in the article (not directly, people should read the article themselves) to sickle cell anemia, which is a disease that occurs in blacks disproportionately.

"It sounded to me as though he was saying that crime to some extent is a function of being black and I think that's monstrous. It's like saying that most of the crime is committed by males, therefore if you are unlucky enough to have a male child, the chances are greater that he will be a criminal.

"I think the Buchanan piece is certainly worth studying. I think it's the worst kind of pandering, stereotyping, and basically disconcerting 'logic.' I put logic in quotes and I think people should be aware of it."

Concluded the governor, "I do think that it is very important to study his thesis about racial implications of crime. It is wrong in my opinion, dead wrong, illogical and unfair to say that crime has anything to do with the fact that you are white or black, or, for example, anything to do with the fact that you might be Italian-American."

But despite Cuomo's reticence to allow anyone to stereotype anyone else on crime, there was this humorous interlude on the show:

AC: What about crime? There's a perception that Democrats are soft on crime?

MC: Republicans commit crime.

Cuomo is quick, real quick. He can take very little and make it into something a lot bigger. Take the time I told him that I had seen Jesse Jackson stepping out of a stretch limousine.

AC: Following up on those lines, Jesse Jackson yesterday came to Albany in a white stretch limousine. I was standing by the Capitol...

MC: [interrupting] A white stretch limousine?

AC: You never saw anything that big in your whole life. I'm standing outside the Capitol and sure enough, this thing rides by and these two rather substantial fellows get out of the front of the car and open up the rear doors. Out of one side steps Deputy Speaker Eve, and on the other side comes Jesse Jackson. I was really struck by the contrast, because you know this guy has really been very articulate about advancing the causes of the poor and here he is getting out of a stretch limo. He got out and went upstairs and did a press conference, and one of the things he said was he thought you ought to be considering running with a minority running mate as lieutenant governor.

MC: If it's someone who can afford a stretch limousine it might make it easier in the campaign.

AC: So, I was wondering, Governor. Last time you tried to do that. You did try to pick someone to run with who is black and he couldn't win that primary.

MC: No, I didn't pick somebody who is black, you're suggesting, because he was black.

AC: No

MC: I picked the former Ambassador to the United Nations...

AC: Yes, but he is black.

MC: Yes, but I think the suggestion that I should pick a black, brown, or Hispanic, or a Jewish person, or an Italian person, or a man or a woman, or an upstater or a downstater —I'm not going to do it that way, and I've said that. I want a person who can serve as governor. I want a person who is competent. I want a person who wants to be lieutenant governor, not because it's the easiest way to get to a high position in a hurry, but because they want to serve with me if I run again. That's what I would want in a lieutenant governor if I run again.

If I have to make a judgment as to what candidate to select, that's what I would be looking for. I wouldn't be looking for balance. Al DelBello and Mario Cuomo ran together, so many vowels it sounded like a symphony, and we won anyway, and I believe that's the kind of state we have. That they're not going to vote for you or against you because of your color. So that's it. That's not going to be my criteria. I said it in the beginning.

Let me tell you who's written to me. This is fascinating. You could do a column on this one, Alan.

You'll love this one, and I can show you the letters. The Polish Community wrote to me and said the lieutenant governor must be Polish, you don't have enough Polish-Americans. I think that's probably right, we don't have as many as I'd like. And they suggested Henry Nowak, Nowak from Buffalo for lieutenant governor. The Hispanic community wrote and said it must be a Hispanic: Herman Badillo. The women's group wrote it must be a woman: Gail Schaefer. Okay, a black group wrote and said it must be a black: Carl McCall. Al Vann, a black assemblyman wrote and said it must be a Hispanic, Herman Badillo, that's Al Vann, the black Assemblyman from Brooklyn.

What have I left out? Irish. An Irish-American group said it should be an Irish-American, John Dearie. I think I have

a letter from an Italian group that said why not? So, that's
what I have. I have the letters for you. Where does it end?
Where does it end? I don't think that's the way one ought
to do it. I really don't. I don't think people ought to vote eth-
nically. Look, Alan, in this state, blacks and whites, Christians and non-Christians, voted for Herbert Lehman more
than once, and for Arthur Levitt, and Louie Lefkowitz."

Perhaps Cuomo's finest performance was in the area of the death
penalty and crime. The governor knew he had a tiger by the tail
on this one. What's more, he knew that I simply didn't agree with
him on this issue. And, yet, those who listened to us argue assured
me that I never laid a finger on him.

In the debate over the death penalty Cuomo took the subject, his greatest challenge, and gave us a lesson that would have
left Winston Churchill holding his head.

To counter the death penalty proponents' immensely appeal-
ing rhetoric, he came up with another argument for protecting
people. He called it "L-WOP" for short (and in private) and by
its proper name, "Life Without Parole," in public.

Cuomo clearly opposed the death penalty on principle. It was
one of those subjects that he simply wouldn't negotiate on. He
believed that death is the province of God, that individuals should
not kill each other and that the state should not set a precedent
and kill people so that others might emulate the state. I believe
in the death penalty, so over the years I became a foil for Cuomo
on the subject. When it got a bit hot Cuomo really let me have
it, suggesting again and again that, "You are for death, Chartock."

No matter how much hysteria was generated by proponents
of the death penalty, Cuomo always came back to Life Without
Parole. Using the radio program as his vehicle he spoke out on
the subject, turning the tables on his opponents suggesting that
it was *they* who would not protect the people by passing a law calling for life without parole. He would always come back to the argu-

ment that the proponents of the death penalty had refused to put killers behind bars for life. He always implied that the reason they didn't was that they were playing some kind of cynical political game. His argument was that if they could pass the death penalty over his veto, that was fine; they were entitled to do that. But if they couldn't, the least they owed the people was to give killers life without parole so that they could not be freed to kill again. Clearly those in the Legislature, like Senator Marino, then the Republican majority leader, did not want life without parole because they were worried that this would be a political victory to be added to Cuomo's string of successes. But they messed up. First of all, they had no one to match Cuomo's rhetoric and style. It would be unthinkable for any of them to go head to head with the governor, even if the governor would allow such a debate. Secondly, the legislators decided to advance the political rather than the meritorious argument to the people. In other words, they suggested to the voters that the governor was playing a cynical and political game by advancing life without parole to destroy the impetus for the death penalty. They may have been right, but the governor just stayed with his unassailable logic. Why not at *least* lock them up. "Don't they want to protect police?" he would ask.

There is yet another example of the "turn the tables" technique which he is unparalleled at administering. Once I told him that I wanted to get his views on the matter of "privatization," the transfer of a formerly public function to a private concern. In order to fully appreciate his ability to debate, it is necessary to remember that I am the Executive Director/Chairman of WAMC, the Albany-based public radio station, a not-for-profit corporation.

So I asked him what his views were about giving over public responsibilities to private companies.

"Whatever they can do as well or better, they should do," was his first answer.

But I pressed on. "Let's take them one by one..."

He wasn't going to let me continue as he interrupted.

MC: How about public radio, and public television. Should we give them all over to the private companies? Privatize public radio?

AC: I would think not in this case...

MC: [interrupting] Why not?

AC: [holding on for dear life knowing what was coming] Well, because in that case if you do that then you are going to a capital base...

MC: [interrupting] Excuse me, excuse me, are you telling me that you do it better than the private companies?

AC: Without question, sir.

MC: Oh, really?

AC: Yes, because we....

MC: [interrupting] So no privatization of public radio. How about more public radio, more public television?

AC: No, I think we are doing very well...

MC: [interrupting] Oh, it's perfect exactly the way it is, Chartock has his nook. Right?

AC: The last man in is what you are saying?

MC: I mean, this giant octopus called government with its insatiable tentacles constantly reaching out to absorb people and institutions to make it part of the monolith. It has gone just exactly far enough with (public) radio, right?

AC: No, not far enough. It could go a little further...

MC: [laughing and interrupting] Stop! Just right. Don't mess with Chartock.

AC: Wait, wait, wait. Again I want to go back. What about privatizing airports?

MC: What about radio?

AC: Well, since I asked you first I think that at least I deserve an answer, and then I'll tell you about radio. I've already told you about radio. The answer to radio is no privatization of public radio and television because then we'll get back to the advertising base and everything will be subject to the needs of companies to show a profit.

MC: [feigning surprise] Oh, I see. On the private side it's all junk. Chartock is perfect.

AC: No, but public radio is much more perfect than the private side. That is correct. You see everything is relative, Governor.

MC: Okay, Alan, we will note, I hope not disrespectfully, your bias as a witness on this subject.

AC: Well, you asked...

MC: [interrupting] We're spending too much time on this subject...

Put succinctly, I had been vanquished once again by the Cuomo treatment.

Then, too, there is the other razzle-dazzle, known as too many wrongs make a right. Take the case of gun control. Gun lobbyists argue that the second amendment to the U.S. Constitution means what it says: that the people shall have the right to bear arms. Cuomo advances his plan to ban guns that hold more than five bullets and he then says, "Now to those people who say that the Constitution gives us an absolute right to guns, not to be limited in any way, under any circumstances, I'd say you'd have to look at the Constitution and see what other rights that's true of. I can't think of any, can you?"

Now Cuomo, at his best, went on to show all the other amendments that were defined by the court to have limits. "The right to practice religion. You're a Jehovah's Witness. Your religion says that your child should not be operated on. You lose that right if the life of the child is at stake. The right to speak? Well, that's about as unfettered as it can be in this society, but it's not perfectly unfettered." And then Cuomo goes on to articulate a law that he says is what the Constitution is all about.

"In all things reasonableness is the ultimate rule of the Constitution."

But Mario Cuomo is capable of arguing both sides of each issue. That's what makes him a great debater. Once I told him that I suspected the judges on our high courts were just making decisions as they went along; that they were really little legislatures. I asked Cuomo what he would do if he were the judge in a particular case.

Cuomo told me, "You don't make decisions that way. There are all the arguments you have to read and all the cases." He suggested that decisions are not made by "...what it smells like, what it feels like—you don't do that."

Cuomo, who has enormous respect for the law, said that there is a difference between being a judge on a court and going to a restaurant.

MC: You do not make constitutional decisions the same way you pick something off a menu. You have nine people who are steeped in history, steeped in law. They read dozens and dozens of pages of records and testimonies and argumentation. Then they talk to their colleagues, they reflect and talk to their law secretaries, and then they reach a conclusion. What you are saying is "forget all of that, make a game of it. Just guess what is going to happen." Alright, if you want to play games, I'll guess.

AC: What you are doing is predicting.

MC: It can't be done that way, it mustn't be done that way.

AC: Why not?...

MC: It has to be done in the context of a particular case, a particular argument. It can't be done apart from the arguments that are made, apart from the briefs that are submitted, apart from the discussion that took place.

I told you he could argue both sides.

Then there was the time I asked the governor about his political versus governmental roles. I wanted to know whether as a governor who serves all the people as their elected leader, he didn't risk alienating the public when he campaigned for candidates of his own Democratic Party.

MC: I don't.

AC: You go down to Yonkers and you campaign for the Democratic candidates. I am not being accusatory.

MC: You are free to be accusatory.

AC: Well, I'm not, though.

MC: You could be accusatory because you do not have anything substantive or concrete to say. I understand.

AC: Now how did this happen? I just asked this philosophical question. Do you lose anything when you do that?

MC: Do I lose anything by being in Albany when I give a speech that says, "Let's meet the state's problems?" Of course not! If I went to Albany and told them one thing and went to Rensselaer and told them a different thing, a separate and contradictory thing, if I went to Long Island and told them something that was good for Long Island and not New York City—I don't do that.

AC: No, no, no. I think you are missing [the point] unless I am much dumber than I think I am.

MC: I don't know. I doubt that. I don't doubt that you are dumber than you think you are.

AC: I think that you are missing the point. In other words, if you go and work for Democratic county executive [candidates] and others, and Republicans vote for you, does that create a problem for you in your capacity as a governor?

MC: Interesting. No, I think not. When I participate, for example, in Chautauqua as I did last weekend, talking about Ted Smith [Democratic candidate for county executive], I never do it as a Democrat who sways votes because the candidate is a Democrat. I say, "You have asked for a judgment and I am telling you to vote for Ted Smith for the following reasons: you need leadership, new leadership... I wouldn't think of saying to New York [City] people, "Vote for David Dinkins because he is a Democrat like you." That is insulting, just because he is a Democrat. There are probably some Republicans I have voted for. Probably some Democrats that I have not voted for and that's true of every thinking Democrat I know.

In sum, the guy never gets enough of debating.

EPILOGUE—EXCERPTS
FROM THE LAST SHOW

AC: There are those who think you could have been sitting on the Supreme Court right now. Do you ever look back on those things?

MC: No. Don't you remember Satchel Paige?

AC: Yes, Satchel Paige.

MC: Don't look back, they may be gaining on you.

AC: So, we have a little over two minutes, Governor. What is the significance, I mean, how do you put the significance into your life so that it counts for each of us? How do we do that?

MC: How do you put significance in your life?

AC: Yes. If significance is the antidote to hell, then how do we— do it?

MC: I'm not smart enough to know—read Somerset Maugham, read *The Razor's Edge*, you know, read all the great books. Get Mortimer Adler, the great, *The Syntopicon* in the great book series in the '60s. It didn't go very far but they started a magazine called *Wisdom Magazine* and in *Wisdom Magazine*, one of the first editions of it, a great large hardcover book with beautiful glossy photographs in it, they did a book on the philosophies and philosophers. They went all the way back and they had them all—they had Buddha, Mohammed, and they had Jesus. And they distill, they took little epitomes of the ancient Hebrew wisdom and all the others—and they said what is the most important thing? And almost always, the great religions and the great philosophies centered on love.

If you want significance, you're supposed to love, you're supposed to share, you're supposed to give, you're supposed to
touch and you're supposed to function. That's the closest I've
been able to come to any essential wisdom. People search a
lifetime. I'm still searching. I read all the time. What is the
significant thing? You make the most of your opportunity in
life. You function everywhere you can, never hurting anybody,
trying as much as you can to help them. Uh, it gets very simple in the end. Do good, avoid evil and you decide what's good
and what's evil. To me it's basic. Try to help people. Make
them smile if you can. Help them if they have AIDS. Get
them a job if they don't. That's what the Chartock show is
all about. I'm going to miss it.

AC: It sure is. He's Governor Mario Cuomo. I'm Alan Chartock.
That's *The Capitol Connection.*

INDEX

Abrams, Robert, 190, 200-201, 233
Allen, Fred, 15
Anderson, Warren, 10-11, 190, 199
Aquinas, St. Thomas, 69
Archie, the dog, 12, 155-156
Atwater, Lee, 199
Axelrod, Dr. David, 55-56, 201, 220-221, 252

Bacon, Sir Francis, 154
Badillo, Herman, 290
Barber, James, 260
Baryshnikov, Mikhail, 90
Belafonte, Harry, 205-206, 208, 283
Belafonte, Julie, 207
Bellamy, Carol, 204-205, 233
Bellamy, Ralph, 89, 91
Benny, Jack, 15
Berger, Simon, 223
Berle, Peter A. A., 130
Berra, Yogi, 143
Bertelli, Angelo, 154
Bishop, Liz, 159-160
Bogart, Humphrey, 276
Bradley, Bill, 206
Brawley, Tawana, 190-191

Breathed, Berk, 135
Breen, Peg, 135
Brooks, Mel, 14, 131
Buchanan, Pat, 225, 289
Buckley, William F., 38
Buddha, 298
Buoniconti, Nick, 154
Burke, Martin, 22
Bush, George, 48-50, 53, 55, 61, 63, 133, 197, 199-200, 260, 271-272

Cagney, James, 88-91, 276
Cagney, Willie, 88
Califano, Joseph, 228
Carey, Hugh L., 15, 66, 129, 158-159, 179, 196, 208
Carideo, Frank, 154
Carter, Jimmy, 139, 210
Castellano, Paul, 177-178
Caufield, Father, 110
Ceausescu, Nicolae, 76
Charles, Bernie, 208
Chartock, Jonas, 7
Chartock, Roselle, 7, 21-22, 118-119, 160
Churchill, Winston, 54, 291
Clinton, Bill, 30
Cohan, George M., 89-90

Craig, May, 148
Crotty, Jerry, 203
Cuomo, Andrea, 253
Cuomo, Andrew, 103-105, 122, 202, 232
Cuomo, Christopher, 104, 122, 125-126, 154-155, 164, 204
Cuomo, Immacolata, 255-256
Cuomo, Madeline, 105
Cuomo, Matilda, 106, 108, 115, 117-120, 122, 126, 128, 139, 164, 189, 231, 246, 252
Cutts, Connie, 152

D'Amato, Al, 22, 53, 217, 222, 224
D'Jardin, Teilhard, 68, 87
Dante, 165
Dearie, John, 290
DelBello, Al, 233, 290
Dente, Matt, 152
Dewey, Thomas E., 49
Dicker, Fred, 160, 164, 166, 180-181
DiMaggio, Joe, 19, 238
Dinkins, David, 85, 172, 224-226, 296
Dole, Robert, 226
Driscoll, Louise, 95
Duffy, Bill, 159
Dukakis, Michael, 16, 64, 133, 197-198, 260, 271-272, 277, 285
Duke, David, 198-99
Dullea, Hank, 201
Duryea, Perry, 151

Eisenhower, Dwight, 117
Erickson, Anne, 10-11
Eve, Arthur O., 93, 211, 289

Falwell, Jerry, 86
Farrell, Denny, 206
Fink, Stanley, 11, 148, 201, 208, 233
Ford, Anne Uzielli, 159
Ford, Gerald, 210, 277
Forman, Milos, 91
Forrester, Alfred A., 249
Fotheringham, Alan, 183

Galletly, David, 22
Garfunkel, Art, 238
Genovese, Kitty, 38
Gephardt, Dick, 218
Gerrity, John, 97
Ginger, the dog, 70, 117-118, 152, 154-156, 264-265
Gingrich, Newt, 23, 27
Giuliani, Rudolph, 223-224, 256-257
Goetz, Bernie, 37-38, 42
Gold, Emmanuel, 154, 204
Goodman, Roy, 15, 157-158
Gorbachev, Mikhail, 49
Gotbaum, Victor, 196
Grant, Bob, 27
Grasso, Thomas, 26
Gugliemi, Ralph, 154
Guiterman, Arthur, 252

Harris, Jean, 275, 277-278
Hart, Gary, 170, 248
Helmsley, Leona, 54, 74
Hepburn, Katharine, 267
Higgins, Colonel, 226-227
Hines, Gregory, 164
Hitler, Adolf, 76
Horowitz, Vladimir, 267
Horton, Willie, 224, 277
Humbert, Mark, 179-180

Jackson, Jesse, 150, 218, 290
Jaffe, Marc, 7
Javits, Jacob, 246
Jesus Christ, 60, 69, 94, 241, 298
Johnson, Lyndon B., 28
Jorling, Thomas, 61, 252
Jung, Carl, 154

Kalikow, Peter, 181
Kaplan, Selma, 7
Kemp, Jack, 136, 288
Kennedy, John F., 16, 32, 71, 148,
    236, 238
Kennedy, Kerry, 103
Kennedy, Robert F., 103
Kennedy, William, 164
Kennedy Jr., John F., 122
King, Dexter Luther, 114
King, Jr., Martin Luther, 114,
    207-208, 236-238
Koch, Ed, 12-13, 15, 58, 88, 143,
    151, 154-155, 158, 190, 195,
    205, 208, 225, 233, 269-270,
    287
Kurlander, Larry, 206

La Duke, Glendy, 152-154
Labretti, Lava, 153
Lautenberg, Frank, 206
Lear, Norman, 208
Lefkowitz, Louie, 291
Lehman, Herbert, 291
Lehrman, Lew, 62-63, 157-158
Levitt, Arthur, 10, 291
Levy, Senator, 161
Limbaugh, Rush, 27
Lincoln, Abraham, 19, 35, 111
Lippman, Walter, 183
Lynch, Dan, 187-188

Madden, Owney, 164
Maddox, Alton, 190
Mandela, Nelson, 238
Marino, John, 105
Marino, Ralph, 190, 228, 270
Martin, Billy, 247
Martinez, Julio, 129, 286-287
Mason, C. Vernon, 190
Maugham, Somerset, 298
McCall, Carl, 290
McGivern, Gary, 277-278
Mello, John, 154
Miller, Melvin, 201, 228, 270
Mohammed, 298
Monahan, Matt, 165
Mondale, Walter, 150-151, 260
Moore, Bishop Emerson, 79
Moore, Emerson, 79
More, Thomas, 111, 247
Murdoch, Rupert, 181

Netanyahu, Benjamin "Bibi", 227
Netanyahu, Jonathan, 266
Nixon, Richard, 53, 210, 217-219,
    277
North, Oliver, 276
Norwood, Scott, 282-283
Novak, 184, 269
Nowak, Henry, 291

O'Connor, Cardinal John J., 73,
    80, 98
O'Rourke, Andrew, 62
Ohrenstein, Manfred, 11, 76
Oreskes, Michael, 17, 148
Ortega, Daniel, 76

Paige, Satchel, 298
Palomino, Fabian, 129, 203-204

Panza, Sancho, 129, 204
Park, 33, 40, 153, 241, 246, 255
Parkinson, A. J., 26, 31, 62, 66,
    154, 162-163
Parkinson, Irving J., 163-64
Pataki, George, 53, 130
Patterson, Basil, 208
Patterson, Floyd, 89-90
Patton, George, 155
Paul, Jean, 134
Petranelli, John, 154
Petrasanti, Nick, 154
Plunkett of Tammany Hall, 51
Poindexter, John, 277

Quayle, Dan, 49, 146
Quinlan, Karen Anne, 263

Rafferty, Charlie, 276
Raft, George, 276
Reagan, Ronald, 26, 29, 33, 49-
    50, 53, 150-151, 178, 189, 199,
    209-210, 212-213, 225, 237,
    260, 275, 281
Reed, Ogden, 130
Regan, Edward (Ned), 222-223
Reiner, Carl, 14
Ritter, Father Bruce, 181
Roberts, Lillian, 196
Robinson, Cleveland, 208, 238
Rockefeller, Nelson, 64
Rockefeller Jr., Nelson, 122
Rogers, Will, 15
Roosevelt, Franklin D., 32, 35, 49
Rosenbaum, Richard, 11
Russe, Charlotte, 260
Russert, Tim, 61, 165
Ryan, Bernie, 12

Samuels, Howard, 151
Savoldi, Jumping Joe, 154
Schaefer, Gail, 290
Schneerson, Rabbi Menachem, 85
Scholefield, Jim "Sparks", 23
Schultz, George, 38
Scruggs-Leftwich, Yvonne, 129
Shakespeare, William, 154
Sharpton, Al, 190-191
Simon, Paul, 238
Simon (Sen.), Paul, 218
Smith, Ted, 296
Spinelli, Joe, 286
Spinks, Leon, 243
Stalin, Joseph, 137
Stanky, Ed, 247
Stengel, Casey, 143-144
Stevenson, Adlai, 16, 232
Stuart, Lyle, 7
Sununu, John, 197
Sweet, Robert, 38

Tarnower, Dr. Herman, 275
Truman, Harry S, 32, 35
Tutu, Bishop Desmond, 85
Tyson, Mike, 243

Valentino, Rudolph, 136
Vann, Al, 290
Vaughn, Bishop Austin, 74

Walesa, Lech, 238
Weprin, Saul, 60, 204
Whitman, Walt, 250
Williams, Henry (Hank), 129-30,
    290
Wilson, Malcolm, 151
Wriston, Walter, 213